# AGAINST MERITOCRACY

Meritocracy today involves the idea that whatever your social position at birth, society ought to offer enough opportunity and mobility for 'talent' to combine with 'effort' in order to 'rise to the top'. This idea is one of the most prevalent social and cultural tropes of our time, as palpable in the speeches of politicians as in popular culture. In this book Jo Littler argues that meritocracy is the key cultural means of legitimation for contemporary neoliberal culture – and that whilst it promises opportunity, it in fact creates new forms of social division.

*Against Meritocracy* is split into two parts. Part I explores the genealogies of meritocracy within social theory, political discourse and working cultures. It traces the dramatic U-turn in meritocracy's meaning, from socialist slur to a contemporary ideal of how a society should be organised. Part II uses a series of case studies to analyse the cultural pull of popular 'parables of progress', from reality TV to the super-rich and celebrity CEOs, from social media controversies to the rise of the 'mumpreneur'. Paying special attention to the role of gender, 'race' and class, this book provides new conceptualisations of the meaning of meritocracy in contemporary culture and society.

**Jo Littler** is a Reader in the Centre for Culture and Creative Industries in the Department of Sociology at City, University of London. She is the author of *Radical Consumption: Shopping for change in contemporary culture* (2009) and co-editor, with Roshi Naidoo, of *The Politics of Heritage: The Legacies of 'Race'* (2005).

# AGAINST MERITOCRACY

Culture, power and myths of mobility

Jo Littler

Routledge
Taylor & Francis Group
LONDON AND NEW YORK

First published 2018
by Routledge
2 Park Square, Milton Park, Abingdon, Oxon OX14 4RN

and by Routledge
711 Third Avenue, New York, NY 10017

*Routledge is an imprint of the Taylor & Francis Group, an informa business*

© 2018 Jo Littler

The right of Jo Littler to be identified as author of this work has been asserted by her in accordance with sections 77 and 78 of the Copyright, Designs and Patents Act 1988.

All rights reserved. No part of this book may be reprinted or reproduced or utilised in any form or by any electronic, mechanical, or other means, now known or hereafter invented, including photocopying and recording, or in any information storage or retrieval system, without permission in writing from the publishers.

*Trademark notice*: Product or corporate names may be trademarks or registered trademarks, and are used only for identification and explanation without intent to infringe.

*British Library Cataloguing-in-Publication Data*
A catalogue record for this book is available from the British Library

*Library of Congress Cataloging-in-Publication Data*
Names: Littler, Jo, 1972- author.
Title: Against meritocracy : culture, power and myths of mobility / Jo Littler.
Description: Abingdon, Oxon ; NewYork, NY : Routledge, 2017. | Includes index.
Identifiers: LCCN 2017002013 | ISBN 9781138889545 (hardback : alk. paper) | ISBN 9781138889552 (pbk. : alk. paper) | ISBN 9781315712802 (ebook)
Subjects: LCSH: Social mobility. | Plutocracy. | Power (Social sciences)
Classification: LCC HT612 .L57 2017 | DDC 305.5/13--dc23
LC record available at https://lccn.loc.gov/2017002013

ISBN: 978-1-138-88954-5 (hbk)
ISBN: 978-1-138-88955-2 (pbk)
ISBN: 978-1-315-71280-2 (ebk)

Typeset in Bembo
by Taylor & Francis Books

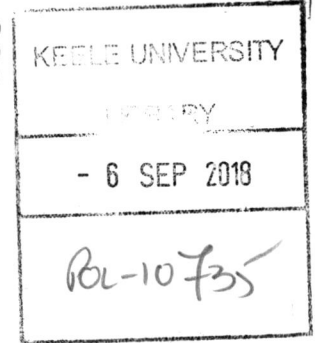

For Jeremy,
For Robin and Isla,
And for everyone who reads it

# CONTENTS

*List of figures* ix
*Acknowledgements* xi

Introduction: Ladders and snakes 1

**PART I**
**Genealogies** **21**

1 Meritocracy's genealogies in social theory 23

2 Rising up: Gender, ethnicity, class and the meritocratic deficit 48

3 Meritocratic feeling: The movement of meritocracy in political rhetoric 78

**PART II**
**Popular parables** **113**

4 Just like us?: Normcore plutocrats and the popularisation of elitism 115

| 5 | #Damonsplaining and the unbearable whiteness of merit | 147 |
| 6 | Desperate success: Managing the mumpreneur | 179 |
| Conclusion: Beyond neoliberal meritocracy | | 212 |

*Index*   *227*

# FIGURES

I.1 'Upward Mobility' by Gloria Pritschet and Tobias Mixer, exhibited at *Grammar of the Elite*, The Gallery Project, Ann Arbor, Michigan, 2012. Photograph by Jennifer Metsker. Reproduced courtesy of the photographer, the artists and the Gallery Project.     6
1.1 Gyanbazi game from Gujarat/Rajasthan, India, late 19th or 20th century. Watercolour on cloth. Reproduced courtesy of the Victoria & Albert Museum, London.     29
1.2 Snakes and ladders board game. Designed in England and manufactured in Germany, *c*.1900. Chromolithographed paper on card. Reproduced courtesy of the Victoria & Albert Museum, London.     30
3.1 UK newspaper *The Sun* announces that Prime Minister Theresa May is offering 'Mayritocracy' through a new wave of grammar schools. Photograph by Nick Ansell / PA Wire / PA Images (PA.28579747). Reproduced courtesy of *The Sun* and the Press Association.     98
4.1 Cover of Duncan Bannatyne, *Anyone Can Do It*. Reproduced courtesy of Orion Books.     122
6.1 Cover of Annabel Karmel, *Mumpreneur*. Reproduced courtesy of the Random House Group Ltd.     181

6.2  'Are You on the Passion Ladder?', *CEO Mums*.
     Reproduced courtesy of Nicola Huelin and *CEO Mums*.   202
C.1  Altgen graphic. Design by Constance Laisné for Altgen.
     Reproduced courtesy of Constance Laisné and Altgen
     via a Creative Commons License.                        223

# ACKNOWLEDGEMENTS

I have always loved acknowledgements in academic books. As an undergraduate they were evidence that these authors were indeed living, breathing, feeling people with lives. They offered slivers of insight into what the existence of this strange breed called *academics* might actually be like. Plus! they seemed to be one of the few ways to find out something of how these books actually got written. My all-time favourite academic preface is in Alan Sinfield's book *Faultlines* (Oxford: Clarendon Press, 1992), where he dissects this miniature paratextual genre with arch wisdom ('we might', he writes, 'call it the higher gossip'). Noting that, at least these days, fewer prefaces end with 'the ultimate solecism: thanking the wife for typing it all', Sinfield thanks his male partner and concludes with a flourish: 'Oh, and I typed it myself.'

I cannot match Alan Sinfield's sardonic prowess and only occasionally stray into the confessional. However, I share the sense that it is useful to expose a little of the process involved in writing, in order to dramatise the palpable fact that books are not the singular product of the name on the spine but the result of multiple apparatuses and flows of communication (although I also typed it myself). There are many thanks to give – indeed, given the nature of interdependent relationality, infinite thanks – but I'll try and keep it brief.

First and foremost I want to thank my partner Jeremy Gilbert, not just for my extensive exploitation of our mutual editing service but for his love and support and for making everyday life more meaningful than I could otherwise imagine. Thanks and lots of love to our daughters Robin and Isla: yes, I *have* finished my work now. At least for the moment. Many thanks to all of my extended family and friends, from Aachen to Swansea, from Lucky Cloud to the locals, who I look forward to seeing more of now the intense stage of completing the book is over.

This book would not have been finished – nor indeed properly started, as at least half of it was written at this time – without a three-month research sabbatical from City, University of London where I have worked for the last few years. It was my first sabbatical for ten years, and it is not a coincidence that is also my first single-authored book in ten years. I would like to thank all my colleagues in Sociology (especially Rachel Cohen, who pointed me in the direction of some useful statistics) and in particular my colleagues in the Centre for Culture and Creative Industries: Debbie Dickinson, Cecilia Dinardi, Ana Gaio, Ros Gill, Jenny Mbaye, Janet Merkel, Andy Pratt, Marisol Sandoval, Alex Williams and Diana Yeh.

A small proportion of this work appeared in earlier versions in previous publications. 'Meritocracy as Plutocracy: The Marketising of "Equality" within Neoliberalism' (*New Formations* 80–81 [2013] pp. 52–72) appears in chapters 1 and 2. I am grateful to Lawrence & Wishart for permission to use this piece. A couple of small (and adapted) paragraphs from 'Consumer Culture and Cultural Studies' (in Deirdre Shaw, Michal Carrington and Andreas Chatzidakis [eds], *Ethics and Morality in Consumer Culture: Interdisciplinary Perspectives* [New York: Routledge, 2016]) and from 'The New Victorians: Celebrity Charity and the Demise of the Welfare State' (*Celebrity Studies* 6[4] [2015] pp. 471–485) appear in chapters 2 and 4. A few paragraphs in chapter 4 thematically update my earlier work on celebrity CEOs that Su Holmes and Sean Redmond supported and published, and I am still grateful to them for that. The writing in this book on *The Apprentice* is indebted to Nick Couldry, for the work we did together to produce our two articles on the subject, back when Donald Trump was but a mere media mogul and corporate CEO. The discussion of *Downton Abbey* in chapter 6 is the result of many conversations with Roshi Naidoo on the matter, and part of a paper we are writing, and I am grateful to Roshi for her laser-like sense of humour and for being a wonderful friend.

I am also grateful for the wit and wisdom of friends, colleagues and casual acquaintances, who now due to my age suddenly seem more numerous: it is hard to compile a comprehensive list. Academia seems like a small world at first, but when you stay a while, suddenly doors open into other academic rooms. So thanks to everyone who was supportive along the way. Particular thanks to those who offered – or who were bribed – to read chunks or chapters of this book: Doreen Massey, Roshi Naidoo, Emma Dowling, Anamik Saha, Gil Rodman, Ros Gill, Milly Williamson, Jeremy Gilbert (who heroically read the entire manuscript) and Sara Hackenberg (who gets a special endurance medal for reading so much of my work over the years). I am extremely grateful for the advice, suggestions, kindness and encouragement you all gave.

At Routledge, many thanks to Natalie Foster for suggesting they publish it and to Sheni Kruger, Kitty Imbert, Stacey Carter and Jamie Askew for putting up with me extending the deadline again (and again). Thanks to Diane Bell at City, University of Library, Fan Yang, Lene Bull Christiansen, Aeron Davis, Joanna Figiel, Dave O'Brien and Ben Little for some very helpful reading suggestions, and to Martin Gilbert for sharing his related writings on the subject. Thanks to all those who invited me to talk on meritocracy at various universities over the past few years, including Brighton, Kings College London, Royal Holloway, Warwick, and Manchester in the UK; University College Dublin, Roskilde University, Denmark and the ACS Institute in Bloemfontein, South Africa.

Special thanks to Trisha Pender for telling me to just write the damn thing already at the beginning and to Bridget Byrne who helped me see that it might be time to stop. Many thanks to Mark and Zöe Fisher for being so enthusiastic about my initial article on meritocracy which formed the basis of chapters 1 and 2. I am also grateful to Judith Watson for being encouraging early on and for sharing her ideas on employment progression with me. For conversations which, whether long or short, really helped, particular thanks to Sarah Banet-Weiser, Rebecca Bramall, Kay Dickinson, James Hay, Toby Miller, Diane Negra, Carol Tulloch, Alison Winch, Helen Wood and to all the students at City who told me exactly what they thought of meritocracy. Thanks to Angela McRobbie, Larry Grossberg, Paul Gilroy and Vron Ware for being kind as well as inspiring. Thanks also to the people who said nice things about work I have done in the final stretch which helped me not give up or press the delete button but continue towards concluding and submitting the manuscript.

All the members of the editorial collective of *Soundings: A Journal of Politics and Culture*, past and present, have in one way or another helped me be able to produce this book.

Meritocracy is a subject that everyone has an opinion on. Within the time that I've had kids it's been brought home to me how we expect children to share nicely, but not the grown-ups. So this is for the grown-ups, as a way to help the arguments, movements, strategic discussions and conversations about how we can share. Because if there was ever a time, it is now.

Jo Littler<br>
London<br>
December 2016

# INTRODUCTION
## Ladders and snakes

> Meritocracy contradicts the principle of equality, of an equalitarian democracy, no less than any other oligarchy.
>
> *Hannah Arendt*[1]

### Meritocracy as plutocracy

Meritocracy today entails the idea that whatever your social position at birth, society ought to offer enough opportunity and mobility for 'talent' to combine with 'effort' in order to 'rise to the top'. This idea is one of the prevalent social and cultural tropes of our time, as palpable in the speeches of politicians as in popular culture. In the UK, Prime Minister Theresa May proclaims that 'I want Britain to be the world's great meritocracy – a country where everyone has a fair chance to go as far as their talent and their hard work will allow' (May 2016). The former US president, Barack Obama, pronounced that 'we are true to our creed when a little girl born into the bleakest poverty knows that she has the same chance to succeed as anybody else'; the new US President Donald Trump argues that 'we must create a level playing field for American companies and workers' (Obama 2013, Trump 2017). In South Africa, President Jacob Zuma is regularly castigated in the press for not being meritocratic enough (James 2012; Soko 2015). Globally franchised TV talent shows like *Idol* and *The Apprentice* promote the idea of a social landscape in which talent, plus effort, 'will out'. As Thomas Piketty recently put it in his economic bestseller

*Capital in the Twenty-First Century*, 'our democratic societies rest on a meritocratic worldview' (Piketty 2013: 297).

This book argues that it is not merely a coincidence that a pronounced lack of social mobility and the continual importance of inherited wealth (Piketty 2013; Dorling 2011; Marmot 2004; McNamee and Miller 2009; Wilkinson and Pickett 2010) co-exist with the common idea that we live in a meritocratic age. On the contrary: the idea of meritocracy has become a key means through which plutocracy – or government by a wealthy elite – perpetuates, reproduces and extends itself. Meritocracy has become the key means of cultural legitimation for contemporary capitalist culture.

In particular, over the past few decades, the language of meritocracy has become an alibi for plutocracy and a key ideological term in the reproduction of neoliberal culture. And in the Global North it has done so by seizing the idea, practice and discourse of greater social equality that gradually emerged in the first half of the twentieth century and the struggles over identity politics and recognition in the late 1960s and marketising them. Meritocracy has long historical roots, but it also has a new face. It proclaims greater equality of opportunity for more people than ever before. We have been encouraged to believe that if we try hard enough we can make it: that race or class or gender are not, on a fundamental level, significant barriers to success. To release our inner talent, we need to work hard and market ourselves in the right way to achieve success.

There are then two significantly new features about the culture of meritocracy today. Firstly, it has drawn on the movements for greater equality that emerged and grew stronger in the Global North over the twentieth century. Secondly, it is characterised by the sheer extent of its attempts to atomise people as individuals who must compete with each other to succeed, by extending entrepreneurial behaviour into the nooks and crannies of everyday life. The interaction between these characteristics is crucial. The attempt to absorb the language of equality and identity politics into entrepreneurial self-fashioning has created lonely forms of selective empowerment, ones profoundly ill-equipped to deal with the wider structural causes of sexism, racism, environmental crisis and economic inequality.

Meritocracy is regularly symbolised in popular and political culture by the image of the ladder. Making a 'ladder of opportunity' available for all to climb is a motif regularly employed by politicians. At the 2013 Conservative Party conference, David Cameron pronounced 'you help people by putting up ladders that they can climb through their own efforts' (Cameron 2013). In the early 2000s, it was a catchphrase of Australian opposition leader Mark Latham, who used it so much that he became known in some quarters as

'Lord of the Rungs' (Hudson 2004). 'The ladder of success is best climbed by standing on the rungs of opportunity' asserts a widely reproduced motivational quote, appearing on multiple fridge magnets and digital memes, often attributed to the twentieth-century right-wing libertarian guru Ayn Rand.[2]

Meritocracy may seem a very contemporary idea, but, as Raymond Williams argued in a book review in 1958, the ladder is a perfect symbol of the bourgeois idea of society, for, while it undoubtedly offers the opportunity to climb, 'it is a device that can only be used individually; you go up the ladder alone'. Such an 'alternative to solidarity', pointed out Williams, has dazzled many working-class leaders and is objectionable in two respects: firstly, it weakens community and the task of common betterment; and secondly, it 'sweetens the poison of hierarchy' by offering advancement through merit rather than money or birth, whilst retaining a commitment to the very notion of hierarchy itself (Williams 1958: 331). This double move is a core characteristic of meritocratic discourse: it promises opportunity whilst producing social division. In the contemporary era, the promises of meritocracy have become increasingly loud and competitive participation has come to be presented as a moral obligation at the same time as the ladders have grown longer.

## What's wrong with meritocracy? Five problems

The drawbacks of meritocracy as an ideal and as an actual social system is the subject of the entire book. For the purposes of this introduction, I will sketch five of its key problems. The first problem with the contemporary meaning of meritocracy is that it endorses a competitive, linear, hierarchical system in which by definition certain people must be left behind. The top cannot exist without the bottom. Not everyone can 'rise'. Unrealised talent is therefore both the necessary and structural condition of its existence. The forms taken by many examples of contemporary celebrity and reality TV talent shows have exemplified this structure, as I explore in chapter 2, dramatising these assumptions through widely consumed forms of public entertainment. Meritocracy offers a ladder system of social mobility, promoting a socially corrosive ethic of competitive self-interest which both legitimises inequality and damages community 'by requiring people to be in a permanent state of competition with each other' (Hickman 2009). The 'fair' neoliberal meritocratic dream rests on the idea of a level playing field, conveniently ignoring systematic inequality, social location and the head start accrued by the children of those at the top or high up the social ladder.

Much empirical and critical work emerged in and around social science since the 2000s on the limitations of and problems with 'social mobility' as a descriptive concept and a normative aim. These limitations have become more apparent as the marketising effects of neoliberalism have ripped through the forms of social protection built up in the Global North in the mid-century and the gap between rich and poor has become increasingly wide. In *The Meritocracy Myth*, for example, American sociologists Stephen McNamee and Robert Miller examine the prevailing belief that 'people get out of the system what they put into it based on individual merit' and conclude that, while US society has reduced some of its prejudicial inequalities structuring the opportunities for women and non-whites, 'the most important factor for determining where people end up economically is where they started in the first place' (McNamee and Miller 2009: 16). 'The simple fact', they write, 'is that there is far more talent, intelligence, hard work, and ability in the population than there are people lucky enough to find themselves in a position to exploit them' (McNamee and Miller 2009: 19). The fact that the expansion of inequality militates against social mobility has become a preoccupation of a number of recent authors (Piketty 2013; Bloodworth 2016; Wilkinson and Pikett 2010).

The second problem is that the contemporary logic of meritocracy frequently (though not always) assumes that talent and intelligence are innate: it depends on an essentialised conception of intellect and aptitude. In other words, it primarily assumes an ability which is inborn and either given the chance or not to succeed. This notion of intelligence is overwhelmingly singular and linear. Its problems are powerfully critiqued in the magnificent multi-authored book *Inequality by Design*, which shows how a particularly narrow notion of intelligence, in the form of psychometric testing of IQs, structured 'the bell curve' debates in the US in the 1990s and became a conduit for renewed racism towards African Americans (Fischer et al. 1996). Conclusively demonstrating that context shapes IQ scores and discussing the history of the IQ test in military planning, they foreground the sheer complexity of the thing we call 'intelligence' and the vast range of methods which are, have been or could be used to measure it. Such techniques include Raymond Cattell's distinction between crystallised and fluid intelligence and Joy Guilford's analysis of at least 120 components of intelligence (Fischer et al. 1996: 26–27). These are conceptions of intelligence as multiple and various: of it as a living phenomena which can change and grow in numerous directions.

Carried to its logical conclusion, a hermetic conception of intelligence as a sealed and singular entity shares, as Michael Young intimated in his classic

1958 work *The Rise of the Meritocracy*, the logic of eugenics (Young 1994). This elitist 'myth of inherent difference' accelerated in intensity in affluent nations during the 1950s. In Britain, as Danny Dorling points out, 'the state enthusiastically sponsored the division of children into types, with the amount spent per head on grammar school children being much higher than on those at the alternative secondary moderns' (Dorling 2011: 870). What Dorling terms 'apartheid schooling' was challenged in the 1960s and 1970s, but it was this 1950s' rising tide of elitist stratification in both schools and society that in part prompted Michael Young's use of the term 'meritocracy' in 1958. All these events were possible because of the ambiguous nature of 'merit'.

The third problem with the contemporary idea of meritocracy is that it ignores the fact that climbing the ladder is simply much harder for some people than others. Gloria Pritschet and Tobias Mixer's art installation 'Upward Mobility', featuring two parts of a ladder with a large gap in the middle, beautifully illustrates this point (Figure I.1; see Metsker 2012). For some people the rungs of the ladder are not as available or as tangible in the same way as for others: the top is placed out of reach. This can be as much about the social context of the time as, for example, the positon of a particular family within it. For instance, as I discuss in chapter 2, the chances of upward social mobility for working-class people in mid-twentieth-century Britain were far greater than for their parents – or for their children in the period since 1980 – due to the expansion and then the contraction of the welfare state and public sector. There was more 'room at the top' for that particular generation at that particular time and in that particular place.

In addition, the availability of material and psychological resources depends on social location. Whether you have the opportunity to touch a musical instrument, spend time practising it or becoming accomplished at it depends on the availability of the instrument and the demands on time as much as anything else (such as physiological facility, self-identity or available tuition). What Fischer and his colleagues term 'the triumvirate of deprivation, segregation and stigma' directly affects performance and life chances, and the realms of housing and education and work opportunities have to be considered together: 'what does a good education mean when there is little surety it will bring a good job? What does a good job mean when choice of neighbourhoods is restricted?' (Fischer *et al.* 1996: 185). As Stuart Hall put it, some people are positioned at the bottom of a number of different ladders and within a multiple series of disadvantages, in terms of, for example, ethnicity, single parenthood or technology (*The Stuart Hall Project* 2013).[3]

**FIGURE I.1** 'Upward Mobility' by Gloria Pritschet and Tobias Mixer, exhibited at *Grammar of the Elite*, The Gallery Project, Ann Arbor, Michigan, 2012. Photograph by Jennifer Metsker. Reproduced courtesy of the photographer, the artists and the Gallery Project.

I explore these permutations and intersections of social position and identity with meritocratic structures and discourse in chapter 2.

The fourth key problem with the contemporary ideology of meritocracy is its uncritical valorisation of particular forms of status, in the hierarchical ranking of professions and status it endorses. Certain professions are positioned at the top, but why they are there – and whether they should be there – tends to be less discussed. Why do singer or entrepreneur become roles to aspire to above those of vet or nurse? Why, today, as income disparity widens, are celebrity-based professions rising in ascribed status? What exactly is being 'made' when we 'make it'? And in what, and whose, interests is it being 'made' for? These are not questions that mainstream commercial or political culture like to ask today. The question of what exactly is being rewarded by social mobility is rarely posed.

The notion of 'escape' introduces an interconnected problem: contemporary meritocracy's frequent validation of upper-middle-class values as norms to aspire to and its rendering of working-class cultures as abject. The language of meritocracy is about moving upwards in financial and class terms, but whilst this may entail, for example, being better fed, it does not mean existing in a 'better' or 'happier' culture. Middle-class suburbs are not usually better places for socialising or connecting with a range of people than housing estates, for instance.[4] Contemporary neoliberal discourses of meritocracy, however, assume that all progressive movement must happen upwards and, in the process, contribute to the positioning of working-class cultures as the 'underclass', as abject zones and as lives to flee from. This is a tendency that has exacerbated since the 1970s under neoliberalism (Tyler 2013; Skeggs 2003; McKenzie 2015), which broadly speaking involves the promotion of corporate power, the marketisation of collective provision and the idea that competition is the organising principle for all areas of life.

The fifth key problem with the contemporary ideology of meritocracy, and the one which moves us into the territory of considering why it has such currency and power, is that it functions as an ideological myth to obscure and extend economic and social inequalities. Recent social-science research into meritocracy and social mobility has picked up on this issue. McNamee and Miller, for instance, have argued that, in America, 'meritocracy' is a word that is both inaccurate and harmful and that its use legitimises inequalities of power and privilege through 'claims that are demonstrably false' (McNamee and Miller 2009: 22). Their book's title *The Meritocracy Myth* has been used (with a slight variation) in a UK context by the political journalist James Bloodworth, whose short polemic *The Myth of Meritocracy* attacked increasing inequality in the UK (Bloodworth 2016). As we will see later, one of the key components of this ideological myth is how 'effort' is over-valued, and social and economic location is not considered or ignored (Khan 2010). The emphasis on effort is the element of meritocracy that has been expanded in recent years. An over-emphasis on merit obscures the unevenness of the social playing field, with its profound dis/advantages of parental wealth and social location. The neoliberal idea of meritocracy as enabling a fair system of social mobility is therefore both profoundly unfair and an ideological sleight of hand, working to justify a system based on greed and extensive structural injustice.

The dominant meaning of meritocracy in circulation today might therefore be broadly characterised as a potent blend of an essentialised and exclusionary notion of 'talent', competitive individualism and the need for social mobility. Neoliberal meritocracy promotes the idea of individualistic, competitive success, symbolised by the ladder of opportunity. This book analyses this particular cultural cocktail, by considering how the claims of meritocracy have worked and circulated in terms of political narrative and public discourse. It argues for abandoning this notion of the individual social ladder altogether and replacing it with the less divisive priorities of mutual progress and egalitarianism.

I explore the theoretical implications of the alternatives more fully in chapter 1 and the practical incarnations of such alternatives more fully in the conclusion. The rest of the book is taken up with a multifaceted analysis of meritocracy. This is partly because meritocracy is strangely under-theorised, and, when it is analysed, it is analysed in a profoundly uni-disciplinary fashion, having predominantly been the concern of academics in educational and social policy and political journalists. I suggest that, in order to understand its strength and potency, we need to draw on other disciplines and tools, on its cultural and political as well as economic and empirical dimensions. Meritocracy needs to be unpacked as an ideologically charged discourse which permeates so many areas from school to work to reality TV.

## Meritocracy as social system and as ideological discourse

It is useful to distinguish between two key forms of meritocracy. Meritocracy firstly refers to a social system which is based around the idea that individuals are responsible for working hard to activate their talent and thus one in which the majority will arrive at social positions for which they are suitable and appropriately rewarded. It has as its core tenets social mobility and equality of opportunity and is therefore legitimated by a very different conceptual structure from that of a social system based around economic and cultural redistribution. However, the uncomfortable fact is that those who 'achieve' pass on more privilege to their children, thus contributing to unequal social starting blocks. Even a 2010 OECD report, pointing out the statistically low levels of social mobility in the US and UK in comparison to the Nordic countries and Canada, concluded that its data showed how 'intergenerational social mobility reflects equality of opportunities' (OECD 2010: 2). Whilst social scientists argue over the details, particularly distinctions between income and occupation, they unequivocally concur that, for most working- and lower-middle-class people in the UK and the US the potential for social mobility has in fact declined over the past few decades (Savage *et al.* 2015: 187–207; Bukodi *et al.* 2015; Goldthorpe 2013; Goldthorpe and Jackson 2007).[5] It is therefore in part what is deemed to be a socially acceptable level of unevenness which either substantiates or threatens a 'meritocratic' order.

The form a meritocratic social system takes is contextually specific. For instance, it took a different form in the civil service examinations conducted in imperial China than in Britain in 1945 when Second World War social provision was expanded into the welfare state, and it takes a different form again in the contemporary education systems of Singapore (Elman 2013; Todd 2015; Talib and Fitzgerald 2015). A meritocratic social system cannot be divorced from an understanding of how it functions in connection with the contextual issues of economic and cultural redistribution and recognition (in terms of, for example, the roles assigned and enabled in terms of physical ability, gender or caste) and with how social success is demarcated and financially and culturally rewarded.

In a second, equally important sense, meritocracy needs to be understood as an ideological discourse, as a system of beliefs which constitute a general worldview and uphold particular power dynamics. This in turn brings us back to the classic 1970s debates on ideology and hegemony (Hall 1986; Grossberg and Hall 1986; Laclau 2002; Lash 2007). As I have discussed elsewhere (Littler 2017) 'ideology' is a charged term: from its original eighteenth-century designation by Desutt de Tracey to mean 'the science of ideas', through Napoleon's influential use of it as a pejorative term, it became adopted by Marx to understand how social relationships work to legitimise capitalism (Williams 1983; Marx and Engels 1987). This meaning of ideology was extended by Althusser and Gramsci to consider its ritual and material functions, psychological effects and role in cultural power struggles (Althusser 2014; Gramsci 2005). Analysing ideology could therefore be used to understand both institutional practice and discursive norms. In their work, greater attention was paid to the instabilities of ideology: to how struggles over meaning were contests to secure hegemony or to secure more dominant forms of social, political and economic power and control. These elements are very useful for understanding meritocracy.

The term 'discourse' in its cultural rather than linguistic sense was used by social theorists, particularly Michel Foucault, from the 1980s, to bypass some of the problems involved in the implication of 'false consciousness' that ideology carried, particularly when crudely applied (Foucault 1981; Hall 1997; Mills 1997). 'Discourse' meant a set of shared meanings in a historically specific 'discursive formation', and it could be conveyed through institutions, imagery and behaviour as well as language. Particular discourses lay claims to truth and work through institutions to set the boundaries of acceptable behaviour. Yet this usage also lost its connection to and stake in understanding how political power dynamics and vested interests were reproduced (thus chiming with this apolitical critical era of postmodern relativism). Here then I tend to use the term 'ideological discourse' in the same spirit that cultural studies, in its CCCS-derived manifestation, implicitly tended to: in order to retain the power of both of these critical terms whilst being alert to the reductive possibilities of each, and using them to offset each other's limitations (Hall 1986; Grossberg and Hall 1986; McRobbie 1978). When I use the phrases 'meritocratic ideology' or 'meritocratic discourse' in this book it is in the vein of this critical spirit and set of theoretical writings.

Crucially, the meaning of meritocracy as an ideological discourse is contextually specific. The project of this book is to map some of its different key contemporary manifestations, and so chapter 1 develops a schema of different contextual moments, explaining how 'social democratic meritocracy' is a very different formation from 'neoliberal meritocracy'. This schema is, of course, not conclusive and is geographically restricted by my own resources and knowledge. But what considering meritocracy as an ideological discourse also does is to enable us to analyse how ideas come to gain traction and to hold sway, and how a social system can be built and endorsed around it: because meritocracy as a social system and meritocracy as an ideological discourse are intimately connected. For instance, most contemporary large-scale sociological surveys of public attitudes in the UK indicate that whilst the majority of the public believes that society is unequal, they also believe there is enough meritocratic opportunity for people to get on if they really want to. Factors such as family wealth and ethnicity in the 2009 British Social Attitudes survey were regarded as important to getting ahead by only 14% and 8% respectively, a drop from 21% and 16% in 1987 (BSA 2009). By contrast, 84% of the interviewed public believed that hard work was important, and 71% believed that ambition was. In later findings carried out for the Joseph Rowntree Foundation, 69% of the public agreed with the statement: 'Opportunities are not equal in Britain today, but there is enough opportunity for virtually everyone to get on in life if they really want to. It comes down to the individual and how much you are motivated'. Only 14% disagreed (Bamfield and Horton 2009: 24).

In other words, in both surveys the majority of people interviewed thought society was unequal but fair, socially mobile and meritocratic enough for the majority to get ahead if they wanted to. Similarly, a 2008 US-based survey indicated that two-thirds of Americans agreed that people are rewarded for intelligence and skill, but only one fifth thought that having a wealthy family was important for getting ahead (McNamee and Miller 2009: 2–3). All these surveys are historically specific, however; and, in the later UK survey, carried out on the cusp of the financial crisis, there were already signs that the degree of acceptable wealth disparity was becoming breached, with excessively large incomes receiving more condemnation. These fluctuating attitudes indicate the imbrication between meritocracy as an ideological discourse and the wider social structure. They also indicate an increasing contemporary dissatisfaction with meritocracy as a persuasive ideological discourse in the Global North since the financial crisis, an issue borne out by a recent rapid increase in reference to, commentary on and questioning of the subject (Hennessey 2015; Hattenstone 2016; Bloodworth 2016; Frank 2016).

This book shows how different constituencies have been encouraged to adopt meritocratic ideas for a range of historical and cultural reasons, and how they have been persuasive (or not). For instance, chapter 4 shows how those particularly likely to believe in the worth of meritocracy are those sections of the super-rich who have experienced upward social mobility, unlike vast swathes of the population. Chapter 6 discusses how new mothers are incited to put faith in neoliberal meritocratic solutions due to a combination of their presentation as feminist, their mediated ubiquity and the paucity of other viable solutions. What can be termed 'the cultural pull of meritocratic hope' is therefore produced by highly specific vested interests, the successful affective resonance of meritocratic narratives, and the limited range of available options in a given social context.

Considering how the cultural pull of meritocracy is expressed in its various incarnations across media forms is therefore a key part of this project. But equally I am not interested in mediated meritocracy as a free-standing entity sealed off from politics and geography and society. I want to explore how meritocracy operates across a number of interconnected realms to get a better sense of what it is doing and what it means. This for me is the strength of the approach of cultural studies: to consider how 'everything connects to everything else' in order to evaluate the power dynamics that constitute meritocracy. This book therefore uses a multifaceted, transdisciplinary cultural studies approach to analyse how the contemporary discourse of neoliberal meritocracy works and how it has come to achieve dominance. The analysis of this book will nonetheless be partial and specific – as all works are – but the aim is to provide a different and multifaceted lens to understand the uses of this concept.

## How this book is organised

This book is split into two halves. Part I explores some of the different genealogies of meritocracy in terms of changes in social and cultural theory, identity politics and political discourse. Part II considers case studies which present and disrupt meritocratic myths of mobility and popular parables of progress. These explore gender and work (by analysing the figure of the 'mumpreneur'); racialisation in media production (by analysing the 'Damonsplaining' incident that blew up in 2015); and different media representations of the ultra-rich. Whilst the chapters can all be read in fairly self-contained form, the narrative and theorisation also builds throughout.

Part I of the book therefore explores meritocracy's contemporary genealogies. Chapter 1 begins this process by discussing the complexity of meritocracy's historical and geographical lineages and examining some contemporary definitions of the term. The bulk of the chapter is concerned with the changing uses of the concept since the word was introduced in academic social theory in the mid-twentieth century. It traces the journey of the word in English from its first use by radical industrial sociologist Alan Fox as a wholly negative term, through Michael Young's affably disparaging deployment of the word to describe a dystopia in his 1958 bestseller *The Rise of the Meritocracy*, to Hannah Arendt's critique of meritocracy in the context of UK education. It then charts Daniel Bell's approving adoption of the concept in the 1970s, its popularity in the new-right think tanks of the 1980s and its significant presence in the work of sociologist Anthony Giddens in the late 1980s and early 1990s. For whilst the *volte-face* of the term's meaning – like Michael Young's notorious claim that later politicians who used the term approvingly had not read his book – have been fairly widely cited, surprisingly scant attention has actually been paid to how and why the connotations of the term mutated to such a degree (Dench 2006; Young 2001).

The second chapter turns its attention to the idea of 'rising up' the social hierarchy in relation to the structural, yet frequently disavowed, disadvantages of gender, race and class. It terms this disavowed disadvantage 'the egalitarian deficit' to indicate how those not at the top of the social pyramid are often doubly or trebly disadvantaged by neoliberal narratives of meritocracy whilst being particularly incited to climb it. Taking a broader historical view, it considers the reasons both for such parables of progress and the intersectional inconsistencies they tend to hide, in the process drawing on a wide range of examples from *Mad Men* to the civil service. The chapter argues that a problematic but quasi-democratic post-war language and practice of egalitarianism was filleted and marketised for corporate gain, popularising the idea of the 'level playing field' whilst perpetuating many problems of inbuilt and structural prejudices in terms of race, class, gender and ability. In other words, discourses of post-racism, post-sexism and what could be termed 'post-classism' – the idea that inequalities of race, gender and class are a thing of the past – have over the past few decades worked hand in hand with neoliberal meritocracy to fuel each other and give each other strength. The chapter also discusses the selective shifts in the characteristics of this formation in recent years, from disavowing the feminist and civil-rights movement to attempting to channel it and poach its imagery in the service of a reinvigorated neoliberal settlement. This formation identifies an egalitarian deficit as a 'meritocratic deficit' and prescribes not equality but individualising, neoliberal capitalism. The book describes this discourse as offering what I call 'neoliberal justice narratives'.

Chapter 3 considers how the idea of meritocracy has come to be mobilised as a key feature of contemporary neoliberal rhetoric and public discourse. It illustrates this process by examining the resonance of the term in relatively recent British political discourse: from a Thatcherite anti-establishment version, through the explicit Blairite adoption of the concept as a means to legitimise a competitive and individualistic ethos, to its recent life in the British coalition government and Conservative discourse as part of David Cameron's 'Aspiration Nation'. It then considers the different discourse around 'Aspiration for All' offered by the opposition Labour Party and the xenophobic demotic populism mobilised by the far (and near) right. The chapter examines the differences and continuities in political discourse in relation to meritocracy. In doing so, it provides an account of how what the book terms 'meritocratic feeling' (drawing on Raymond Williams' work on 'structures of feeling', alongside more recent work on affect) has taken various forms in different political regimes of neoliberal culture.

Part II of the book, 'Popular Parables', uses case studies to explore in detail the contemporary workings of neoliberal meritocracy alongside its

14  Introduction

failures and disruptions. Chapter 4 asks: How do plutocratic elites use discourses of meritocracy to maintain and reproduce their privilege? It considers this question by identifying particular motifs and themes deployed in the mediated presentation of the super-rich and characterising them as particular social types. These are, first, the 'normcore plutocrat', when elites are presented as 'just like us'; second, the 'kind parent', when they are positioned as the benevolent custodians of society; and third, the 'luxury-flaunter', when they show off their material excess. The chapter traces these motifs across a range of media, considering examples such as celebrity CEOs, the rehabilitation of the royal family, *Rich Kids of Instagram, Downton Abbey* and *The King's Speech* and analysing them in relation to changes in both the demographics of the international super-rich and to the fluctuating meanings of 'meritocracy'. It argues that in such populist modes of presentation, elites are actively mobilising the widely felt injustices of 'post-democracy' and rechannelling them for their own benefit and that plutocratic elites believe in neoliberal meritocracy because they are the ones benefitting from it most. The chapter concludes by considering how the rich have variously presented themselves after capitalist crises through an analysis of various historical versions of the film *Annie*. Whereas plutocratic excesses were curbed in the post-war period, today they have not been: the super-rich have been permitted to flourish, which makes it much more pressing for them to appear 'just like us'.

Chapter 5 considers neoliberal meritocracy's racialisations. It uses the specific case study of the brief 2015 media furore over an incident on *Project Greenlight*, a US reality-TV talent show programme where film-makers compete for the chance to make their first feature film and thus break into an industry that is notoriously difficult to access for those without wealth and connections. During one episode of *Project Greenlight* the white film actor Matt Damon interrupted the black film producer Effie Brown to explain the meaning of diversity to her. Damon's comments were widely ridiculed on Twitter through the hashtag #Damonsplaining. This chapter has several components: first, drawing on David Theo Goldberg's work on the post-racial, it discusses the racialisation of merit as an abstract category; second, it considers these processes in relation to the ascribed merit of cultural products; third, it relates this incident to the racialised exclusions of cultural production in the media industries; and finally, it analyses the viral status of this event. The chapter reads the Damonsplaining incident as both an arch example of a discourse of neoliberal post-racial meritocracy and also of its rupture. In doing so, it explores in detail the question: How is meritocracy racialised in contemporary neoliberal culture and what are the meanings of its disruption?

Chapter 6 uses its analysis of the 'mumpreneur' – a mother who becomes an entrepreneur, starting a business at home while her kids crawl under the kitchen table – as a springboard into discussing the gendering of neoliberal meritocracy and its structuring of academic texts as well as working lives, popular culture and social possibilities. It opens by considering how the relationship between gender, work and childcare has, for a long time, been spectacularly inequitable and how, since the 2008 financial crisis, these old inequalities have been situated within a newly challenging economic setting. Being a mumpreneur is presented as a solution for these combined difficulties: offering self-realisation through entrepreneurialism, a solution for the problems of childcare and the sop for the inadequacies of the labour market. Yet it often works to heap unmanageable pressure on women despite and through its narrative of liberation. The chapter argues that the mumpreneur predominantly operates through a motif of what I call 'desperate success': a motif and a coping strategy which often negates the potential for more collective forms of co-operation that were raised by second-wave feminism. Later, it moves to consider what this example reveals about wider genderings of entrepreneurialism as a category (in academia as well as a lived gendered reality), discussing recent work on neoliberalism alongside earlier work on gender and enterprise coming out of cultural studies in the 1980s and 1990s. Finally, it analyses the specificity of the contemporary 'post-post-Fordist' conjunction between gender and enterprise by following the mumpreneur online and examining the now seemingly indispensable dynamic of the 'branded self'. The chapter ends by considering what discourses and alternatives might be useful resources to find routes out of the mumpreneur's pragmatic yet constrained worldview.

Having attempted to track some of meritocracy's contemporary journeys and meanings, the conclusion considers what the alternatives are. It disaggregates the concept of meritocracy to see what might be worth salvaging. Then it considers the contemporary status of meritocracy in terms of its ideological fluctuation, discussing which constituencies no longer believe in neoliberal meritocracy and why.

I have been working on this subject off and on for the past decade, because it has seemed to me that while meritocratic ideology is one of the key drivers of late capitalism, its historical mutations, its cultural forms and its emotional pull have not been very extensively analysed. It is a curiously formative and yet under-theorised ideological engine of late capitalism.

However, as I have indicated, today it is also more noticeably under attack: whilst writing this book there has also been an increase in the number of voices critiquing the idea and practice of meritocracy. It is becoming much more commonplace for media articles and politicians to mention, or even to foreground, its problems: that meritocracy is not working, or is problematic, is now more widely acknowledged (*The Economist* 2013; Hayes 2012; Bloodworth 2016; Frank 2016). This is because the aftermath of the 2008 crisis has overwhelmingly worked to bolster the position of financial elites, rather than to move toward greater equality, and thus, in many ways, the neoliberal meritocratic dream has perhaps never looked so tenuous.

At the same time, capitalism is persistent, and, as I outline in chapters 2 and 3, new versions of neoliberal meritocracy are emerging, both in the shape of right-wing populist nationalisms and through forms of neoliberal meritocracy that selectively draw on the rhetoric of social justice movements or 'neoliberal justice narratives'. From the billionaire Donald Trump's claims to speak for the hardworking oppressed masses in the US, to Prime Minister Theresa May's vision of making Britain 'the great meritocracy of the world' whilst re-introducing educational segregation through grammar schools, the centrality of narratives of meritocracy is being aggressively re-established in new guises. The active refashioning of these stories make this a crucial moment to examine the meritocratic dream in all its variations: to expand our critical understanding of what it means, and the abuses to which this term is put, in order to contribute to reshaping popular narratives around it and working toward more egalitarian societies.

## Notes

1. Arendt 2006: 176–177.
2. The quote has been extensively reproduced, but I have not yet been able to find the original source.
3. *The Stuart Hall Project* shows a clip of Stuart Hall on a TV discussion programme. He says: 'We can now begin to identify a range of different processes which do tend in particular kinds of societies to deliver a certain number of people at the bottom of a number of different ladders. Some of them are technological, some of them have to do with race and ethnicity, some of them have to do with single parenthood. Although the causes are multiple, what seems to be important is that they deliver a certain number of people to a multiple series of disadvantages. And then, the question of permanence comes in: how on earth do people like that get themselves out? Well, they don't get themselves out of being stuck in that way by being thrifty or getting on their bikes or any of those things' (*The Stuart Hall Project* 2013).
4. As author Zadie Smith pointed out on *Start the Week* (BBC 2013). Thanks to Doreen Massey for alerting me to this programme and discussing these issues with me.

5 While social-mobility statistics are continually contested and in process, the majority of quantitative analysis has pointed to a decline in the possibility for upward social mobility for working and lower-middle classes (particularly men) in the more unequal countries in the Global North. Research by Jo Blanden and her colleagues in the UK, for instance, examining incomes of people in comparison to that of their parents found a clear decline in income mobility between cohorts born in 1958 and 1970 (Blanden *et al.* 2004). Other work, particularly in teams including John Goldthorpe, has complicated what they see as an overall 'decline narrative', but their arguments still end up concluding that opportunities for the working class are declining. For particular attention to gender analysis, see Bukodi *et al.* 2015; I discuss the significance of this in relation to meritocracy in chapters 2 and 6.

## References

Althusser, Louis (2014) *On the Reproduction of Capitalism: Ideology and Ideological State Apparatuses*. London: Verso.

Arendt, Hannah (2006) *Between Past and Future: Eight Exercises in Political Thought*. London: Penguin Books.

Bamfield, Louise, and Tim Horton (2009) *Understanding Attitudes to Tackling Economic Inequality*. London: Joseph Rowntree Foundation, www.jrf.org.uk/report/understanding-attitudes-tackling-economic-inequality. Accessed 1 December 2016.

BBC (2013) *Start the Week*, Radio 4, 24 June.

Blanden, Jo, Alissa Goodman, Paul Gregg and Stephen Machin (2004) 'Changes in Intergenerational Mobility in Britain', in Miles Corak (ed.) *Generational Income Mobility in North America and Europe*. Cambridge: Cambridge University Press, pp. 122–146.

Bloodworth, James (2016) *The Myth of Meritocracy: Why Working-Class Kids still Get Working-Class Jobs*. London: Biteback Publishing.

BSA (2009) *British Social Attitudes 27th Report*. London: National Centre for Social Research.

Bukodi, Erzsébet, John H. Goldthorpe, Lorraine Waller and Jouni Kuha (2015) 'The Mobility Problem in Britain: New Findings from the Analysis of Birth Cohort Data', *British Journal of Sociology* 66(1) pp. 93–118.

Dench, Geoff (ed.) (2006) *The Rise and Rise of Meritocracy*. Oxford: Wiley-Blackwell.

Dorling, Danny (2011) *Injustice: Why Social Inequality Still Persists*, Kindle edn. Bristol: Policy Press.

*The Economist* (2013) 'Repairing the Rungs on the Ladder: How to Prevent a Virtuous Meritocracy Entrenching Itself at the Top', 9 February, www.economist.com/news/leaders/21571417-how-prevent-virtuous-meritocracy-entrenching-itself-top-repairing-rungs. Accessed 1 December 2016.

Elman, Benjamin A. (2013) *Civil Examinations and Meritocracy in Late Imperial China*. Boston: Harvard University Press.

Fischer, Claude S., Michael Hout, Martín Sánchez Jankowski, Samuel R. Lucas, Ann Swidler and Kim Voss (1996) *Inequality by Design: Cracking the Bell Curve Myth*. Princeton: Princeton University Press.

Foucault, Michel (1981) 'The Order of Discourse', in Robert Young (ed.), *Untying the Text: A Post-Structuralist Reader*. London: Routledge, pp. 48–78.

Frank, Thomas (2016) *Success and Luck: Good Fortune and the Myth of Meritocracy*. Princeton: Princeton University Press.

Goldthorpe, John H. (2013) 'Understanding – and Misunderstanding – Social Mobility in Britain: The Entry of the Economists, the Confusion of Politicians and the Limits of Educational Policy', *Journal of Social Policy* 42(3) pp. 431–450.

Goldthorpe, John H., and M. Jackson (2007) 'Intergenerational Class Mobility in Contemporary Britain: Political Concerns and Empirical Findings', *British Journal of Sociology* 58 pp. 526–546.

Gramsci, Antonio (2005) *Selections from the Prison Notebooks*, trans. Quintin Hoare and Geoffrey Nowell-Smith. London: Lawrence & Wishart.

Grossberg, Lawrence, and Stuart Hall (1986) 'On Postmodernism and Articulation: An Interview with Stuart Hall', in David Morley and Kuan-Hsing Chen (eds), *Stuart Hall: Critical Dialogues in Cultural Studies*. London: Routledge, pp. 131–150.

Hall, Stuart (1986) 'The Problem of Ideology: Marxism without Guarantees', in David Morley and Kuan-Hsing Chen (eds), *Stuart Hall: Critical Dialogues in Cultural Studies*. London: Routledge, pp. 24–45.

Hall, Stuart (1997) 'The Work of Representation', in Stuart Hall (ed.), *Representation: Cultural Representation and Signifying Practices*. London: Sage, pp. 41–63.

Hattenstone, Simon (2016) 'Is the New Meritocracy a Sham?', *The Guardian*, 10 August, www.theguardian.com/society/2016/aug/10/is-the-new-meritocracy-a-sham. Accessed 1 December 2016.

Hayes, Christopher (2012) *Twilight of the Elites: America After Meritocracy*. New York: Crown Publishing Group.

Hennessey, Peter (2015) *Establishment and Meritocracy*. London: Haus Publishing.

Hickman, Rebecca (2009) *In Pursuit of Egalitarianism: And why Social Mobility cannot get Us There*. London: Compass.

Hudson, Phillip (2004) 'Analysis: Latham's Ladder: Eight Rungs make a Right', *The Age*, 1 February, www.theage.com.au/articles/2004/01/31/1075340894078.html?from=storyrhs. Accessed 1 December 2016.

James, Wilmot (2012) 'The Language of Meritocracy', *Inside Politics*, 5 March, https://inside-politics.org/2012/03/05/the-language-of-meritocracy. Accessed 1 December 2016.

Khan, Shamus (2010) *Privilege: The Making of an Adolescent Elite at St Paul's School*. Princeton: Princeton University Press.

Laclau, Ernesto (2002) *On Populist Reason*. London: Verso.

Lash, Scott (2007) 'Power after Hegemony: Cultural Studies in Mutation?', *Theory, Culture and Society* 24(3) pp. 55–78.

Littler, Jo (2017) 'Ideology', in Laurie Ouellette and Jonathan Gray (eds), *Keywords for Media Studies*. New York: NYU Press, pp. 98–101.

McKenzie, Lisa (2015) *Getting By: Estates, Class and Culture in Austerity Britain*. Bristol: Policy Press.

McNamee, Stephen J., and Robert K. Miller (2009) *The Meritocracy Myth*. Lanham: Rowman & Littlefield.

McRobbie, Angela (1978) 'Jackie: An Ideology of Adolescent Femininity', CCCS Stencilled Occasional Paper, University of Birmingham, http://epapers.bham.ac.uk/1808. Accessed 1 December 2016.

Marmot, Michael (2004) *Status Syndrome: How your Place on the Social Gradient Directly Affects your Health*. London: Bloomsbury.

Marx, Karl, and Friedrich Engels (1987) *The German Ideology*. London: Lawrence & Wishart.

May, Theresa (2016) 'Britain, the great meritocracy: Prime Minister's speech', 9 September. https://www.gov.uk/government/speeches/britain-the-great-meritocracy-prime-ministers-speech. Accessed 1 January 2017.

Metsker, Jennifer (2012) 'Lost Ladder – Middle Section Broken – Last Seen 1967', *Art Hopper*, 31 October, http://arthopper.org/lost-ladder-middle-section-broken-last-seen-1967. Accessed 1 December 2016.

Mills, Sara (1997) *Discourse*. London: Routledge.

Obama, Barack (2013) 'Inaugural Address of Barack Obama', 31 January, www.whitehouse.gov/the-press-office/2013/01/21/inaugural-address-president-barack-obama. Accessed 1 December 2016.

OECD (2010) *Economic Policy Reforms: Going for Growth*, www.oecd.org/eco/growth/economicpolicyreformsgoingforgrowth2010.htm. Accessed 1 December 2016.

Piketty, Thomas (2013) *Capital in the Twenty-First Century*. Cambridge, MA: Belknap Press.

Savage, Mike, Niall Cunningham, Fiona Devine, Sam Friedman, Daniel Laurison, Lisa McKenzie, Andrew Miles, Helene Snee and Paul Wakeling (2015) *Social Class in the Twenty First Century*. Milton Keynes: Pelican.

Skeggs, Beverley (2003) *Class, Self, Culture*. London: Routledge.

Soko, Mills (2015) 'South Africa Needs a Meritocratic Civil Service, not a Political One', *Rand Daily Mail*, 14 May, www.rdm.co.za/politics/2015/05/14/sa-needs-a-meritocratic-civil-service-not-a-political-one. Accessed 1 December 2016.

*The Stuart Hall Project* (2013) dir. John Akomfrah. London: BFI.

Talib, Nadira, and Richard Fitzgerald (2015) 'Inequality as Meritocracy: The Use of the Metaphor of Diversity and the Value of Inequality within Singapore's Meritocratic Education System', *Critical Discourse Studies* 12(4) pp. 445–462.

Todd, Selina (2015) *The People: The Rise and Fall of the Working Class, 1910–2010*. London: John Murray.

Trump, Donald (2017) 'Congress Speech (full text) 1 March, CNN Politics transcript'. http://edition.cnn.com/2017/02/28/politics/donald-trump-speech-transcript-full-text/ Accessed 10 March 2017.

Tyler, Imogen (2013) *Revolting Subjects: Social Abjection and Resistance in Neoliberal Britain*. London: Zed Books.
Wilkinson, Richard, and Kate Pickett (2010) *The Spirit Level: Why Equality is Better for Everyone*. London: Penguin.
Williams, Raymond (1958) 'Democracy or Meritocracy?', *Manchester Guardian*, 30 October, p. 10.
Williams, Raymond (1983) *Keywords: A Vocabulary of Culture and Society*. Oxford: Oxford University Press.
Young, Michael (1994) *The Rise of the Meritocracy* [1958], 2nd revd edn. London: Transaction Publishers.
Young, Michael (2001) 'Down with Meritocracy', *The Guardian*, 29 June, www.theguardian.com/politics/2001/jun/29/comment. Accessed 15 December 2016.

# PART I
Genealogies

# 1
# MERITOCRACY'S GENEALOGIES IN SOCIAL THEORY

> The idea of meritocracy may have many virtues, but clarity is not one of them.
>
> *Amartya Sen*[1]

## Never start with the dictionary

> Government by persons selected on the basis of merit in a competitive educational system; a society so governed; a ruling or influential class of educated people. Hence **meritocrat** *sb* and *a.*; **meritocratic** *a.*
>
> *(Oxford English Dictionary 2001: vol. IX, p. 635)*

Lecturers often tell students never to start with a dictionary definition. They do this for a reason: the temptation to treat dictionary definitions as immutable empirical truths flung from a faceless, ahistorical summit of scientific rationality. But these definitions are also gravitated towards because they are attempts to condense shared understandings of what a word means at the time the dictionary was put together. When Raymond Williams produced his book *Keywords*, he solved this problem by taking significant words in everyday use, situating them in broader contexts and tracing the longer evolutions of their meaning across time and space (Williams 1983). 'Meritocracy', unfortunately, is not one of the words examined by Williams in *Keywords* (although, as I discuss below, he did have some very powerful and important points to make about meritocracy in a book review). We will therefore have to do some of this genealogical work ourselves.

It is only too easy to see from the dictionary entry above why meritocracy is such a charged, 'of the zeitgeist' subject. Just look at the issues it connects to: the question of who governs society, the issue of a small group having influence over the many, competitiveness in general and within education in particular, the thorny problem of what it means to have 'merit' and the promise (and, less conspicuously, the pitfalls) of social mobility. These are core themes and problems of our time. Noticeably, however, other dictionary definitions have slightly different emphases. Some foreground meritocracy's emphasis on individual advancement through wider social structures. To take the widely used online Free Dictionary's current version:

Meritocracy:

1. A system in which advancement is based on individual ability or achievement.
2.
    a. A group of leaders or officeholders selected on the basis of individual ability or achievement.
    b. Leadership by such a group.

*(Free Dictionary 2016)*

Here meritocracy is a system structured around advancement of people who are selected on the basis of individual achievement; and, as I show throughout this book, its emphasis on the *individual* is important. The '-ocracy' of 'meritocracy' derives from the Greek word for government, and, as this definition illustrates, the word can with modifications ('meritocrat') refer to an elite group of people who govern and who have been able to arrive at such a position 'on the basis of individual ability or achievement'. Whereas 'a meritocracy' refers to a social system where people are selected by some undefined source according to their merit, 'the meritocrats' can also mean an elite group of rulers who have risen up through this system. There is an immediate palpable contrast and chasm between the elite cadre of rulers and the 'open' system of access to that elite, a gap that is bridged by the image of travelling up the ladder.

As we have seen already, 'meritocracy' has been a word used to describe both a social system and a set of discourses, cultural meanings, associations, ideas, judgements, presumptions and emotions about it. These definitions and distinctions (much like terms like 'government' or 'economy') can be difficult to separate given the extent to which they have shaped each other. Furthermore, as this chapter discusses, contemporary definitions of meritocracy often rest on some problematic foundations in terms of what they cite as the first use of the word. As Amartya Sen wrote, 'the idea of meritocracy may have many virtues, but clarity is not one of them' (Sen 2000: 7).

In the introduction I suggested that it is useful to separate the meaning of the social system from meritocracy as an ideological discourse and to rigorously contextualise both of them. This chapter discusses the slippage between meritocracy-as-a-social system and meritocracy-as-a-discourse in a number of ways. It considers how meritocracy has changed in meaning, tracing its etymology, mapping the stunning U-turns the word has undertaken in its journey from negative slur to positive axiom of modern life. It suggests that particular conceptual categories might be created to help understand the mutations of the word. To these ends this chapter traces a journey from what it terms the 'socialist critique of meritocracy' through 'social democratic meritocracy' and then finally to 'neoliberal meritocracy'. It traces these historical formations through the usage of the word in social theory, from Alan Fox, Hannah Arendt, Michael Young, Daniel Bell and Anthony Giddens. Social theory does not exist in a vacuum, and so the discussion gestures to the lines of traffic between these writers and the wider cultural and political climate that they helped form and which formed them, contexts which are explored in more detail in later chapters. But to begin with it is useful to consider what happened to meritocracy before it was coined as a word.

## Early genealogies, histories and geographies

The meanings of 'meritocracy' were, of course, not just born with the invention of this word in English in the 1950s. As a complex concept it can be connected to much longer historical and geographical genealogies, an extensive discussion of which is beyond the scope of this book. The discourse and social systems this book discusses are primarily those which have been mobilised in the West or the Global North and particularly as manifest in relatively recent Anglo-European culture, with a pronounced bias towards my own standpoint as a British citizen. However, as we have already begun to see, this discourse has a wider resonance beyond this zone. What this book terms a recognisable discourse of neoliberal meritocracy has been noted in South Africa, Singapore and South Korea, with pronounced specific geocultural variations (James 2012; Soko 2015). For instance, the language of diversity, meritocracy and opportunity have been used to help entrench economic inequality in Singapore's educational system and its wider society between the 1970s and the present, despite and alongside its novel attempts to tackle racialised forms of discrimination (Quinn Moore 2000; Talib and Fitzgerald 2015). In terms of wider histories of the concept, we might cite a number of different international examples, such as the early example of the exams introduced in the civil service in imperial China providing 'access for all' to the profession (Elman 2013). And at the same time the meaning of meritocracy, as I discuss it here, has been shaped by Western histories and values which themselves were shaped through past and present transnational imperialisms.

In the West the expansion of the potential for 'social mobility' has been a key feature of ideological narratives, if not of widespread social reality, in different ways and forms ever since the establishment of industrial capitalism and the Enlightenment, which emphasised the supposedly equal potential of those it qualified as 'human'. For instance, after the Paris Commune of 1871 – which overthrew the French monarchy – was crushed, the re-established republic announced that it was now a regime in which 'careers were open to talents' (Ross 2002).[2] These developments were echoed in the British Victorian self-help tradition, most famously represented in the bestselling books by Samuel Smiles (e.g. *Self-Help*, 1859). Smiles had been a Chartist but later jettisoned his commitment to socialism in favour of an enthusiastic embrace of capitalism and the Protestant work ethic and the perceived potential of the individual to pull themselves up by their bootstraps (Lindemann 2013: 121–122; Hobsbawm 1988: 255). The gradual expansion of the democratic franchise and educational provision in the UK in the nineteenth and early twentieth centuries was also justified and rendered acceptable to conservatives and capitalists on the basis that it would facilitate the movement of a small pool of talented people into the Establishment, and into the capitalist class, rather than on the basis of increasing equality (Todd 2015).

In the US, where '[p]eople understand the idea of the American Dream as the fulfilment of the promise of meritocracy' (McNamee and Miller 2009: 2) a similar set of tenets was mobilised. The basis of the American Dream was that, as Thomas Jefferson famously put it, an 'aristocracy of talent and virtue' was replacing the aristocracy of birth that characterised a degenerate European social order. From this perspective, rejecting aristocratic hereditary privilege and striving through the Protestant work ethic meant 'freedom', and it was exactly this shake-up of the European social order and the break with feudalism that so struck the French diplomat, historian and political scientist Alexis de Tocqueville who wrote about it in his book *Democracy in America* (De Tocqueville 1994).

A narrative of social mobility enabling a talented few to rise to the top has then been a discourse which is extremely compatible with capitalism for a couple of centuries. Indeed a dominant strand of the Western liberal capitalist tradition is that we are 'taught to scorn equality of property whilst aspiring to equality of condition', as Steve Cross put it (Cross and Littler 2010). This division is reflected in how the phrases 'equality of opportunity' and 'equality of outcome' became political terms. 'Equality of opportunity' became synonymous with liberal capitalism, and 'equality of outcome' became associated with socialism (Schaar 1997). To some extent these terms echo classic sociological theory. 'Equality of opportunity' echoes Emile Durkheim's idea of a society providing 'free space for all merits': that the most social harmony will be achieved if people can find work according to their natural ability (Durkheim 2013). 'Equality of outcome' echoes Marx's emphasis on dissecting capitalism's exploitations to argue for equality in distribution of wealth, a theory taken up across the wide political spectrum on the left, from vicious authoritarian communists through social democrats to libertarian anarchists (Marx and Engels 2004).

In general, 'equality of opportunity' has been used by right-wing and liberal or neoliberal governments. 'Equality of outcome' is a left-wing idea, although it is not a term which has been used rhetorically in the same way as 'equality of opportunity' and it has little if any popular resonance. Indeed, politicians who are actually arguing for 'equality of outcome' have mainly tended simply to use the language of 'equality', which has also blurred the debate. In the neoliberal era formerly left-wing parties have switched sides: an important strand of the New Labour government in the UK of the 1990s (which Margaret Thatcher described as her greatest success) was jettisoning the idea of equality of outcome in favour of equality of opportunity, as we will see in the next chapter. 'Opportunity' can sound excitingly open and undetermined; 'outcome' can sound fairly defined and final. In part what this book does is to examine how this language of equality of opportunity has been used to justify rampant and increasing social inequality; and, whilst arguing for equality of outcome in terms of greater parity of material resources and expenditure of effort, it also argues that it is crucial to both factor in, and to mobilise, the diversity, malleability and variability of flourishing that 'opportunity' has historically been associated with.

## Ladders and level playing fields

As we saw earlier, the 'ladder of opportunity' is a key metaphor for meritocracy. At times the ladder is also used metonymically to stand for the whole of society. In the collaborative sociological study *Inequality by Design*, the authors discuss how, whereas some societies or nations can be understood as being short, broad ladders, with lots of room for many people all the way to the top, other societies (particularly the US and South Africa) have tall, narrowing ladders: ladders with vast distances between top and bottom rungs (Fischer *et al.* 1996: 7, 12). A connected problem of the long social ladder is that once people get to the top they tend to pass on their privilege to their children, as I discuss in the conclusion. This 'social ladder' imagery also has a resonance in imperialistic accounts of development, whereby 'developed' countries are placed at the top of the global social ladder and 'other' or 'undeveloped' countries below them (Kothari 2005).

It is therefore important to remind ourselves that this key emblem or motif of individual people going up single ladders is historically and contextually specific. There is an interesting resonance here in the evolution of the board game Snakes and Ladders. The earliest examples known are Hindu, Jain and Islamic versions from India, Nepal and Tibet, where they were developed as religious instruction games (Parlett 1999; Topsfield 2006a, 2006b). Figure 1.1 is a Jain version, 'Gyanbazi', from either Gujarat or Rajasthan in the late nineteenth century.[3] The pavilion at the top represents the heavens, where the liberated beings live together. There is no supreme creator god: Jains, like Buddhists and Hindus, believe in a cycle of birth and rebirth influenced by the effects of good and bad deeds and attitudes. The goal is for people to move past the many snakes (symbolising bad behaviour) and to arrive, through good behaviour, at the pavilion at the top.

In later nineteenth-century versions, British imperialism in India resulted in the game being translated into a game of Christian-capitalist moral instruction.[4] In, for example, a British design produced around 1900 and manufactured in Germany, 'Robbery' leads down a snake to a beating, 'Strike while the iron is hot' results in 'Forging ahead', and 'Punctuality' leads up a ladder to 'Opulence' (Figure 1.2). By this stage, 'Opulence' is good.[5] The goal of the game is to reach the 'Scroll of Fame', a zone featuring a list of people well known for their wealth, hard work, genius and virtue, including nurse Florence Nightingale, scientist Isaac Newton and banker-philanthropist George Peabody. This nineteenth-century version is clearly shaped through British imperialism and what C.B. Macpherson termed the

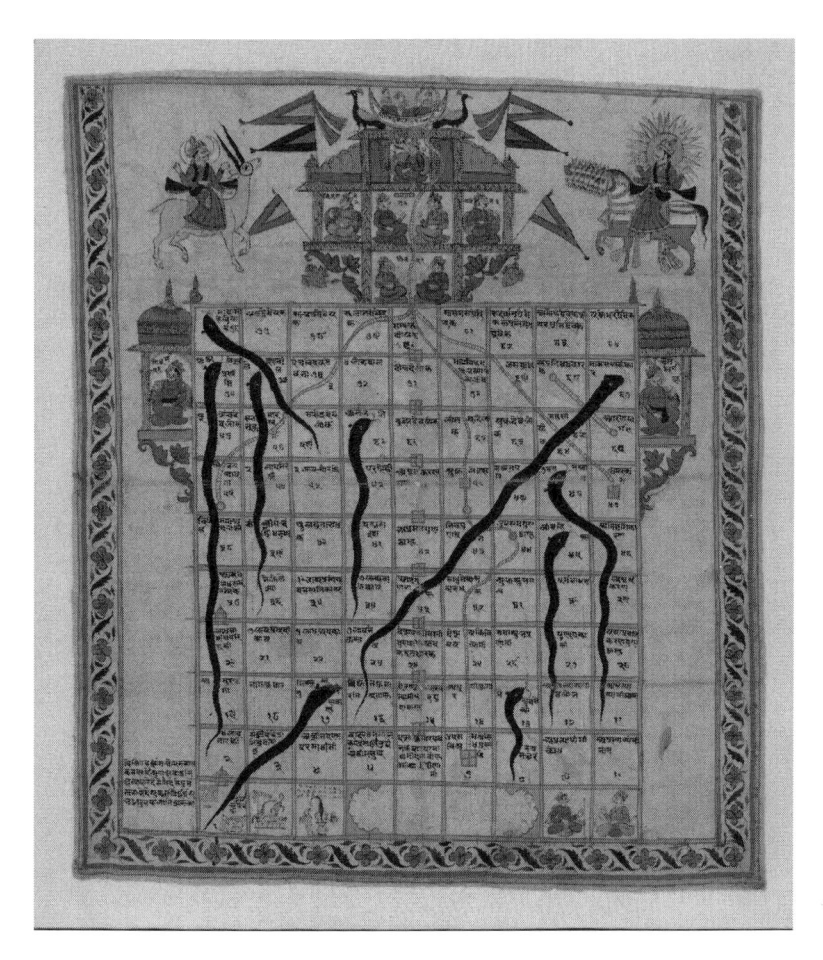

**FIGURE 1.1** Gyanbazi game from Gujarat/Rajasthan, India, late 19th or 20th century. Watercolour on cloth. Reproduced courtesy of the Victoria & Albert Museum, London.

rise of possessive individualism, of the idea of the self as bounded individual subject which arose during capitalist modernity (Macpherson 2010). The Protestant work ethic is here hard at work in fuelling and helping generate individualised forms of capital. Its goal is no longer spiritual enlightenment, but a different mixture of celebrity, virtue and wealth.

Many versions of the game were produced throughout the twentieth century, including the American versions of Chutes and Ladders introduced

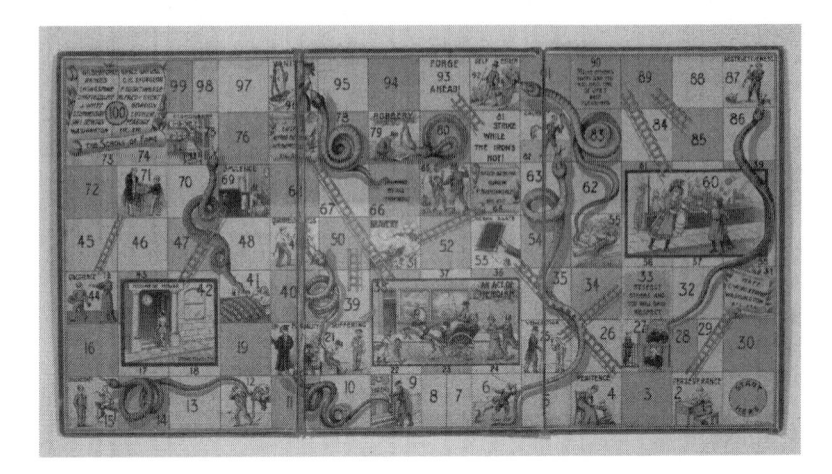

**FIGURE 1.2** Snakes and ladders board game. Designed in England and manufactured in Germany, c.1900. Chromolithographed paper on card. Reproduced courtesy of the Victoria & Albert Museum, London.

in 1943 by board-game manufacturer Milton Bradley. Bradley took the health and safety option of removing the snakes to make the board game appear less dangerous and to popularise it as a game for children (Augustyn 1974: 27; Slesin 1993). The characters on the board were exclusively white until 1974, when black children were finally represented as having a chance to 'climb the ladder' (Slesin 1993). Boards increasingly foregrounded a singular goal of winning. Today, in a recent version for smartphones, the game is streamlined even further – with a single snake being split into squares and the singular aim of attaining wealth symbolised by a treasure chest full of gold.[6]

If this example indicates how meritocracy's symbolism is historically and socially constructed, it also indicates how the symbolism around meritocracy itself is revealing and important. The ladder is not the only image that meritocracy has been associated with; another key example is the 'level playing field'. The sporting imagery of this phrase figures life as a game, its players all starting from an equal footing, not slanted and favouring some over others. It is a handy aphorism, and, whilst it is, of course, a metaphor, metaphors are 'ideas we live by', as Lakoff and Johnson famously put it (Lakoff and Johnson 1980). The phrase 'level playing field' has a particularly obscure history, with agreement only being that it became popularised in the US in the 1980s in business discourse and adopted by Ronald Reagan as a means to argue for deregulation and 'free' trade (Safire 2008: 387–388).

The popular charge of the phrase is dependent on the popularity of sport (and sporting metaphors have a far longer history, as does the notion of 'levelling'). The usage of the term 'level playing field' was further popularised by such management texts as American journalist Thomas Friedman's 2005 business bestseller *The World is Flat*. This book extended the vision of a level playing field to the whole world, arguing that shifts in geopolitics and technology now enabled a dynamic transnational meritocracy to surface from its brave new world of commercial competitiveness (Friedman 2005). Such visions of a level playing field for a mobile cosmopolitan workforce have been enthusiastically embraced by contemporary management literature and neoliberal governmental rhetoric (as I discuss in the following chapter), but just as emphatically criticised by geographers and cultural, educational and political theorists. Educational scholars Brown and Tannock, for instance, critique the idea of a transnational level playing field in education, arguing that it contradicts the fact that 'in reality, economic, social and education inequalities both within and between nations are vast and increasing' (Brown and Tannock 2009: 386). They argue that the construction of a competitive 'global war for talent', as manifested in universities, which is characterised by an increasingly stratified vision of 'hyper-meritocracy' and skewed towards a 'winner takes all' market, greatly exacerbates such inequalities (Brown and Tannock 2009; Frank and Cook 1995; see also Piketty 2013; chapter 4 below).

In both Thomas Friedman's and Ronald Reagan's use of the term, the idea of the level playing field is significant in that it figures 'the ground' as equal, but it is also significant in that it does not take other key forms of differentiation into account. We do not learn, for instance, how the players are selected, how long they have been training and practising beforehand or who is allowed to play against whom. The assumption implies a team victory, thus suggesting more collective forms of egalitarianism, but, as a phrase, it is often applied to an individual's chances in a particular context. The examples here indicate how the application of tropes from the realm of sport, leisure and fun have been used to validate a particular way of organising society and the economy with savagely unequal results. As we will see in the rest of the book, tropes and stories like the ladder and the level playing field have been insistently drawn upon in recent times to popularise neoliberal meritocracy, to promote particularly stratified, individualistic and competitive ways of organising the world in the interests of the few. However, to understand how the meanings of meritocracy were able to move in this direction, we also need to consider its evolution and its stunning U-turn as a term since it was coined in English in the mid-twentieth century.

## Socialist roots and critique

Michael Young is widely regarded as having coined the term 'meritocracy' in his 1958 book *The Rise of the Meritocracy*. However, the term was in fact used two years earlier by Alan Fox in 'Class and Equality' for the journal *Socialist Commentary*, as the British historian David Kynaston recently noted in *Modernity Britain: Opening the Box, 1957–59* (Kynaston 2013: loc. 3666; Fox 1956). As Kynaston is not especially interested in meritocracy, he devotes only a couple of sentences in *Modernity Britain* to the discovery, but in terms of the etymology of the word and its cultural currency, this is a significant and quite remarkable finding.[7]

What is striking about Fox's article is that it makes more extensive critical and politically radical use of the term than Michael Young (whose use of it I discuss below). Alan Fox was to become an influential industrial sociologist whose radical perspective on industrial relations challenged the liberal orthodoxy of the discipline. In 1956 he was a researcher at Nuffield College Oxford, working on a history of British trade unions and a history of the National Union of Boot and Shoe Operatives (*Oxford Dictionary of National Biography* 2013; Fox 2004: 230). The journal the article appeared in, *Socialist Commentary*, was the weekly publication of the Socialist Vanguard Group, a political group to the left of the Labour Party. Indeed, in 1955 the Labour leader and former prime minister, Clement Atlee described *Socialist Commentary* as 'a useful corrective to the *New Statesman* [a more mainstream UK left weekly magazine]' (Douglas 2002: 80).

Fox's article is a careful sociological summary of the policies, social apparatuses and ideologies that cause stratification. It considers the role of 'the four scales' – income, property, education and occupation – in solidifying inequality of position. It discusses how these factors are interconnected, with, for example, low incomes having made it impossible for workers 'to break out of the vicious circle which cramped their lives' (Fox 1956: 12). Because of the era and his specific research interests, Fox tended to focus on industrial work. He suggests that we might understand social inequality by looking at extremes of occupational status and ways of categorising their social standing ('Is it dirty and laborious or the reverse of those things? Is it carried out under discipline and supervision, or under conditions permitting personal independence, initiative and discretion?' [Fox 1956: 11]). Whilst he raises the hope that mechanisation and workers' demands on the shop floor would make blue-collar lives better, he suggests that this is only part of the story. For even if mechanisation improves and unionisation succeeds, social stratification will remain. For Fox, inequality

> will remain as long as we assume it to be a law of nature that those of higher occupational status must not only enjoy markedly superior education as well but also, by right and of necessity, have a higher income into the bargain. As long as that assumption remains – as long as violations of it are regarded as grotesque paradoxes – then so long will our society be divisible into the blessed and the unblessed – those who get the best and most of everything, and those who get the poorest and the least. This way lies the 'meritocracy'; the society in which the gifted, the smart, the energetic, the ambitious and the ruthless are carefully sifted out and helped towards their destined positions of dominance, where they proceed not only to enjoy the fulfilment of exercising their natural endowments but also to receive a fat bonus thrown in for good measure.
>
> This is not enough. Merely to devise bigger and better 'sieves' ('equality of opportunity') to help the clever boys get to the top and then pile rewards on them when they get there is the vision of a certain brand of New Conservatism; it has never been the vision of socialism.
> (Fox 1956: 13)

I quote this at length because it is both a remarkable and remarkably unquoted passage. It indicates the radical origins of critiques of meritocracy – roots that have been obscured – alongside the extent to which it has travelled as a term. For Fox, 'meritocracy' is a term of abuse. It denotes a society in which 'the gifted, the smart, the energetic, the ambitious and ruthless' not only reap the rewards for their (dubious or admirable) skills but receive too much: these 'fat bonus[es]', the rewards piled on them are excessive and mean that others suffer.

As a result of this analysis, Fox suggests 'cross-grading' as a route towards greater equality. 'Cross-grading' is conceptualised not only in financial terms, but also in terms of time, education and leisure. He makes pointers towards policies of redistribution; these

> might mean, perhaps, refusing to accept the idea that to prolong the education of secondary modern pupils beyond the age of fifteen is 'a

waste of time'. It might mean that those who perform the dull and repetitive jobs in which our economy abounds receive substantially more leisure than the rest.

*(Fox 1956: 13)*

Fox's remarkable article in which the earliest use of 'meritocracy' to be recorded to date appears is therefore an explicitly socialist argument against the very logic of meritocracy. These origins were forgotten, however, until 2013, in favour of Michael Young's playful, dystopian social satire, *The Rise of the Meritocracy*.

## Social democratic meritocracy

*The Rise of the Meritocracy* was published in 1958 and set in 2034. It is voiced by a pompous narrator who draws on the PhD thesis of the now-deceased social scientist 'Michael Young' – who (we learn at the end) died in a ferocious battle caused by the problems with the new social system of meritocracy. 'Meritocracy' here is understood as produced through the formula I + E = M, or 'Intelligence combined with Effort equals Merit'. The first half of the book depicts early twentieth-century Britain from the vantage point of a science-fiction future. It charts the demise of the old class-bound nepotistic order, in which kinship triumphs over skill and the rich bequeath their social worlds to their children, as a world overthrown by movements for greater social equality. The second half relates the ascendancy of the new system of merit, which turns out to lead not to an equal society but rather to a new caste system in which IQ determines social station. In this world, the lower rungs are occupied by both ex-rich and ex-poor who are dim-witted and, to borrow contemporary terminology, 'socially excluded'; careers tend to dip after people reach 40 or 50; and there is a roaring black-market trade in brainy babies. The book concludes by gesturing towards the 2034 'Battle of Peterloo' when an alliance of housewives and 'populists' fight back on May Day against meritocracy. We learn that it was in this battle that 'Michael Young' died.

Rejected by a number of publishers, including one who wanted it refashioned into a novel in the style of Aldous Huxley's *Brave New World* – which Young did, although that particular version, intriguingly, never got published – *The Rise of the Meritocracy* eventually became a UK bestseller. This was in itself indicative of what Mike Savage has described as the unprecedented power of sociology in mid-twentieth-century Britain

(Savage 2010).[8] The book portrays a hidebound, class-bound British society as grossly unfair and registers the seismic post-war moves towards a more egalitarian society and the redistribution of resources by the welfare state. But it is also, clearly, a book in which meritocracy is not depicted as a problem-free goal that such class-bound societies should strive for. On the contrary, it is presented as an ideology or organising principle that will become a problem, by leading to new inequalities of power and forms of social stratification.

Through its satire, *The Rise of the Meritocracy* was both questioning the way the social order was being re-made and connecting to older political–philosophical debates around merit. These debates included, for example, Emile Durkheim's vision of society providing 'free space to all merits'; those of the US structuralist–functionalists of the 1940s and 1950s, who sought to update his ideas; and the scepticism of British social democratic radicals of the interwar period like Tawney, Cole and Hobson, who argued that the production of 'merit' needed to be understood instead as a more egalitarian, co-operative process (Beck 2008). Young's political–philosophical position was closer to the latter. As a key writer of the 1945 Labour Party manifesto *Let Us Face the Future* and Labour's director of research, Young wrote *The Rise of the Meritocracy* in part as a warning shot to his party against newly emergent forms of social division (Briggs 2006). The book is critical of tendencies toward over-valorising innate ability and the emergence of new hierarchies. As Raymond Williams argued in a review of Young's book, 'we think of intelligence as absolute and limited because we have been told to think so, by this kind of society. It seems increasingly obvious, in practice, that our concepts of intelligence are peculiarly unintelligent' (Williams 1958).

'Meritocracy' came to move away from this overtly satirical meaning to such an extent that, notoriously, by the 1990s UK's New Labour under Tony Blair had adopted a non-satirical idea of a meritocratic society with gusto. Shortly before his death, Young wrote of how the term had been adopted by Blair and widely disseminated in the US but not in the way he intended. It had been misunderstood, and so New Labour should stop using the term, he argued in an oft-quoted article for *The Guardian*. For Young, the unironic way 'meritocracy' was now deployed, which worked by 'sieving people according to education's narrow band of values [using] an amazing battery of certificates and degrees' meant that social stratifications had hardened, those demoted to the bottom of the social pile were deemed unworthy and demoralised. 'No underclass', he wrote, 'has ever been left as morally naked [as this one]' (Young 2001).

I will come to the issue of how 'meritocracy' changed in value from the 1960s onward below, but it is worth considering how Young's book itself – or rather, the text and its author's paratextual framings of it – may have contributed, despite themselves, to such misreadings.[9] For, whilst *The Rise of the Meritocracy* is a text which is known for being disparaging of meritocracy, there is also a fair amount of ambiguity on this issue within both the text itself and in Michael Young's comments on it. Its author claimed that *The Rise of the Meritocracy* was 'intended to present two sides of the case – the case against as well as the case for a meritocracy' (Young 1994: xvii). In the book, whilst 'meritocracy' is valued for its ability to dismantle inherited privilege, it is also damned for its power to create new, unfair social divisions. The fictional 'Chelsea Manifesto' is the clearest expression of an alternative to both, with its often powerful arguments for equality, for valuing 'kindliness and courage, sympathy and generosity' over narrow conceptions of intelligence; and yet this alternative vision is truncated and cut off. Neither was the author's paratextual activity always consistent. For instance, Young stated that he supported the ideal of a classless society; yet when asked in the 2000s whether the book was arguing to promote 'the comprehensive idea' in education, he replied with an unexpansive but unequivocal 'no' (Dench 2006: 74).

Young, who was director of the Institute of Community Studies at the time of writing the book, later became a founder and co-founder of a variety of institutions key to post-war British life and progressive social education, including the Open University, the Consumer's Association and the University of the Third Age. He was deeply committed to formations which enabled innovative forms of participation and engagement with political and social structures. It is for this reason that his legacy is held in such high regard in the UK today. This is a political–conceptual lineage which connects Young's work with that of contemporary advocates of participatory democracy; the tentative conclusion of the book's story, in which the housewives and other populists rise up together, is symptomatic of this tendency.

Yet, whilst arguing against 'the big organisation', Young's primary model or template for participation was the nuclear family. As Hilary Land makes clear in her essay about *The Rise of the Meritocracy*, the book, whilst anticipating a feminist critique of merit, does not particularly challenge conventionally gendered divisions of labour (Land 2006: 59); nor, we can add, its heteronormativity, nor its singular means of conceptualising 'social closeness'. We can also note that Young's antipathy towards large organisations involved being decidedly ambivalent / hostile towards nationalised industries. At its most left wing, this involved promoting mutual aid and 'neighbourly socialism'. At its least, it involved joining the liberal Social Democratic Party (SDP) and not making any explicit critique of capitalism. The emphasis on economic and cultural redistribution, which is foregrounded in Fox's account, is very much downplayed in Young's.

What this means is that, whilst *The Rise of the Meritocracy* clearly critiques an essentialised and individualised notion of merit and implicitly eugenicist approaches to intelligence, its relationship to comprehensive provision, and indeed to capitalism, is somewhat less clear. There is a slide away from a more explicitly socialist critique into a more ambiguous, social democratic version. In this particular articulation, its gendered nature begins to be questioned, although this line of questioning is not pursued but rather foreclosed and returned to the bosom of the heteronormative nuclear family. And whilst responsibility for what happens to any concept, book or term cannot obviously be laid at the feet, the brain or the typewriting fingers of the author, the persistence of such textual lacunae is a key factor in how the term later became deployed. The paradoxical nature of Young's historical position is also apparent in the tendency of commentators to describe him as the original 'social entrepreneur' (Briggs 2006), a phrase which has now become decidedly ambivalent, reflecting not only innovative brilliance at creating socially beneficial initiatives (at which Young excelled), but also what was to become a wider saturation of the field of social policy by neoliberal entrepreneurialism.

## The critique of educational essentialism

On the other side of the Atlantic in 1958, the same year that *The Rise of the Meritocracy* was published, Hannah Arendt published a scathing essay 'The Crisis in Education' (Arendt 1958). Designed to have wider applicability than a US audience, it was based on a lecture she had recently given in Germany and had had translated (Wild and Posten 2010; Nordquist 1997). The essay took as its starting point the media anxiety and commentary in the US over falling educational standards, which Arendt expressed as 'the puzzling question of why Johnny can't read' (Arendt 2006: 171). Contending that both progressive and traditional education were failing to address the key issues, Arendt's critical perspective broadens out to consider the social context of American education in relation to that offered in Europe, and philosophises about what effective pedagogy would involve (Arendt 2006:

171). On the one hand, she suggests that schools need to hold back on didactic moralising ('the function of the school is to teach children what the world is like and not to instruct them in the art of living' [Arendt 2006: 192]). On the other, she revisits the issue of authority, making the connection between a lack of parental authority and the problem of a lack of democratic involvement or adults who 'refuse to assume responsibility for the world into which they have brought children' (Arendt 2006: 187) thus failing to 'prepare them in advance for the task of renewing a common world' (Arendt 2006: 193).

Arendt therefore argues that most American secondary schools do not educate well enough for college but rejects the idea that this is an automatic result of mass education. Indeed, in the process, she is scathing of the new 'English example' of selecting a small proportion of those considered to have enough ability to attend grammar schools. For

> there at the end of primary school, with students at the age of eleven, has been instituted the dreaded examination that weeds out all but some ten per cent of the scholars suited for higher education. The rigor of this selection was not accepted even in England without protest; in America it would have been simply impossible. What is aimed at in England is 'meritocracy', which is clearly once more the establishment of an oligarchy, this time not of wealth or of birth but of talent. But this means, even though people in England may not be altogether clear about it, that the country even under a socialist government will continue to be governed as it has been from time out of mind, that is, neither as a monarchy nor as a democracy but as an oligarchy or aristocracy – the latter in case one takes the view that the most gifted are also the best, which is by no means a certainty. In America such an almost physical division of the children into gifted and ungifted would be considered intolerable. Meritocracy contradicts the principle of equality, of an equalitarian democracy, no less than any other oligarchy.
> 
> *(Arendt 2006: 176–177)*

It is striking to read that Arendt at this time states that a division between 'gifted and ungifted would be considered intolerable' in America, given the ubiquity of 'gifted and talented' programmes in the US today and, indeed, the extent to which it has become synonymous with US education.

## A 'just meritocracy'? the beginnings of neoliberal meritocracy

In 1973, in his classic text *The Coming of Post-Industrial Society*, Daniel Bell – an American sociologist and friend of Michael Young – pronounced that 'the post-industrial society, in its logic, is a meritocracy' (Bell 1973: 409). The impact of the 1960s movements and struggles by those disenfranchised by the hierarchies of the Fordist settlement – women, non-whites, gay people – challenged and partially ruptured the existing patterns of social stratification. For example, after the 1963 Equal Pay Act in the US and the 1970 Equal Pay Act in the UK, it was no longer legal to pay men and women differently for doing the same job, even if the struggle over equal pay for work of equal value – and against cultural prejudices against what it is possible for a woman or a man to do – remained necessary.

These challenges to social mobility were engendered through and alongside the shift to a 'post-industrial', post-Fordist society and culture. Post-Fordist culture and society has involved a range of notable cultural, social, economic and political developments. These developments have included the rapid growth in consumer-oriented production, branding and the service sector; the mobilisation of just-in-time production and ICTs in the service of 'the creative industries'; industrial downsizing and the contracting-out of manufacturing overseas; and the neoliberal erosion of workers' rights, and the social provisions of the welfare state, in favour of privatised solutions and social risk borne by 'the individual' (Beck and Beck-Gernsheim 2001; Lash and Urry 1993; Bauman 2000; Boltanski and Chiapello 2007; Crouch 2004).

In *The Coming of Post-Industrial Society*, Bell uses 'meritocracy' to refer primarily to the new forms of social mobility which are engendered within allegedly 'post-industrial' society. This is important, as use of the term 'meritocracy' in Bell's text works to neutralise and erase those more problematic (or 'dystopian') aspects of the term present in Young's work and powerfully criticised in Fox's essay. Bell elaborates upon his ideas about meritocracy in a now more obscure text: a 1972 article, 'On Meritocracy and Equality', in the journal *Public Interest*. This article is fascinating as it forms a mid-point in the journey of meritocratic ideology from object of satirical scorn (in *The Rise of the Meritocracy*) to central and explicit tenet of neoliberalism (as in the pamphlet which I consider in the following section). *Public Interest* was a quarterly American public policy journal aimed at journalists, academics and policy makers founded by Daniel Bell and Irving Kristol in 1965. Irving Kristol, writer, journalist and publisher, was dubbed 'the godfather of neoconservatism' when he featured on the cover of *Esquire* magazine in 1979, a moniker he later adopted and adapted in his books including *Reflections of a Neoconservative, The Neoconservative Persuasion* and *Two Cheers for Capitalism*. Bell dropped his involvement with the journal from the late 1970s, as it lurched further to the right (Buhle 2011).

Bell's interpretation of meritocracy was therefore a meeting point between Young's social-democratic version – Young explicitly refers to Bell as 'a friend' in the 1994 Introduction to *Rise of the Meritocracy* – and neoconservatism (Young 1994: xv). This is palpable in the article. It is a thorough, carefully written piece, in which Bell argues for a distinction between 'equality of opportunity' and 'equality of result'. There has been a conceptual confusion between these positions, the article argues, drawing on the work of John Rawls. Which do we want? Bell claims that 'equality of result' is a socialist ethic, whereas 'equality of opportunity' is a liberal one (Bell 1972: 48). In the process, he questions the value of affirmative action programmes and comes, eventually, to argue for a 'just meritocracy' which is 'made up of those who have earned their authority', as opposed to an 'unjust' one which 'makes those distinctions invidious and demeans those below' (Bell 1972: 66).

In this text the usage of 'meritocracy' comes to take the lineaments of the form we are familiar with today. It is an unambiguously positive and valorised term. It is also one which argues in favour of 'opportunity'. This is familiar territory to a contemporary readership. However, what distinguishes it from current usage are two important contextual points. First, the terrain on which meritocracy operates is one of high confidence in economic growth, as evidenced by virtue of Bell being able to debate whether or not 'we have reached the post-scarcity state of full abundance'. This is clearly a moment before either the 1970s recession (and before extensive anxiety about the finite nature of natural resources). Second, and relatedly, the position from which Bell speaks is defined by a political context in which widespread support for the Keynesian consensus has not yet collapsed, a context that has resulted in 'a steady decrease in income disparity between persons' (Bell 1972: 64).[10] To put it bluntly: putting a competitive vision of meritocracy into play is not hugely conspicuous or controversial at a time when there is a strong social safety net.

Bell was writing at a time in the Global North when the Fordist welfare settlement was offsetting the worst extremes of capitalist inequality and its attendant social squalor and from a time when there was high confidence in expanding economic growth. From this position meritocracy is, for Bell, to be conceived as a social system in which 'just' rewards and small gradations of privilege and position can be given to differential talent. From here, it might even be used as a motor for greater growth:

> And there is no reason why the principle of meritocracy should not obtain in business and government as well. One wants entrepreneurs and innovators who can expand the amount of productive wealth for society.
>
> *(Bell 1972: 66)*

And so the ambiguities of *The Rise of the Meritocracy* are resolved in favour of a specific usage which is quite different from Young's. For Bell, IQ is far less problematic than for Young. He is not so interested in the potential of local or participatory power or the extent of social levelling proposed by Fox. He is interested in achieving a social order in which the excesses of capitalism are curbed by the state, and hopes that meritocracy can be recalibrated in such a way as to avoid it solidifying into the new caste system imagined by Young, instead providing an incitement-engine for a dynamic yet just society. Here meritocracy starts to become posited as an engine of 'productive wealth'.

## Meritocracy in the neoliberal laboratory

Bell's vision of meritocracy emerged from a historical situation characterised by the presence of a strong welfare state which could offset the most extreme effects of market-produced social inequality. In this context, meritocracy could be imagined as a dynamic engine both of 'opportunity' for social mobility, shaking up an ossified class system, and for ambiguously imagined 'productive wealth' – a term vague enough to be used by actors across the political spectrum. By the 1990s, however, this ambiguity was being aggressively exploited by the right, as the concept of 'meritocracy' became mobilised in explicit opposition to social democracy.

In Britain, a 1995 pamphlet by Adrian Wooldridge from the Social Market Foundation, *Meritocracy and the 'Classless Society'*, argued for a vision of meritocracy which was explicitly pitted against comprehensive education, student grants, housing benefit and any other kind of collective provision. Meritocracy is here opposed to what Wooldridge calls the 'niceness revolution' of the 1960s and 1970s. As part of this, it is explicitly opposed to 'community' (Wooldridge 1995: 45) and to the welfare state, which is figured as 'an obstacle' to spreading meritocratic values (Wooldridge 1995: 43). Meritocracy in Woolridge's version then is explicitly bound up with the logic of a capitalist market and with entrepreneurialism and very much against the collective provision of social democracy and the welfare state. Here meritocracy fully embraces the liberal idea of equality of opportunity and renders it synonymous with economic growth, capitalist competition and marketisation. Meritocracy is marketised, and marketisation is good.

We can understand the development of this framework more capaciously by drawing on Michel Foucault's series of distinctions between liberalism and neoliberalism in his prescient 1978–1979 Collège de France lecture series (which forms the backdrop to his account of the emergence of biopolitics, published in French in 2004 and English in 2008). Foucault is insistent on the need to grasp the distinctions between liberalism and neoliberalism, to grasp their singularity, to 'show you precisely that neoliberalism is really something else' (Foucault 2008: 130). For Foucault, the 'something else' neoliberalism became was a situation in which 'the overall exercise of political power can be modelled on the principles of a market economy' (Foucault 2008: 131). In other words, it was not just that the market became dominant but that, since the 1970s, it had begun to structure the way political power itself works.

Foucault describes how, to create this regime, classical liberalism had to be subjected to a number of transformations. A key transformation is that whilst classical liberalism accepts monopolies, neoliberalism does not: competition under neoliberalism is not considered natural, but structured (Foucault 2008: 134–137). Moreover, the only 'true' aim of social policy for neoliberalism can be economic growth and privatisation; thus, the multiplication of the 'enterprise' form within the social body, Foucault states, is what is at stake in neoliberalism, and it is what comes to constitute the 'formative power of society' (Foucault 2008: 148).

In Wooldridge's formulation, meritocracy becomes a means of actively intervening to multiply the enterprise form within the social body. For example, he saw danger both in the hereditary interests of the House of Lords and in Thatcher's inability to 'undermine the comprehensive principle in state schools' (Wooldridge 1995: 9). The vision, in other words, is of a starkly stratified society, one in which people can travel according to their inborn 'merit'. It considers vast inequalities of wealth and poverty to be legitimate as long as the potential to travel through them for those savvy enough is maintained. The distaste for the masses, towards the 'all and sundry' model of comprehensive education, combines revulsion toward 'standardisation' and toward the masses who fall out of view when the socially mobile are focused upon. These terms are elided.

Interestingly, Woolridge's pamphlet was produced by the Social Market Foundation, an ostensibly cross-party think tank. The very name 'Social Market Foundation' bears out Foucault's claim that neoliberal rhetoric works to incite marketisation throughout the social body, while strongly echoing Michael Young's language of social entrepreneurialism: neoliberalism as analysed by Foucault and Young's own political discourse here become almost wholly intertwined. In this influential pamphlet, a product of several decades of new right thinking, 'meritocracy' is unambiguously posited as an engine of competition against supposedly debilitating forms of social collaboration. Neoliberalism has competition as a central organising principle, as William Davies amongst others has analysed (Davies 2014). Meritocracy as an ideology is a key contributor to the success and tenacity of neoliberalism, as a seemingly 'fair' means through which competition is expressed and extended.

It was not only narratives associated with the political right which were to embrace this new, neoliberal meaning of meritocracy. The theoretical work of British sociologist Anthony Giddens was also used by the British New Labour government in the development of its 'Third Way' politics, in which 'meritocracy' became a key term and was used for simultaneously socially liberal and neoliberal ends. The story of this political adoption and its similar politics to the Clinton government in the US are taken up in chapter 3; how social liberalism became so malleable is discussed in the next chapter.

'Meritocracy', therefore, is a word with a short etymological history – under 60 years – but during this time it has gradually and dramatically shifted in its meaning and value. It has moved from a negative, disparaging criticism of an embryonic system of state organisation which was creating problematic new hierarchies by using a controversial notion of 'merit' in education, to a positive, celebratory term, one connecting competitive individualism and 'talent' with a belief in the desirability and possibility of social mobility in an increasingly unequal society. Initially mobilised as a critical term through a radical socialist discourse, it mutated through left-liberal social democracy, and then, by the 1980s, 'meritocracy' became a wholly positive term. It was mobilised gradually into having a positive charge through and by neoliberalism, although this has happened in diverse, sometimes erratic ways. It has been and continues to be shaped as a discourse by diverse constituencies, agents and sites including popular culture, social theory and political rhetoric. The next chapter considers the relationship between 'rising up' the social hierarchy in relation to work and to the structural, yet frequently disavowed, disadvantages of gender, ethnicity and class.

## Notes

1 Sen 2000: 7.
2 It also enshrined equality before the law whilst only allowing property-owners to vote.
3 Hindi versions were known by other names including Moksha-Patamu.
4 They appeared in Britain at the end of the nineteenth century, and 'the end of Victoria's reign saw the gradual loss of moral exhortations' (Parlett 1999: 92–93).
5 Notably, 'Self-esteem' (or pride) leads to a fall in this board game: a trope which was not to be a feature of twenty-first-century meritocracy, where self-esteem is a precondition for action.
6 Published by Agatco. You can see the image on iTunes, but I was unable to secure copyright permission to publish it (https://itunes.apple.com/gb/app/sna kes-and-ladders/id300205243?mt=8. Accessed 16 December 2016).
7 The *Oxford English Dictionary*'s entry on meritocracy and its earliest use has been updated during the time I have been writing this book (*Oxford English Dictionary* 2016).
8 In this book, Young is simultaneously noted as being influential whilst *Rise of the Meritocracy* is absent from the discussion.
9 Young stated in the introduction to the 1994 edition that 'the most influential books are always those which are not read' (Young 1994: xv) and later wrote that he did not think that Blair had actually read his book (Young 2001). Clare Donovan has argued, somewhat tenuously, that many academics who have cited it have not read it either (Donovan 2006). Various reviewers have also argued that its style is problematic (e.g. Hoggart 1958; Barker 2006: 3).
10 'Traditionally, the market was the arbiter of differential reward, based on scarcity or on demand. But as economic decisions become politicized, and the market is replaced by social decisions, what is the principle of fair reward and fair difference?' (Bell 1972: 63).

## References

Arendt, Hannah (1958) 'The Crisis in Education', *Partisan Review* 25(4) pp. 493–513.
Arendt, Hannah (2006) *Between Past and Future: Eight Exercises in Political Thought*. London: Penguin Books.
Augustyn, Frederik J., Jnr (1974) *Dictionary of Toys and Games in American Popular Culture*. Philadelphia: Haworth Press.
Barker, Paul (2006) 'A Tract for the Times', in Geoff Dench (ed.), *The Rise and Rise of Meritocracy*. Oxford: Wiley-Blackwell, pp. 36–44.
Bauman, Zygmun (2000) *Individualisation*. Oxford: Polity Press.

Beck, John (2008) *Meritocracy, Citizenship and Education: New Labour's Legacy*. London: Continuum.
Beck, Ulrich, and Elizabeth Beck-Gernsheim (2001) *Individualization: Institutionalised Individualism and its Political Consequences*. London: Sage.
Bell, Daniel (1972) 'On Meritocracy and Equality', *Public Interest* 29 (Fall) pp. 29–68.
Bell, Daniel (1973) *The Coming of Post-Industrial Society: A Venture in Social Forecasting*. New York: Basic Books.
Boltanski, Luc, and Eve Chiapello (2007) *The New Spirit of Capitalism*. London: Verso.
Briggs, Asa (2006) 'The Labour Party as Crucible', in Geoff Dench (ed.), *The Rise and Rise of Meritocracy*. Oxford: Wiley-Blackwell, pp. 17–26.
Brown, Phillip, and Stuart Tannock (2009) 'Education, Meritocracy and the Global War for Talent', *Journal of Education Policy* 24(4), pp. 377–392.
Buhle, Paul (2011) 'Daniel Bell: Obituary', *The Guardian*, 26 January, www.guardian.co.uk/education/2011/jan/26/daniel-bell-obituary. Accessed 1 November 2016.
Cross, Steve, and Jo Littler (2010) 'Celebrity and Schadenfreude: The Cultural Economy of Fame in Freefall', *Cultural Studies* 24(3) pp. 395–417.
Crouch, Colin (2004) *Post-Democracy*. Oxford: Polity Press.
Davies, William (2014) *The Limits of Neoliberalism*. London: Sage.
De Tocqueville, A. (1994) *Democracy in America*. London: Fontana Press.
Dench, Geoff (ed.) (2006) *The Rise and Rise of Meritocracy*. Oxford: Wiley-Blackwell.
Donovan, Paul (2006) 'The Chequered Career of a Cryptic Concept', in Geoff Dench (ed.), *The Rise and Rise of Meritocracy*. Oxford: Wiley-Blackwell, pp. 61–72.
Douglas, R.M. (2002) 'No Friend of Democracy: The Socialist Vanguard Group 1941–1950', *Contemporary British History* 16(4), pp. 51–86.
Durkheim, Emile (2013) *The Division of Labour in Society*, 2nd edn, ed. Stephen Lukes, trans. W.D. Halls. Basingstoke: Palgrave Macmillan.
Elman, Benjamin A. (2013) *Civil Examinations and Meritocracy in Late Imperial China*. Cambridge: Harvard University Press.
Fischer, Claude S., Michael Hout, Martín Sánchez Jankowski, Samuel R. Lucas, Ann Swidler and Kim Voss (1996) *Inequality by Design: Cracking the Bell Curve Myth*. Princeton: Princeton University Press.
Foucault, Michel (2008) *The Birth of Biopolitics: Lectures at the Collège de France, 1978–1979*, trans. Graham Burchell. Basingstoke: Palgrave Macmillan.
Fox, Alan (1956) 'Class and Equality', *Socialist Commentary*, May, pp. 11–13.
Fox, Alan (2004) *A Very Late Development*. 2nd revd edn. Coventry: BUIRA.
Frank, Thomas H., and Philip J. Cook (1995) *The Winner-Take-All-Society: Why the Few at the Top Get So Much More than the Rest of Us*. New York: Simon & Schuster.
Free Dictionary (2016) 'Meritocracy', www.thefreedictionary.com/meritocrat. Accessed 1 November 2016.
Friedman, Thomas (2005) *The World is Flat*. New York: Farrar, Straus and Giroux.
Hobsbawm, Eric (1988) *The Age of Capital: 1848–1875*. London: Abacus.
Hoggart, Richard (1958) 'IQ plus Effort = Merit', *The Observer*, 2 November.

James, Wilmot (2012) 'The Language of Meritocracy', *Inside Politics*, 5 March, https://inside-politics.org/2012/03/05/the-language-of-meritocracy. Accessed 1 November 2016.
Kothari, Uma (ed.) (2005) *A Radical History of Development Studies*. London: Zed Books.
Kynaston, David (2013) *Modernity Britain: Opening the Box, 1957–1959*, Kindle edn. London: Bloomsbury.
Lakoff, George, and Mark Johnson (1980) *Metaphors We Live By*. Chicago: University of Chicago Press.
Land, Hilary (2006) 'We Sat Down at the Table of Privilege and Complained about the Food', in Geoff Dench (ed.), *The Rise and Rise of Meritocracy*. Oxford: Wiley-Blackwell, pp. 45–60.
Lash, Scott, and John Urry (1993) *Economies of Signs and Space*. London: Sage.
Lindemann, Albert (2013) *A History of Modern Europe From 1815 to the Present*. Oxford: Wiley.
McNamee, Stephen J., and Robert K. Miller (2009) *The Meritocracy Myth*. Lanham: Rowman & Littlefield.
Macpherson, Crawford B. (2010) *The Political Theory of Possessive Individualism from Hobbes to Locke*. Oxford: Oxford University Press.
Marx, Karl, and Friedrich Engels (2004) *Marx and Engels Collected Works*. London: Lawrence & Wishart.
Nordquist, Joan (1997) *Hannah Arendt (II): A Bibliography*, Social Theory: A Bibliographic Series, 46. Santa Cruz: Reference and Research Services.
*Oxford Dictionary of National Biography* (2013) http://oxforddnb.com/. Accessed 1 November 2016.
*Oxford English Dictionary* (2001) Oxford: Clarendon Press.
*Oxford English Dictionary* (2016) www.oed.com. Accessed 28 February 2017.
Parlett, David (1999) *The Oxford History of Board Games*. Oxford: Oxford University Press.
Piketty, Thomas (2013) *Capital in the Twenty-First Century*. Cambridge, MA: Belknap Press.
Quinn Moore, R. (2000) 'Multiracialism and Meritocracy: Singapore's Approach to Race and Inequality', *Review of Social Economy* 58(3) pp. 339–360.
Ross, Kristin (2002) *May '68 and its Afterlives*. Chicago: University of Chicago Press.
Safire, William (2008) *Safire's Political Dictionary*. Oxford: Oxford University Press.
Savage, Mike (2010) *Identities and Social Change in Britain since 1940: The Politics of Method*. Oxford: Oxford University Press.
Schaar, J. (1997) 'Equality of Opportunity, and Beyond', in L. Pojman and R. Westmoreland (eds), *Equality*. Oxford: Oxford University Press, pp. 137–147.
Sen, Amartya (2000) 'Merit and Justice', in Kenneth Arrow, Samuel Bowles and Steven Durlauf (eds), *Meritocracy and Economic Inequality*. Princeton: Princeton University Press, pp. 5–16.
Slesin, Suzanne (1993) 'At 50: Still Climbing, Still Sliding', *New York Times*, 15 July, www.nytimes.com/1993/07/15/garden/currents-at-50-still-climbing-still-sliding.html. Accessed 1 November 2016.

Soko, Mills (2015) 'South Africa Needs a Meritocratic Civil Service, not a Political One', *Rand Daily Mail*, 14 May, www.rdm.co.za/politics/2015/05/14/sa-needs-a-meritocratic-civil-service-not-a-political-one. Accessed 1 November 2016.

Talib, Nadira, and Richard Fitzgerald (2015) 'Inequality as Meritocracy: The Use of the Metaphor of Diversity and the Value of Inequality within Singapore's Meritocratic Education System', *Critical Discourse Studies* 12(4) pp. 445–462.

Todd, Selina (2015) *The People: The Rise and Fall of the Working Class, 1910–2010*. London: John Murray.

Topsfield, Andrew (2006a) *The Art of Play: Board and Card Games of India*. Bombay: Marg Publications.

Topsfield, Andrew (2006b) 'Snakes and Ladders in India: Some Further Discoveries', *Artibus Asiae* (66)1 pp. 143–179.

Wild, Thomas, and Anne Posten (2010) 'For the Sake of What is New', Hannah Arendt Center, Bard College, www.hannaharendtcenter.org/?tag=denver-lindley. Accessed 18 March 2016.

Williams, Raymond (1958) 'Democracy or Meritocracy?', *Manchester Guardian*, 30 October, p. 10.

Williams, Raymond (1983) *Keywords: A Vocabulary of Culture and Society*. Oxford: Oxford University Press.

Wooldridge, Adrian (1995) *Meritocracy and the 'Classless Society'*. London: Social Market Foundation

Young, Michael (1994) *The Rise of the Meritocracy* [1958], 2nd revd edn. London: Transaction Publishers.

Young, Michael (2001) 'Down with Meritocracy', *The Guardian*, 29 June, www.guardian.co.uk/politics/2001/jun/29/comment. Accessed 1 November 2016.

# 2

# RISING UP

## Gender, ethnicity, class and the meritocratic deficit

> The enemies of '68 have never forgotten how much was unhinged in that period.
>
> Stuart Hall[1]

### See where your talent takes you

> We strongly believe that work is the way each of us can put our passion and energy into creating value. And we're convinced that choosing a career requires careful consideration, as it will inevitably lead to challenges as we embark upon a journey of personal and professional transformation.
>
> Our goal is to release those energies. We know it's not easy, and can often be stressful: that's why, at Meritocracy, we make job-seeking a rich, rewarding experience. We give candidates the power to grasp the vision of a London-based charity, explore the spaces of Swedish market leader in the packaging industry, or discover the values of a Korean multinational connecting millions of people worldwide daily, before making their next move. Be curious, see where your talent takes you.
>
> (Meritocracy n.d.)

There is an online job agency called Meritocracy. It aims to help companies recruit 'millennials' – young people born between 1980 and 2000 – and to help these millennials find jobs.[2] Meritocracy, whose clients include Tetra-Pak, Samsung, Coca-Cola, Moleskine and JustGiving, encourages companies to upload photos and details of their working environments alongside job specs to the site. Meanwhile, applicants can see at-a-glance statistics about the number of company employees and its gender ratio alongside photos of beaming members of staff in funky environments, embedded films featuring workers discussing why they love working there, and icons indicating 'benefits', such as games rooms, pensions or laptops. In the talent economy Meritocracy promises to transform the stressful business of job-seeking into a bold, adventurous experience, helping release passions to 'create value'. Its weightless, generalising adjectives conjure up a young, affluent, passion-driven cosmopolitan imaginary. The agency workers are based in London and Italy but, like their clientele, they do not like to be pinned down by geography. 'It might sound odd, annoying even, but on Meritocracy you can't select locations, only ambitions. Above all, we want to offer the best opportunities for each of you. Wherever they may be' (Meritocracy n.d.).

It is the affective work experience here which is paramount, in terms of surroundings, colleagues, benefits and feeling like you are 'creating value' (rather than having values and creating things out of them). These experiences are most important, presenting an exciting alternative to, and/or extension of, current surroundings and networks. The envisaged cosmopolitan corporate work-subjects are young, and are not imagined as parents: family-related provision notably doesn't figure in the 'associated benefits' section. Meritocracy here connotes the freedom to work – not so much hard as 'boldly' and 'passionately' – in order to unlock inner talent and rise up the global ladder of opportunity to corporate cosmopolitan nirvana.

The ideology of meritocracy has, as we saw in chapter 1, long been yoked to the idea of career advancement from egalitarian beginnings. But here it takes a specific form as an ideologically loaded brand name for a commercial agency, one seeking itself to create profit by drawing on an image of egalitarian opportunity and talent-activation as the route to climb the global ladder. In the process, it harnesses rhetoric about the transnational meritocratic winners of a 'global war for talent' (Brown and Tannock 2009) that has been popularised by recent management literature, as we saw in chapter 1 and, as the next chapter shows, has also been sanctioned by neoliberal governments. It is also indicative of how meritocracy has been more widely positioned as a discourse with a 'cool' value, a social system suggesting boundless and limitless opportunity for the transnationally gifted. It represents what we might call 'neoliberal meritocracy as corporate liberation'.

The images being mobilised here gain traction by having some vestiges of truth. It is possible for some young people to have working lives involving a sizeable amount of travel and a variety of forms of self-realisation. But on the Meritocracy website these messages are massaged into relentlessly glamorous forms and the substantial negative aspects of such work are elided. In a wider context such messages accrue along with others like them to gain a mythic status and become a widely disseminated truth-claim about contemporary 'no-collar' work. The term 'no-collar work' refers to formerly 'white-collar' professions repackaged under post-Fordism as attractive and casual, combined with new professions, particularly in the tech sector and the creative industries (Ross 2004; Sennett 2006; Friedman 2005). Jobs advertised on the Meritocracy website span a wide range of roles and sectors – including administration, creative, technological, branding, sales, production, retail and management work – and all are promoted through exactly this creative, cool, no-collar, youth-oriented aesthetic. The clue that there just might be a problem with the image is to be found when you click on an image of their core staff, who are overwhelmingly white and male.[3]

The pervasive branding of no-collar labour as cool, informal, fun and open access has been facilitated by the cultural and creative industries which prefigured and set a template for an image of the future of work and for conditions across other sectors (Gill 2002; Gregg 2011; McGuigan 2009; McRobbie 2016; Ross 2010). Yet a sizeable quantity of research has now shown that, alongside the image of carefree enjoyability that anyone talented and purposeful enough can access, there has in all of these sectors simultaneously been an erosion of working conditions both in terms of job security (the cutting of sick pay and pensions, a rise in fixed-term, permatemp and zero-hours contracts) and of the ability to access and progress through the sector by those who are not rich, white, male or well-connected enough. To use two ugly, but extremely useful neologisms, contemporary work in the private and increasingly in the public sector has overwhelmingly moved in the direction of offering 'flexploitation' (flexibility + exploitation) rather than 'flexicurity' (flexibility + security) (Ross 2010).

As we have seen, meritocracy today, in its neoliberal form, tends to endorse a competitive, linear system of social mobility and to function as an ideological myth to obscure inequalities, including the role this discourse of meritocracy itself plays in actually curtailing social mobility. Its myth of mobility is used to create the idea of a level playing field that does not exist. As chapter 1 tracked, meritocracy has travelled a long way from a term of abuse to a normalised principle. By taking a broader historical view, focusing on worlds of work and using a series of cultural snapshots, this chapter considers the historical reasons for both such parables of progress and the intersectional inconsistencies they hide. It shows how a quasi-democratic, but problematic, post-war language and practice of egalitarianism was filleted and marketised for corporate gain: popularising the ideas of a level playing field and that we can all 'rise up' at work, whilst perpetuating particular inbuilt and structural prejudices in terms of race, class, gender and ability. It terms these structural, yet frequently disavowed, disadvantages of gender, race and class the 'egalitarian deficit'.

The second half of the chapter considers how this egalitarian deficit has been dealt with. It argues that over the past few decades, the idea that we are 'over' disparities of race, gender and class – or post-racism, post-sexism and what could be termed 'post-classism' – have worked hand in hand with neoliberal meritocracy to fuel each other and give each other strength. Those experiencing the egalitarian deficit, who do not start out at the top of the social pyramid, are often doubly or trebly disadvantaged by neoliberal narratives of meritocracy whilst being particularly incited to climb it. They have been encouraged to feel the pressures of inequality as, overwhelmingly, a personal failing. But the chapter also identifies selective shifts in the characteristics of this formation in recent years: from ignoring inequality to selectively noticing injustice, an injustice positioned as a 'meritocratic deficit'; and from disavowing the feminist and civil-rights movements to attempting to re-articulate their imagery in the service of a reinvigorated neoliberal settlement. These 'neoliberal justice narratives', as I term them, attempt to redress some forms of inequality whilst perpetuating others.

## Partial progression and painful ladders: mid-century welfare

A key reason why neoliberal meritocracy has been able to gain ideological traction is because of its use of the powerful residual effects and affects of changes in the high point of social democracy during the mid-twentieth century, particularly in terms of opening up access to occupations. Lauren Berlant's book *Cruel Optimism* suggests that an affective relationship to the promise of the post-war social democratic moment is both a constitutive feeling of the present and an impasse to our future, given that its social solidarities are being eroded away and sold by neoliberalism. The very optimism of the post-war moment is abused and channelled into becoming 'an obstacle to our flourishing' (Berlant 2011).

It is important to consider the nature of the meritocracy which was on offer at this mid-century moment. Social democratic welfare states were neither globally ubiquitous nor a uniform phenomenon. In many countries, this formation did not appear at all, and its manifestations across countries that were affected was variable. Nonetheless the term 'welfare states' indicates a range of systems of social provision and protection – including universal healthcare, education and pensions – that developed most markedly in Western Europe and the Nordic countries, and significantly in the US in the shape of the New Deal, from the end of the Second World War up into the 1970s. (Certain aspects can be dated earlier: in the UK, for example, the arrival of social democracy is often dated from the reforms of the Liberal government in the 1900s [see Wahl 2011: 4].)

The swathe of entitlements generated by the introduction of welfare states offered multiple routes to rising up or increased forms of social mobility for many, including sick pay, maternity pay, holiday pay, universal education, healthcare, pensions and legislation against discrimination. As the inclusion of the word 'healthcare' in this list makes clear, these forms of protection were extremely variegated between countries: there were stark differences between universal public healthcare in Denmark and its non-existent or bony skeletal structure in the US. Esping-Anderson described these differences as being part of the 'three worlds' of welfare capitalism. In this typology universal provision was most pronounced in the social-democratic Nordic countries, 'middling' in Christian-democratic areas like France and Germany and much weaker in liberal regimes such as the USA and Japan (Esping-Anderson 1990).

The phrase 'welfare capitalism' itself indicates how this system was a compromise – a fraught and heated compromise – between states and capital. Such tensions are captured in the term Yiannis Gabriel and Tim Lang provide for this settlement, 'the Fordist Deal': a phrase evoking car manufacturer Henry Ford's argument that his workers needed to be able to afford to buy the goods they were making. The Fordist Deal promised 'ever-increasing standards of living in exchange for a quiescent labour force' (Gabriel and Lang 2015: 10) and for those within its national borders, offered substantial levels of social protection within a profoundly hierarchical and patriarchal structure.

At this time, a very significant opportunity for rising up the social ladder of employment was provided by the expanded numbers of people employed in the public sector, such as the civil service, hospitals, schools and libraries. As the Nuffield Mobility Study 1968–1971 demonstrated, the public sector had grown alongside the service sector, there was much more white-collar work on offer: more 'room at the top' (Bukodi *et al.* 2015;

Savage *et al.* 2015: 190). We can translate this phenomenon into terms compatible with academic research on social mobility, which usually differentiates between 'absolute' and 'relative' social mobility (Hickman 2009: 11; Goldthorpe, Llewellyn and Payne 1980). Absolute social mobility refers to the movement in occupational classes from one generation to the next. In the UK there was a high level of movement in absolute terms between 1945 and the mid-1980s due to the growth in professional employment in the public sector (especially in education and health) and in service sector employment.

The phenomenon of partial and expanding mid-century upward mobility has since reduced with the combined effects of public sector spending cuts since the 1980s and shrinkage in the service economy. Measuring relative social mobility involves comparing rates at which those from 'lower down' move up, compared to how many 'higher up' fall down. As Vikki Boliver and David Byrne have argued, not only has there been 'little if any sign of [people] becoming any more equal over time' but now with a crumbling middle class, 'upward mobility increasingly necessitates downward mobility' (Boliver and Byrne 2013; see also Dorling 2011). In other words, the 'room at the top' generated by an expanding public sector has shrunk.

Such patterns help explain both the mid-century cultural validation of professional occupations and the expanding late-twentieth-century focus on entrepreneurialism and celebrity. Since the late 1970s, these public welfare systems have been under sustained and incremental attacks and erosion from national and international policies and marketisation (Foucault 2008; Harvey 2005; Wahl 2011). The forms of social protection offered by welfare states have been subject to repeated assaults by various permutations of neoliberal practice as part of a longer unravelling since the late 1970s, now well documented in a range of texts on the effects of neoliberalism (Brown 2015; Foucault 2008; Harvey 2005). Neoliberalism has had 'uneven geographical developments', as David Harvey discusses in *A Brief History of Neoliberalism*. Naomi Klein and her team also provide a usefully detailed account of global differentiation in *The Shock Doctrine*, tracing connections between the compromises twisted into the legislation in post-apartheid South Africa, Chile and the UK (Klein 2008). In recent years, amidst neoliberal austerity, jobs and provision offered by the public sector have been one of the first targets for extensive cuts. Cutting back the protections offered by social democracy has disproportionately affected women, non-whites and the working class (Stephenson 2011; Pearson and Elson 2015; Wilkinson and Pickett 2010).

## Pulling rank: problems with welfarist rising up

However, there were also problems with both the extent, and the character, of these forms of rising up, of social mobility at the high point of the social democratic welfare state. Whilst it reduced poverty and squalor for all, the Anglo-American model of social democracy was disproportionately helpful at opening up progress and access to work for men, and especially white men. Whilst it provided more forms of social protection for all, the welfarist model in many countries was not particularly attuned to wider equalities in terms of social reproduction (as I explore in chapter 5). In the Anglo-American model of welfare capitalism the emphasis in paid work in the public sector like many private companies was still very much on the male worker as breadwinner. The question of reducing work hours for men and women so that they could share equal parenting, for example, was never on the agenda of the UK or US welfare state, unlike the Nordic model of welfare capitalism, a settlement which was more oriented towards this model (Fraser 2013). For example, in Sweden, equal pay was introduced in 1947 and paid maternity leave in 1948, whereas in the UK similar acts were only introduced in 1975 (by which time Sweden had made its parental leave unisex).

Neither did it integrate women, ethnic minorities or the working class with proportional egalitarianism into its employment structures. Covert discrimination continued to flourish. One good example of this is the British civil service. In the 1960s, the UK civil service employed nearly a million workers and, much like the administrative wing of imperial China mentioned in chapter 1, 'required examinations for promotions in order to privilege talent over connections', thus being known as a 'fair field with no favour' (Hicks 2016: 29). Whilst it was a more open system, the entrance exam still favoured some forms of experience over others, a fact recognised by the 1968 Fulton report which argued that the civil service entry exam was 'rooted firmly in the educational standards of Oxbridge and the curricular preferences of middle-class public schools' (Pilkington 1999: 20).

Moreover, as Marie Hicks' historical archive work on women and technology shows, there was a marked misogyny to how such employment positions and ranks were classified (Hicks 2010, 2016). Hicks writes of how, in the UK civil service, thousands of women working with early computers were given the employment classification of 'operators': jobs coded as menial and given low pay rates. As computing grew in importance and prestige, these tasks were recoded as skilled work, but instead of women rising alongside the new-found esteem of the labour task, they ended up training the very men who rose above them. Instead of rising up the ranks, women were structurally repositioned in terms of both pay and prestige away from the higher grades of work. Therefore, rather than inviting people to 'work their way up' employment hierarchies, Hicks concludes,

> we should look at the larger cultural and historical reasons why so many more women than men, and so many more black women than white women, have to start from the very bottom and often get stuck there.
>
> (Hicks 2016: 33)

It is also interesting to consider the model of 'progression' itself, and particularly the extent of what we could call the 'verticality' of the dominant model of employment in terms of pay and prestige. Undoubtedly the vast terrain of work includes very different tasks and responsibilities: different jobs require different skills, some jobs require more skills or are particularly complex, not everybody can do everything, experience needs to be valued. Yet the way work can be rewarded is variable. It can be rewarded through, for example, more time off after a certain length of service (as in Australian universities, where academics get a term off after a decade served) or as compensation for a particularly unattractive task (as in Alan Fox's idea of 'cross-grading' discussed in chapter 1, where rubbish collectors get extra leisure time due to the nature of their work).

To adapt a model so often applied to politics and social movements, the structure of ranks within a workplace can be differently organised in horizontal and vertical terms. An extremely hierarchical, vertical model will require little collaboration between ranks; an extremely horizontal model will require endless collaboration. The civil service was often taken as offering an excellent example of meritocracy. It was also a means through which competitive hierarchies of progression became more widely disseminated in the world of employment from the nineteenth century.[4] Its model, combining open recruitment with progressing through different ranks on the basis of merit rather than seniority, had been borrowed from the Indian civil service as it mutated from the East India Company (O'Toole 2006: 46–60). An imperialist militaristic corporation was then the template for what became the Northcote–Trevelyan report and the modern civil service. Notably the Northcote–Trevelyan report also sought to revoke a model in which progression was coterminous with seniority and explicitly advocated hiring more young men on the grounds that they were cheaper and would compete for better wages (O'Toole 2006: 57). This combination of open competition and pronounced, competitive hierarchical ranking was therefore normalised as a desirable labour practice. It is not that progressing, developing and the flourishing of capabilities are not necessary or useful – of course, they are vital – but their channelling and normalisation through an extremely vertical, competitive ladder-like system are noteworthy here. To what extent is this pronounced vertical ladder system, of competing to move up ranks, a system which perpetuates financial and classed differences and prevents, rather than fosters, flourishing?

At the high point of the welfare state, the expansion of professional jobs, particularly in the public sector, offered a route up the ladder, a means of social mobility. At the same time such social mobility was frequently painful. For some, like Richard Hoggart's working-class 'scholarship boy' who entered the middle-class domain of grammar school in the 1950s or the middle-class suburban women from working-class backgrounds interviewed by Steph Lawler in the 1990s, it led to a cultural isolation, a dissociation from support networks and/or 'imposter syndrome' alongside the longed-for material ease and opportunity (Hoggart 1957; Lawler 1999). Contemporary sociological work such as Sam Friedman's study of social mobility amongst comedians shows that a similar lack of cultural validation and affective dissonance remains acutely felt today (Friedman 2013). The point is not that people should somehow stay in an allotted, essentialised place, but rather that the classed, competitive hierarchies of 'a ladder of opportunity' leaves people behind.

## Selling 1968

A later and equally pivotal influence on the idea of meritocracy and rising up was the effects of the mid-to-late-twentieth-century liberation movements. The increasingly insistent demands for greater equality in terms of gender, race and sexuality from the 1960s in the Global North came to be widely culturally accepted as demands that were right and just. Whilst the realities of progress have been uneven and problematic, the argument that societies should be equal in terms of gender, race and sexuality was largely won. Significant acts and moments of progress were made in many respects on all fronts: for example, from the Equal Pay Act in UK in 1970 (1963 in the US) outlawing men and women being paid different amounts for the same job, through legislation outlawing discrimination on grounds of race or ethnicity in the UK Race Relations Act of 1976 (in the US, the Civil

Rights Act was passed in 1964) and to the wave of legalisation of gay marriage across most of Europe, New Zealand and Mexico in the early twenty-first century. Such dreams of equality have not exactly come to complete fruition. The move towards progressive social change is not, as liberal discourse would have it, automatically moving upwards on a steadily increasing curve. It is erratic and has to be continually fought for. These egalitarian movements, including demands for sexual liberation, anti-Vietnam War protests and worker reforms are sometimes referred to under the 'sign of 1968', the year of public uprisings, when 9 million people went on strike in France (Ross 2002; Gilbert 2008). The victories of this generation are enormously significant in terms of both their material gains and in terms of their colonisation of hegemonic common sense about what a 'just' society should be.

Yet these gains were also seized upon by corporate business discourse. The liberation movements for rights on the basis of gender, race, sexuality and environmentalism was seized upon by capitalism, its marketing gurus selling the dream of equality back to us as something we could have and possess if only we just bought this product. This process is dramatised at the end of the US HBO TV series *Mad Men*. The main character, advertising executive Don Draper, is featured channelling his recent experience in a Californian hippy retreat into creating Coca-Cola's famous hands-around-the-world corporate equal-opportunities anthem, 'I'd Like to Buy the World a Coke'. A real advert inserted into this fictional drama and sung to the tune of 'I'd Like to Teach the World to Sing', the footage of the famous advert features a self-consciously wide range of people singing who are supposed to represent the diversity of the world's population and marks the sucking-up of holistic environmentalism and multicultural universalism to refresh the corporate brand identity of a fizzy brown sugary drink.

The process of hijacking strands of 1960s-and-onwards progressive social movements was (and remains) not complete but uneven and continually contested. Liberation movements were themselves ideologically complex and multifaceted but were notably often produced through strong commitments to greater economic equality alongside that of race, sexual orientation and gender and often in innovative intersectional forms. The Black Panthers in the US, for example, set up both breakfast clubs to feed local kids and healthcare clinics in their communities (Nelson 2011; Cleaver and Katsiaficas 2001). In the UK, sections of the environmental and women's liberation movement joined with workers from heavily masculine trade unions to create the innovative 'Alternative Plan' for socially useful production when the

Lucas Aerospace plant was threatened with closure (Wainwright 2009; Rowbotham, Segal and Wainwright 2012). The corporate embrace of the new movements for equality was also complex and inventive, a mixture of carrot and stick: of being forced to comply with equal rights through legislation, and an eager embrace of the new marketing opportunities jacking your product to the promise of liberation might bring. What more potent advertising jingle than that offered by freedom?

Understanding the processes through which corporate discourse embraced these movements whilst simultaneously eroding workers' rights, the security of the full-time job and ultimately the welfare state has been a preoccupation of many scholars and activists for a couple of decades now (Frank 1998; Brooks 2001; Boltanski and Chiapello 2005; Hardt and Negri 2000; McGuigan 2009). Luc Boltanski and Eve Chiapello examine how management absorbed and reused the 'aesthetic critique', the imagery, rhetoric and vitalism of the 1968 counterculture to generate new forms of exploitation as part of what they termed *The New Spirit of Capitalism* (Boltanski and Chiapello 2005). After the Protestant work ethic that animated the industrial revolution from the eighteenth century and the bureaucratic spirit which marked the centralised uniformity of mid-twentieth-century Fordism and its 'company man' came this new rebel spirit, from the 1970s, forged in the networked knowledge economy. In his book on American politics and society, *Twilight of the Elites*, Christopher Hayes usefully argues that this moment can be understood as promising a 'second age of equality', as offering

> liberation from the unjust hierarchies of race, gender and sexual orientation, but swapped in their place a new hierarchy based on the notion that people are deeply unequal in ability and drive.
> 
> *(Hayes 2012: 22)*

As public funding for the public sector has been cut, sections sold off and marketised, and working conditions throughout the private sector have been weakened, the structural problems that were not addressed – the extremely hierarchical nature of the social ladder, the continued prejudice against and lack of opportunities for many women and those who were not white and the large majority of working-class people – have in a variety of ways become exacerbated. The picture is undoubtedly complex: the success of movements against sexism and racism allowed some mobility, particularly in terms of the entry of women into professional workplaces, but ongoing prejudice combined with structural economic inequality has kept the majority down. Meanwhile, the stories of the ones who 'made it', their 'inner talent' and drive causing them to rise up against the odds, are spotlighted, awarded a mediated power, and packaged into parables of progress through which to shame the rest.

## Parables of progress: luminous media fables

Rising up the social hierarchy is a narrative with considerable history, tending to appear – in different forms and with different articulations – wherever there is social inequality (Littler 2004). But it has been reinvigorated as a form within neoliberal culture and calibrated through an insistent emphasis on the self-fashioning of the entrepreneurial, self-promotional working subject. Stories about 'working really hard' to activate your talent form the structural template of many media texts, from self-help books through magazines to reality TV, presenting the journey of 'ordinary subjects', who become spotlighted, or made 'luminous', to borrow Angela McRobbie's inspired use of Deleuze (McRobbie 2009), and fashioned into moralising parables of meritocracy.

Indeed, mediated forms of competitive self-improvement are now ubiquitous. Perhaps nowhere has climbing the ladder of competitive individualism been represented so vividly as in the crystalline example of the genre of reality TV shows that are structured around 'making it', and so it is worth considering this example here in a little more detail. Wildly successful transnational franchises such as *Idol, The Apprentice, Voice, Got Talent* and *Top Model* repeatedly address ordinary subjects who can 'make it to the top' of their particular profession, particularly in the performing arts and business, through hard work and self-fashioning (Banet-Weiser 2012; Couldry and Littler 2008, 2011; Ouellette and Hay 2008; Stahl 2004; Turner 2010). The extent to which this subgenre of reality TV has provided a space through which work can be represented as above all a ruthless struggle between competing people for scarce prizes is remarkable. *The Apprentice*, for example, naturalises competitive individualism – in which all teamwork is a temporary means to an individualistic end – by offering itself up as a dramatic but essential truth of the harsh realities of how work 'just is' (Couldry and Littler 2008, 2011).

The degree to which both reality TV and its 'making it' subgenre have become small-screen staples makes it harder to remember the novelty of the format when it was so swiftly developed. *The Apprentice*'s promotion of entrepreneurialism as accessible for all, for instance, has long roots in the

Thatcherite enterprise culture that I discuss in the next chapter. But these terms have also been carefully cultivated and expanded, through the valorisation of entrepreneurialism as a significant factor of all employment, by the framing of the programme as 'educational' and its use in embedding entrepreneurialism as a subject children should be taught in schools. In the UK, the presenter Sir Alan Sugar was appointed 'Enterprise Tsar' for the government in 2009 and 2016 (Couldry and Littler 2008, 2011; BBC 2009, 2016). The glossy, meritocratic parables of rising up offered by the TV show and their surrounding media commentary are a key means through which entrepreneurialism, as both a discourse and a practice, has not simply been 'continued' but has been reinvigorated and extended into new domains, including, in the US, presidential candidacies.

Reality TV shows like *Idol* and *The Apprentice* offer dramas of rising up starring 'real' people. Reality television can be read and decoded in a variety of ways, and some critiques can harbour elitist snobberies (Skeggs and Wood 2011, 2012). The eruption of representations of ordinary, previously non-famous people (or 'civilians' in celebrity parlance) has for some critics been an invigorating sign of progressive representation of ordinary lives, or, in John Hartley's phrase, 'democratainment' (Hartley 1999). Yet for others, reality TV has been only too full of problems, problems which might be divided into two thematic areas. Firstly, it has been widely observed that the representation of ordinary people on reality TV has often been not only less than flattering, but has routinely involved ridicule and public forms of shame and humiliation (McRobbie 2009: 124–129; Ouellette and Hay 2008; Skeggs and Wood 2011, 2012; Biressi and Nunn 2005). In Milly Williamson's terms, 'ordinariness is circumscribed' on the majority of reality TV shows: instead of opening up a wide range of representations of ordinary people, it denigrates a large swathe of them whilst glorifying the winners (Williamson 2016).

Secondly, its economic basis, production and labour has been analysed and condemned as exploitative. The genre that Graeme Turner astutely described as involving a 'demotic turn' (Turner 2010) – or the increased representation of working- and lower-middle-class people – expanded from the 1990s primarily because such formats were cheap to make (Chalaby 2016) enabling employers to cut labour costs whilst the owners of the production companies harvested huge profits (Skeggs and Wood 2011: 2). In the process, as Milly Williamson puts it,

> Reality TV contributed significantly to the restructuring of the television industry, which, rather than opening up the industry democratically,

has resulted in attacks on the conditions of those who work in the industry and those who try to enter the ranks of fame by this means.

*(Williamson 2016: 102)*

Reality TV's promotion of ordinary people therefore came at the expense of shutting down access routes to employment and good conditions for workers in the TV industry. On the one hand, then, the trajectory of people winning competitions and fulfilling their latent talent was being made 'luminous', was being spotlighted as a model route to success by reality TV shows. On the other – whether through helping to close the doors to employment or to socially denigrate the working class – it functioned, in terms of both production and cultural discourse, to reduce career possibilities and to help make the process of actually accessing and progressing through the creative industries more difficult (Williamson 2016). As such they have become a vivid example of neoliberal meritocracy: for the majority, they present fables of progress whilst restricting possibilities.

## Not so cool: unequal employment

These restricted possibilities have begun to be more widely publicised. Over the past few years, the difficulties of entering the most publicly visible sections of the creative industries has become increasingly noted by workers, consumers, journalists and academics, as what has begun to be called 'the class ceiling' becomes more and more conspicuous. In the UK, actor Julie Walters, for instance, stated that working-class actors like herself who were able to attend drama school because their fees were paid and they received a full student maintenance grant from the government 'wouldn't get a chance today' in an era of vastly reduced public spending (Hattenstone and Walker 2015). Articles noting the predominance of upper-class actors on screen have been joined by others noting the affluent backgrounds of many pop stars, with conspicuous markers being either having attended expensive fee-paying schools or their status as offspring of other pop stars (Hensher 2013; Price 2014). In 2015, the UK shadow arts minister, Chris Bryant, stated that if he became a government minister, one of his priorities would be to encourage cultural organisations 'to hire from a wider variety of backgrounds. ... We can't just have a culture dominated by [actor] Eddie Redmayne and [singer] James Blunt and their ilk.' This statement prompted a furious reaction ('that classist, prejudiced wazzock') from the expensively educated singer James Blunt and a burst of media commentary on the increasingly conspicuous nature of class privilege in acting and singing (Furness 2015).

A related wave of scholarly attention over the past decade has foregrounded the lack of diversity in terms of gender, ethnicity and class in the no-collar, technology and cultural industries (e.g. Banks, Conor and Mayer 2015; Hesmondhalgh and Baker 2010; Hesmondhalgh and Saha 2013; Conor, Gill and Taylor 2015). For example, in their analysis of the 2014 British Labour Force Survey, Dave O'Brien and his colleagues argue that, despite considerable variation across the creative industries, there is a general underrepresentation of people from working-class origins across the sector, a phenomenon which is particularly pronounced in publishing and music; and that a 'class origin pay gap' persists (O'Brien et al. 2016). Taking a longer historical view and a more specific sector-based focus, Kate Oakley and Mark Banks have examined how art schools offered an alternative space for working-class youth and a flourishing incubator for creative production in the post-war period. As these art schools have been cut back and incorporated into the traditional university sector, and as student grants and social security benefits have been slashed, this supportive context has unravelled, decimating an important space of expression for working-class youth (Banks and Oakley 2016).

The continuing problems of covert and overt forms of racism, sexism and class prejudice in acting, the technology sector and the gaming industry have therefore received escalating media and academic coverage (e.g. Ross 2016). Rosalind Gill's work on European freelance new-media workers highlighted the disparities between men and women in terms of both payment and of difficulty of gaining jobs through 'clubbable' networks of male sociability (Gill 2002). The mythologised features of flexibility and informality work to bolster inequality, and these characteristics combined with 'the rejection by most new media workers of any discourse that makes gender visible' mean 'you have a situation in which patterns of discrimination are naturalised and inequality and injustice wear an egalitarian mask' (Gill 2002: 86). There has also been significant analysis of the varieties of forms taken by sexism in the online gaming industry, from overt abuse through homosocial nepotism to what Alison Harvey and Stephanie Fisher describe as the subtle forms of profession paternalism known as 'dadding' (Harvey and Fisher 2016: 655–656). And to take yet another instance, the film industry in the US and UK has come under renewed fire for its paucity of female directors and scriptwriters (Conor 2014; Geena Davis Institute on Gender in Media 2017).

The problem of the overwhelming whiteness of the film industry erupted into the consciousness of mainstream media commentary in 2015 with the popularisation of the #OscarsSoWhite hashtag on Twitter and the associative boycott of the Oscars by a range of stars, as I explore in chapter 5. The lack of non-white actors in general has been honed in on by pressure groups including the Act for Change Project.[5] The paucity of people of colour in prominent positions or positions of power in journalism has been imaginatively responded to by new sites of cultural production such as Media Diversified (a non-profit organisation and platform 'which seeks to cultivate and promote skilled writers of colour' in print and online).[6] And the small numbers of non-white workers (and audiences) in museums and galleries has prompted events including a recent single evening event showcasing contemporary artforms within London's Victoria & Albert Museum, curated by black women's collective gal-dem which attracted four thousand visitors (Okolosie 2016; Littler and Naidoo 2005).[7]

Of course, all of these problems of work access and progression in the cultural industries and no-collar sectors are not evenly distributed and have some highly specific characteristics (Conor, Gill and Taylor 2015). Art galleries, for example, have a high proportion of female workers, yet most managers and senior authority figures are male (Malik 2012). Publishing and PR are known for being industries particularly dominated by the white and upper-middle classes (Edwards 2013). The gaming industry is particularly patriarchal both in terms of the sexism directed at its female employees and the statistical proportion of women gaining entry to it. Yet a key point here is that all these inequalities and difficulties – whilst being highly specific in their complexity and particularity – are nonetheless happening, in the broader sense, simultaneously on the levels of gender, race and class. And these proven difficulties are in opposition to the dream that we have a level playing field, to the parables of progress, or to the liberal idea that equality is slowly, but surely, advancing on all fronts.

The realities, then, are that for those not at the top of the social pyramid it is harder to access these forms of social mobility through work, and yet the prevailing mythos has been that they are accessible to anyone. On the one hand, we only too clearly do not have a level playing field; on the other hand, we are told that we do.

## Selling inequality: post-feminism, post-race ... post-class?

How can we theorise these intersectional inequalities in contemporary neoliberal meritocracy? Attempts by neoliberal capitalism to commodify the impulses and desires of liberation movements have slowly started to be discussed by work in a range of disciplinary areas. But whilst work focusing on gender and neoliberalism, class and neoliberalism, or ethnicity and neoliberalism often share an analytical focus, they also use different languages or terminology. Therefore it would seem to be useful and important to consider how they are differently discussed and to put them more closely together in the same frame, in order to consider relational commonalities as well as the differences that are undoubtedly easier to identify.

Perhaps the area where the corporate hijacking of social demands for equality in order to extract the elements compatible with capitalism has received the most thorough ongoing analysis is in relation to feminism. There is now a sizeable body of theoretical and cultural work considering the corporate or neoliberal use of strands of feminism. For example, Nancy Fraser's recent collection *Fortunes of Feminism* foregrounds neoliberal borrowings from feminism, and the largely successful inciting of women to be complicit in individualising, privatising formations of gender: an updated twist on liberal feminism in the service of neoliberal capital (Fraser 2013, see also 2015). Angela McRobbie's incisive work has considered a variety of cultural modes through which women are encouraged to succeed, ostensibly as equals, by embracing individualised corporate rhetoric and behavioural norms in work and leisure, whether though 'being creative' in the cultural industries or through the cultural instruction of TV programmes like *What Not to Wear* (McRobbie 2009, 2016).

Whilst the terms 'neoliberal femininism', 'marketised feminism' and 'corporate feminism' have all been mobilised to gesture toward or analyse the articulation of feminism to neoliberal forces and agents, in academia 'post-feminism' remains the most ubiquitous term of choice to refer to these processes. 'Post-feminism' is used to refer to a widely distributed 'common sense', roughly from the 1980s and 1990s, that the movement for gender equality has been achieved: that the need for feminism is finished and we have a level playing field through which we need to progress (McRobbie 2009; Gill 2006, 2007; Gill and Scharff 2011; Banet-Weiser 2012). It therefore often involves a distancing from or disavowal of the feminist movement, heightened individualism and a resurgence of ideas of 'natural' sexual difference, often through a focus on self-surveillance and make-over culture as 'empowerment': a constellation which for Rosalind Gill is best understood as a 'sensibility' (Gill 2006). It can often harbour overtly 'retrosexist' discourse which is compatible with an anti-feminist backlash (Whelehan 2000). In similar fashion the marketplace's embrace of gay rights and the spending power of the 'pink pound' has produced formations of neoliberal sexuality that move away from queer socialism into gay and lesbian corporatism (Hennessey 2000). Post-feminist discourse can at times be conspicuously white, given that it often addresses wealthier women most directly in attempting to solicit their spending, replicating the structural prejudice of the systemic inequalities. Yet it is far from exclusively so, as work on post-feminist interpellations of women in, for instance, Nigeria shows (Dosekun 2015).

How do these analyses of gender relate to the theorisation of neoliberalism's use of demands for racial or ethnic equality? Again no singular terminology is uniformly mobilised; rather, a range of terms are used to describe and interrogate various dimensions of this dynamic. In critical race theory there has been an analytical focus on the widespread dissemination in the neoliberal era of the idea that we are now in a post-discrimination moment: that we are 'post-race', that we have a level playing field and that anyone can get on if they try hard enough (I explore this formation in more detail in chapter 5). David Theo Goldberg's work, for example, has extensively elaborated upon, critiqued and popularised the notion of 'post-race' (Goldberg 2015). Racialised neoliberalism, in the form of ethnically marked mobilisations of empowerment, is the subject of Jean Comaroff and John Comaroff's book *Ethnicity, Inc.* It is discussed both in terms of particularly ethnicised populations' entrepreneurial self-branding and in terms of corporations' use of racialisation to open up new markets. As they put it, 'despite the fact that it was supposed to wither away and die with modernity', ethnicity is 'becoming more corporate, more commodified, more implicated than ever before in the economics of everyday life' (Comaroff and Comaroff 2009: 1). Paul Gilroy's instructive work providing 'fragments for a history of black vernacular neoliberalism' traces the histories of the insistent interpellations to American black subjects to make themselves rich – through such routes as the popular self-help money-making/masculinity guide *Rich Dad, Poor Dad* (Gilroy 2013).

There is then an obvious semantic synchronicity and conceptual 'family resemblance' between the analytical categories of post-feminism and post-race, although this family resemblance is surprisingly under-discussed. Interestingly, 'post-class' has not been mobilised as a term in the same way. To some degree this is because the corporate co-option of struggles for equality and liberation, of anti-racism and anti-sexism, to sell products to produce profit, has involved targeting people with enough wealth to buy the products. Class is not always so easy a target in this regard as post-feminism – easily the most conspicuously discussed of these 'posts-' – has been.[8] Put bluntly, this is because women are a large consumer market. Post-Fordist neoliberalism adopted the aspects of late-twentieth-century liberation movements that it found compatible, absorbing many women and non-white people into the workplace, making them professional. And the increased spending power of women – obviously not all women, but still a large proportion following the influx of women into paid work – has made feminism a particularly ripe zone for corporations to poach, package and brand.

In the 1980s and 1990s, for many people identifying on the political left, as well as the right, in the Global North, class was often presumed to be less relevant than gender or ethnicity, as we shall see in the next chapter. This particular worldview was helped along by the ambiguities of the meaning of 'class'. 'Class' refers to financial income and social location in relation to wider stratifications and exploitations, particularly in relation to individual/ family occupation. Most famously, for Marx, it is defined by position in the relations of production (Marx and Engels 2004); for Weber, it also needs to be understood in terms of status. Class also tends to refer to a constellation of cultural attributes, dispositions and subjectivities which are formed in relation to a particular habitus (Skeggs 2004; Steedman 1986; Crompton 2008). As Steph Lawler puts it, 'class is not simply an "objective" position which one occupies, but becomes configured into subjectivity' (Lawler 1999: 6). The slippage between financial positon and socio-cultural identification and behaviour has aided the ambiguities of class in relation to meritocracy. The welfare state did reduce inequality, expanding social protection, introducing greater levels of financial egalitarianism for all, both engendering social mobility and helping reduce the length of the ladder in financial terms. An expanding middle class, combined with the effects of new social movements and the 'decline of deference' also produced considerable ambiguity about social standing.

As post-Fordist marketing identified and targeted ever more particularised 'lifestyle demographics', the broad certainties of class looked to many less certain. At the zenith of the post-Fordist retail boom, class often became neglected as a category in academia, in part in favour of what were perceived as more interestingly hybrid categories, in part due to challenges from the feminism to the masculinism of class analysis, and in part due to the emphasis on consumption (Crompton 2008). Rosemary Crompton's different introductions to the reissues of her classic text *Class and Stratification* is telling here: she discusses the fluctuating academic fortunes of class as an analytical category, from avid debates in the 1960s to having to justify why class should still be considered an important category at all in the 1980s and

1990s, a moment when the end of class was regularly proclaimed. But by the end of the decade of the 2000s the effects of neoliberal inequality meant it was increasingly apparent to even the most apolitical sociologist that class could not be ignored (Crompton 2008: ix–x).

The dream of classlessness, the idea of it, was taken up by post-Fordist capitalism through the promotion of many of its products even while its production found new means to exploit the labour power of its workers and extract profit from their labour. The phrase which for me captures most vividly this yoking of the selling of the idea of a new classlessness to the desire to accumulate capitalistic profits is Anthony Barnett's phrase 'corporate populism' (Barnett 2003). To Barnett, 'corporate populism' foregrounds how an image of popular democracy was foregrounded by Blairism in the Labour Party in the 1990s, at the very moment when democratic politics – the meaningful involvement of more and more people in decision-making over their own futures – was being emptied out, in a 'post-democratic' landscape, in favour of corporate hierarchies (Crouch 2004).

Whilst 'post-class' is not popularised as an analytical term, then, the dream or ideology of classlessness has definitely been mobilised as a selling point in the service of corporate capital. Just as the idea of empowerment through freedom from discrimination on the basis of ethnicity, gender or sexuality has been mobilised, so too has a certain discourse used the idea of freedom from the constraints of class in the service of corporate profit. We saw this above in relation to what Graeme Turner analysed as the 'demotic populism' of media forms such as reality TV, and Jim McGuigan analysed as 'cool capitalism' (Turner 2010; McGuigan 2009). To bring it into line with the terms 'post-race' and 'post-feminism', we can term this formation – this idea that we are beyond class – 'post-class'.

## Neoliberal justice narratives

These recent strands of academic work analysing 'post-class', 'post-feminism' and 'post-race' have many resemblances. Putting these terms side by side helps highlight how they share a logic, whilst being simultaneously moulded through their own particular, ascribed formations (as well as being hybrid and interwoven with each other). All these terms foreground the neoliberal, entrepreneurial, corporate market-based logic that suggests it offsets and rectifies inequalities of class, race and gender. Their persuasive currency is undoubtedly rooted in the fact that they do offer the partially privileged more privilege. Neoliberal meritocratic post-feminism, for example, can work well for you if you are a professional woman with no children. Neoliberal post-racism, for example, can work well for you if you are wealthy and brown or wealthy and white. These discourses do not work for those with less social and economic capital: for those who are insistently told to pull themselves up by their bootstraps when they are unable to afford the boots to begin with.

Such ideological discourses work on an individualised level, for the already privileged, whilst foreclosing any challenges using collective action, universal provision or democratic organisation (and creating further and different forms of inequality). Neoliberal meritocracy has played the cards of identity politics by creating and exploiting the meritocratic deficit. Putting these discourses side by side helps indicate just how much neoliberal meritocracy is fed by and sources its galvanising energies from post-feminism, post-racism and post-classism. These phenomena are sophisticatedly detailed, to be sure, but they are also connected through neoliberal meritocracy and crucially work together to give each other strength.

As we will see, in recent years there have been changes within this post-class/feminism/race formation, with the widespread acceptability of the idea that we are now beyond inequalities of class, race and gender. For the extent to which such narratives simply do not fit with the tangible material reality of the majority of people's experience has become increasingly apparent and hard to ignore. Neoliberalism's post-crash interregnum has produced a new formation which recognises intersectional injustice but promotes neoliberal marketisation as the solution: what I call the 'neoliberal justice narrative'. Whereas a pivotal component of post-feminism and post-race sensibilities involve a distancing from (and disavowal of) the feminist and anti-racist movements, neoliberal justice narratives recognise and draw on them whilst prescribing capitalist meritocracy as the cure for their ills. The idea of feminism has been more sympathetically and overtly drawn upon for commercial purposes, promising forms of commoditised 'empowerment' in, for example, adverts for Always sanitary towels, which took stereotypical misogynistic slander about 'throwing like a girl' to task, or in the adverts for Dove featuring differently sized 'real women' (Banet-Weiser 2012: 15–50). Such forms of 'commodity feminism' or 'femvertising' are now routinely (if still, overall, marginally) discussed in journalism and academia. Andi Zeisler's *We Were Feminists Once: From Riot Grrl to Cover Girl* (2016), for instance, attacks the 'selling out' of the feminist movement (located later than usual) into marketplace feminism, in which commercial companies are involved in selling empowerment as a means to attractively package their brand. Such corporate use of feminist symbolism is a significant shift from post-feminism: as in post-feminism, the temporal distancing from the feminist movement is a key feature and, indeed, one signified through the term itself. They are both variants of neoliberal feminism, but they have different temporal and affective relationships to the feminist movement.

Similarly, there have been recent high-profile commercial activities which do not suggest that the social playing field in relation to ethnicity is level – but rather loudly proclaim that it is anything but. Beyoncé's powerful mobilisation of the iconography of the Black Power movement at the US Superbowl in 2016, the foregrounding of Black Lives Matter and the institutional racism of the response to Hurricane Katrina in New Orleans in the song and incendiary video 'Formation' and her album *Lemonade* are much-discussed cases in point here (London 2016). They have had the highest media profile of any recent examples of anti-racism in US popular culture, and they have a powerful charge in a time of resurgent racism. They are also very obviously commercial products. Indeed, Beyoncé positions her accumulation of vast wealth as an anti-racist 'fuck-you' badge of pride, with the lyrics to the song 'Formation' proclaiming: 'I just might be a black Bill Gates in the making.' This is a commercial song and persona with a profoundly anti-racist yet profoundly capitalist message, a form of powerful and neoliberal anti-racism and feminism. It has a different relationship to racism than that of the neoliberal post-racial.

Whilst post-feminism, post-race and post-class are all recognisably evoked discourses, then, they have been joined by newer variants of neoliberal feminism, anti-racism and populism. This formation takes a slightly different angle of approach to neoliberal meritocracy. It does not disrupt its basic tenets of competitive individualism and effort (or the end result of the production of greater inequality). Instead, it is propelled by recognisable and profound intersectional injustices to climb harder up the ladder. This is neoliberal meritocracy as social justice narrative. Neoliberal justice narratives recognise existing unjust social dynamics in relation to ethnicity, gender and class, and suggest that neoliberal marketisation will solve these problems to produce greater meritocracy.

## Egalitarian and meritocratic deficits

In the Global North, then, for very well-discussed historical reasons, the positions of greatest social and economic power have tended, and still tend to be, occupied by rich white men. Inequality disproportionately affects those from the working or lower-middle classes, who are not white and who are female.[9] This is not exclusively the case and is not by any means uniform. (Therefore chapter 4, on meritocracy and elitism, considers examples which disrupt this pattern, and chapter 6 discusses middle-class women.) Yet notably it is often people who face significant disempowerment in terms of the extent of their resources and the range of available choices who are most intensely incited to construct a neoliberal meritocratic self. In other words, people who are not part of the elite and who are not rich white men start from positions of reduced power, and, at the same time, they are simultaneously incited to address their lack of privilege themselves, individually, through cultural discourses of neoliberal meritocracy which deploy particular languages and accents of gender, race and class. Less privileged constituencies are then positioned as particularly amenable to a meritocratic discourse of empowerment by becoming 'entrepreneurial selves', whilst, at the very same time, these constituencies continue to face far greater difficulties in terms of both recognition and redistribution. This gap, in the face of the demand to move upwards, is a double penalty: they face a double egalitarian deficit.

The idea of the double egalitarian deficit foregrounds how progressing upwards is not the easy task that the various permutations of the meritocratic myth would have us believe. It indicates the extent of the ingrained and structural obstacles in the way of people who do not have the economic, social and cultural power of those at the top of the pile and who are incited to work hard individually to overcome them. To understand the reasons for the double egalitarian deficit and the mythic structure of neoliberal meritocracy in relation to work, this chapter looked in two directions. Firstly, the ideal of 'progression' itself as an employment category was traced to the growth in democratic career opportunities during the high point of the Fordist welfare state with its simultaneous expanded opportunities and 'blindspots' (or exploitations). The limited and incomplete nature of this progression was discussed using the example of the civil service which, whilst significantly open in many ways, also remained severely limited in terms of access and movement up the career hierarchy to women, ethnic minorities and working-class people. It considered the limitations of what such progression meant – in terms of who was included, of the extended competitive verticality of rank and the wider terrain of social reproduction – alongside the vast possibilities it opened up.

Secondly, the chapter looked at the corporate exploitation of identity politics and liberation demands from the 1960s and 1970s: at how the emergence of neoliberalism extrapolated and re-appropriated selective discourse from wider movements for equality in the name of gender, race, class, environmentalism and sexuality. Today, progression up the social ladder is selectively presented in media fables which make stories of everyday stratospheric upward job mobility both ordinary and luminous (McRobbie 2009). But there is now ample evidence of the decidedly unmeritocratic nature of contemporary work in many of these 'desirable' jobs despite their 'cool, creative and egalitarian' image (Gill 2002). The image of work as 'hip' and egalitarian can therefore be situated in relation to the wider context of the decline of deference and the 'rebel' 'spirit of capitalism' that Luc Boltanski and Eve Chiapello have identified as the animating aspect of the dominant contemporary corporate ethos (Boltanski and Chiapello 2005). Such an aesthetic of corporate rebellion borrowed from the demands of the 1968 generation for gender, racial and sexual equality, accepting selective elements compatible with liberal capitalism whilst helping perpetuate, and generate new forms of, structural inequality.

These historical developments were traced to theorisations of post-race, post-feminism and post-class. All these discourses deny that there are any longer any inequalities that matter at the level of race, class or gender. They feed neoliberal meritocracy by suggesting there is a level playing field and inciting those who face a greater uphill battle for success with greater degrees of 'responsibilisation'. More recently neoliberal meritocracy has been extended through the addition of neoliberal justice narratives, which, unlike post-feminism, post-race and post-class, recognise injustices at the level of race, gender and class, but like them suggest that it is the responsibility of neoliberal marketisation and the individual to redress these inequalities. Neoliberal justice narratives recognise the egalitarian deficit as a meritocratic deficit and prescribe competitive neoliberal meritocracy as the solution, which in turn produces more inequality.

All these discourses of neoliberal meritocracy are powerful and, as I show in chapter 6, frequently work by being 'internalised'. There is often a different tenor and expenditure of energy to them than to the meritocratic discourses inhabited by elites (as I discuss in chapter 4). They inhabit a similar neoliberal entrepreneurial logic but at very different points on the scale: occupying different affective positions and positions of power. The position occupied by elites inhabits, externalises and radiates outwards the privileges proffered by the neoliberal meritocratic system. But this is qualitatively different from how less privileged constituencies are able to relate to neoliberal meritocracy: they are always in a particularly exploited process which has to labour harder and harder to offset the structural inequalities which are there to begin with; and they are also, as we will see in chapter 6, often marked by a tenor of desperation. Whilst the elite access meritocracy through a rapid express elevator, these constituencies have to run hard just to keep on the same spot.

To consider in more detail how disempowered constituencies have been positioned as especially amenable to a meritocratic discourse of empowerment, chapters 4 and 5 therefore focus on case studies where the incitement to internalised meritocratic subjects is taking place: in the form of racialisation on the reality TV show *Project Greenlight* and through the emergent social figure of the mumpreneur. But before we turn to the case studies, we need to ask: how was the neoliberal meritocratic political settlement achieved? This chapter has focused on the relationship between meritocracy, intersectional inequalities and worlds of work. The next chapter considers how this settlement was achieved through political discourse.

## Notes

1 *The Stuart Hall Project* 2013.
2 'Meritocracy is your ideal partner for finding and attracting top Millennials' (Meritocracy n.d.).
3 There are eight men and two women depicted on the management team: they could all pass as white (Meritocracy n.d.).
4 I am grateful to Judith Watson and Ben Little for sharing their knowledge of these histories with me.
5 www.act-for-change.com. Accessed 1 December 2016.
6 https://mediadiversified.org. Accessed 1 December 2016.
7 www.gal-dem.com. Accessed 1 December 2016.
8 Post-class discourse and its lack of critical definition is also, of course, because the new left's socialist egalitarianism, which Kristin Ross calls 'the properly 1960s aspiration to equality' (K. Ross 2002: 10) was defeated. And it is also because socialism is harder to extract elements from for neoliberal purposes, given that they are antithetical, even though projects like the UK prime minister David Cameron's 'Big Society', which sought to offset public sector cuts by encouraging volunteering and using a language of solidarity, or the neoliberal encouragement in Italy of social family networks to replace state provision, for example, have tried hard (Muehlebach 2012).
9 There is, of course, an endlessly proliferating diversity of intersectional positions in and around such social identities. The position of a middle-class black woman in Birmingham is not the same as a brown transsexual in Helsinki or a white working-class woman in Detroit.

## References

Banet-Weiser, Sarah (2012) *AuthenticTM*. New York: NYU Press.
Banks, Mark, and Kate Oakley (2016) 'The Dance Goes on Forever? Art Schools, Class and UK Higher Education', *International Journal of Cultural Policy* 22(1) pp. 41–57.

Banks, Miranda, Bridget Conor and Vicki Mayer (eds) (2015) *Production Studies, the Sequel! Cultural Studies of Global Media Industries*. New York: Routledge.
Barnett, Anthony (2003) 'Corporate Populism and Partyless Democracy', in A. Chadwick and R. Hefferman (eds), *The New Labour Reader*. Oxford: Polity Press.
BBC (2009) 'Sir Alan Hired in Government Role', *BBC News*, 5 June, http://news.bbc.co.uk/1/hi/business/8085254.stm. Accessed 1 November 2016.
BBC (2016) 'Lord Sugar Re-hired as Government Enterprise "Tsar"', *BBC News*, 25 May, www.bbc.co.uk/news/uk-politics-36376161. Accessed 1 November 2016.
Berlant, Lauren (2011) *Cruel Optimism*. Durham, NC: Duke University Press.
Biressi, Anita, and Heather Nunn (2005) *Reality TV: Realism and Revelation*. New York: Columbia University Press.
Boliver, Vikki, and David Byrne (2013) 'Social Mobility: The Politics, the Reality, the Alternative', *Soundings* 55 (December) pp. 50–59.
Boltanski, Luc, and Eve Chiapello (2005) *The New Spirit of Capitalism*. London: Verso.
Brooks, David (2001) *Bobos in Paradise: The New Upper Class and How They Got There*. New York: Simon & Schuster.
Brown, Phillip, and Stuart Tannock (2009) 'Education, Meritocracy and the Global War for Talent', *Journal of Education Policy* 24(4) pp. 377–392.
Brown, Wendy (2015) *Undoing the Demos*. Cambridge, MA: MIT Press.
Bukodi, Erzsébet, John H. Goldthorpe, Lorraine Waller and Jouni Kuha (2015) 'The Mobility Problem in Britain: New Findings from the Analysis of Birth Cohort Data', *British Journal of Sociology* 66(1) pp. 93–118.
Chalaby, Jean (2016) *The Format Age*. Cambridge: Polity Press.
Cleaver, Kathleen, and George Katsiaficas (eds) (2001) *Liberation, Imagination and the Black Panther Party: A New Look at the Black Panthers and their Legacy*. New York: Routledge.
Comaroff, John L., and Jean Comaroff (2009) *Ethnicity, Inc.* Chicago: University of Chicago Press.
Conor, Bridget (2014) *Screenwriting: Creative Labour and Professional Practice*. London: Routledge.
Conor, Bridget, Rosalind Gill and Stephanie Taylor (eds) (2015) *Gender and Creative Labour*. London: Wiley-Blackwell.
Couldry, Nick, and Jo Littler (2008) 'The Work of Work: Reality TV and the Negotiation of Neoliberal Labour in *The Apprentice*', in Thomas Austin and Wilma de Jong (eds), *The Documentary Reader*. Maidenhead: Open University Press.
Couldry, Nick, and Jo Littler (2011) 'Work, Power and Performance: Analysing the "Reality" Game of The Apprentice', *Cultural Sociology* 5(2) pp. 263–279.
Crompton, Rosemary (2008) *Class and Stratification*, 3rd edn. Oxford: Polity Press.
Crouch, Colin (2004) *Post-Democracy*. Oxford: Polity Press.
Dorling, Danny (2011) *Injustice: Why Social Inequality Still Persists*. Kindle edn. Bristol: Policy Press.

Dosekun, Simile (2015) 'For Western Girls Only? Postfeminism as Transnational Media Culture', *Feminist Media Studies* 15(6) pp. 960–975.

Edwards, Lee (2013) 'Institutional Racism in Cultural Production: The Case of PR', *Popular Communication* 11(3) pp. 242–256.

Esping-Anderson, Gøsta (1990) *The Three Worlds of Welfare Capitalism*. Princeton: Princeton University Press.

Foucault, Michel (2008) *The Birth of Biopolitics: Lectures at the Collège de France, 1978–1979*, trans. Graham Burchell. Basingstoke: Palgrave Macmillan.

Frank, Thomas (1998) *The Conquest of Cool: Business Culture, Counterculture and the Rise of Hip Consumerism*. Chicago: University of Chicago Press.

Fraser, Nancy (2013) *Fortunes of Feminism*. London: Verso.

Fraser, Nancy (2015) 'The Fortunes of Socialist Feminism: Jo Littler Interviews Nancy Fraser', *Soundings* 58 (January) pp. 21–33.

Friedman, Sam (2013) 'The Price of the Ticket: Rethinking the Experience of Social Mobility', *Sociology* 47(6) pp. 352–368

Friedman, Thomas (2005) *The World is Flat: A Brief History of the Twentieth Century*. New York: Farrar, Straus and Giroux.

Furness, Hannah (2015) 'James Blunt Pens Letter to "Classist, Prejudiced Wazzock" Chris Bryant MP over Privilege Claims', *Daily Telegraph*, 19 January, www.telegraph.co.uk/news/11355123/James-Blunt-pens-letter-to-classist-prejudiced-wazzock-Chris-Bryant-MP-over-privilege-claims.html. Accessed 1 November 2016.

Gabriel, Yiannis, and Tim Lang (2015) *The Unmanageable Consumer*, 3rd edn. London: Sage.

Geena Davis Institute on Gender in Media (2017) https://seejane.org. Accessed 1 March 2017.

Gilbert, Jeremy (2008) 'After '68: Narratives of the New Capitalism', *New Formations* 65 pp. 34–53.

Gill, Rosalind (2002) 'Cool, Creative and Egalitarian? Exploring Gender in Project-Based New Media Work in Europe', *Information, Communication and Society* 5(1) pp. 70–89.

Gill, Rosalind (2006) *Gender and the Media*. Cambridge: Polity Press.

Gill, Rosalind (2007) 'Postfeminist Media Culture: Elements of a Sensibility', *European Journal of Cultural Studies* 10(2) pp. 147–166.

Gill, Rosalind, and Christina Scharff (eds) (2011) *New Femininities: Postfeminism, Neoliberalism and Subjectivity*. Basingstoke: Palgrave.

Gilroy, Paul (2013) 'We Got to Get Over before We Go Under': Fragments for a History of Black Vernacular Neoliberalism', *New Formations* 80–81, pp. 23–38.

Goldberg, David Theo (2015) *Are We All Postracial Yet?* Cambridge: Polity Press.

Goldthorpe, John, Catriona Llewellyn and Clive Payne (1980) *Social Mobility and Class Structure in Modern Britain*. London: Transaction.

Gregg, Melissa (2011) *Work's Intimacy*. Cambridge: Polity Press.

Hardt, Michael, and Antonio Negri (2000) *Empire*. Cambridge, MA: Harvard University Press.

Hartley, John (1999) *Uses of Television*. London: Routledge.

Harvey, Alison, and Stephanie Fisher (2016) 'Growing Pains: Feminisms and Intergenerationality in Digital Games', *Feminist Media Studies* 16(4) pp. 648–662.
Harvey, David (2005) *A Brief History of Neoliberalism*. Oxford: Oxford University Press.
Hattenstone, Simon, and Peter Walker (2015) 'Julie Walters: Lack of Working-Class Actors is Sad', *The Guardian*, 23 January, www.theguardian.com/culture/2015/jan/23/julie-walters-lack-working-class-actors-sad. Accessed 1 November 2016.
Hayes, Christopher (2012) *Twilight of the Elites*. New York: Crown Publishing Group.
Hennessey, Rosemary (2000) *Profit and Pleasure: Sexual Identities in Late Capitalism*. New York: Routledge.
Hensher, Philip (2013) 'Do We Really Want Pop Stars from Public School?', *The Independent*, 29 March, www.independent.co.uk/voices/comment/do-we-really-want-pop-stars-from-public-school-8554501.html. Accessed 1 November 2016.
Hesmondhalgh, David, and Sarah Baker (2010) *Creative Labour: Media Work in Three Cultural Industries*. London: Routledge.
Hesmondhalgh, David, and Anamik Saha (2013) 'Race, Ethnicity, and Cultural Production', *Popular Communication* 11(3) pp. 179–195.
Hickman, Rebecca (2009) *In Pursuit of Egalitarianism: And Why Social Mobility Cannot Get Us There*. London: Compass.
Hicks, Marie (2010) 'Meritocracy and Feminization in Conflict: Computerization in the British Government', in Thomas Misa (ed.), *Gender Codes: Why Women are Leaving Computing*. Oxford: Wiley-Blackwell, pp. 96–114.
Hicks, Marie (2016) 'Against Meritocracy in the History of Computing', *CORE: The Magazine of the Computer History Museum*, http://s3.computerhistory.org/core/core-2016.pdf. Accessed 1 March 2017 .
Hoggart, Richard (1957) *The Uses of Literacy*. Harmondsworth: Penguin.
Klein, Naomi (2008) *The Shock Doctrine: The Rise of Disaster Capitalism*. Harmondsworth: Penguin.
Lawler, Steph (1999) 'Getting Out and Getting Away', *Feminist Review* 63 pp. 3–24.
Littler, Jo (2004) 'Making Fame Ordinary: Intimacy, Reflexivity and "Keeping it Real"', *Mediactive* 2 pp. 8–25.
Littler, Jo, and Roshi Naidoo (eds) (2005) *The Politics of Heritage: The Legacies of 'Race'*. London: Routledge.
London, Dianca (2016) 'Beyoncé's Capitalism, Masquerading as Radical Change'. *Death and Taxes*, 9 February, www.deathandtaxesmag.com/280129/beyonce-capitalism-black-activism. Accessed 2 March 2017 .
McGuigan, Jim (2009) *Cool Capitalism*. London: Pluto Press.
McRobbie, Angela (2009) *The Aftermath of Feminism: Gender, Culture and Social Change*. London: Sage.
McRobbie, Angela (2016) *Be Creative: Making a Living in the New Culture Industries*. Cambridge: Polity Press.
Malik, Suhail (2012) 'Survey on Gender Ratios in Curating Programmes', *Red Hook Journal*, www.bard.edu/ccs/redhook/survey-on-gender-ratios-in-curating-programs. Accessed 1 November 2016.

Marx, Karl, and Friedrich Engels (2004) *Marx and Engels Collected Works*. London: Lawrence & Wishart.
Meritocracy (n.d.) https://meritocracy.is/en/manifesto. Accessed 1 October 2016.
Muehlebach, Andrea (2012) *The Moral Neoliberal: Welfare and Citizenship in Italy*. Chicago: University of Chicago Press
Nelson, Alondra (2011) *Body and Soul: The Black Panther Party and the Fight Against Medical Discrimination*. Minneapolis: University of Minnesota Press.
O'Brien, Dave, Daniel Laurison, Andrew Miles and Sam Friedman (2016) 'Are the Creative Industries Meritocratic? An Analysis of the 2014 British Labour Force Survey', *Cultural Trends* 25(2) pp. 116–131.
Okolosie, Lola (2016) 'People of Colour are Painfully Absent from Our Museums: Let's Change That', *The Guardian*, 4 November, www.theguardian.com/commentisfree/2016/nov/04/people-of-colour-absent-museums. Accessed 10 December 2016.
O'Toole, Barry (2006) *The Ideal of Public Service: Reflections on the Higher Civil Service in Britain*. London: Routledge.
Ouellette, Laurie, and James Hay (2008) *Better Living Through Reality TV*. Malden, MA: Wiley-Blackwell.
Pearson, Ruth, and Diane Elson (2015) 'Transcending the Impact of the Financial Crisis in the United Kingdom: Towards Plan F, a Feminist Economic Strategy', *Feminist Review* 109(1) pp. 8–30.
Pilkington, C. (1999) *The Civil Service in Britain Today*. Manchester: Manchester University Press.
Price, Simon (2014) 'How My Research into Pop's Posh Takeover was Hijacked', *The Guardian*, 23 February, www.theguardian.com/music/2014/feb/23/research-pops-posh-takeover-hijacked-stars-privately-educated. Accessed 1 October 2016.
Ross, Andrew (2004) *No Collar: The Humane Workplace and its Hidden Costs*. Philadelphia: Temple University Press.
Ross, Andrew (2010) *Nice Work if You Can Get It: Life and Labor in Precarious Times*. New York: NYU Press.
Ross, Kristin (2002) *May '68 and its Afterlives*. Chicago: University of Chicago Press.
Ross, Tracey (2016) 'The Unsettling Truth about the Tech Sector's Meritocracy Myth', *Washington Post*, 13 April, www.washingtonpost.com/news/in-theory/wp/2016/04/13/the-unsettling-truth-about-the-tech-sectors-meritocracy-myth. Accessed 1 December 2016.
Rowbotham, Sheila, Lynne Segal and Hilary Wainwright (2012) *Beyond the Fragments: Feminism and the Making of Socialism*, 3rd revd edn. London: Merlin Press.
Savage, Mike, Niall Cunningham, Fiona Devine, Sam Friedman, Daniel Laurison, Lisa McKenzie, Andrew Miles, Helene Snee and Paul Wakeling (2015) *Social Class in the Twenty First Century*. Milton Keynes: Pelican
Sennett, Richard (2006) *The Culture of the New Capitalism*. New Haven: Yale University Press.
Skeggs, Beverley (2004) *Class, Self Culture*. London: Routledge.

Skeggs, Beverley, and Helen Wood (2011) *Reacting to Reality Television*. London: Routledge.
Skeggs, Beverley, and Helen Wood (eds) (2012) *Reality Television and Class*. Basingstoke: Palgrave.
Stahl, Matt (2004) 'A Moment Like This: American Idol and Narratives of Meritocracy', in Chris Washburne and Maiken Derno (eds), *Bad Music: The Music We Love to Hate*. New York: Routledge, pp. 212–232.
Steedman, Carolyn (1986) *Landscape for a Good Woman: A Story of Two Lives*. London: Virago.
Stephenson, Mary-Ann (2011) *Women and the Cuts*. London: TUC.
*The Stuart Hall Project* (2013) dir. John Akomfrah. London: BFI.
Turner, Graeme (2010) *Ordinary People and the Media: The Demotic Turn*. London: Sage.
Wahl, Asbørn (2011) *The Rise and Fall of the Welfare State*. London: Pluto Press.
Wainwright, Hilary (2009) 'A Real Green Deal', *Red Pepper*, October, www.redpepper.org.uk/a-real-green-deal. Accessed 1 October 2016.
Whelehan, Imelda (2000) *Overloaded: Popular Culture and the Future of Feminism*. London: Women's Press.
Wilkinson, Richard, and Kate Pickett (2010) *The Spirit Level: Why Equality is Better for Everyone*. London: Penguin.
Williamson, Milly (2016) *Celebrity: Capitalism and the Making of Fame*. Cambridge: Polity Press.
Zeisler, Andi (2016) *We Were Feminists Once: From Riot Grrl to Cover Girl*. New York: PublicAffairs Press.

# 3

# MERITOCRATIC FEELING

The movement of meritocracy in political rhetoric

> There is no value-free definition of meritocracy.
>
> Ronald Bénadou[1]

## Meritocratic feeling

So far, this book has considered how the discourse of neoliberal meritocracy emerged and mutated in social theory and how it has been shaped through the changing dynamics of work and through the legacies of 1960s social movements. In this chapter, the book turns its attention to how such changes in the meaning of meritocracy were made possible in the political sphere. It pays particular attention to the rhetorical and discursive strategies used by major figures in mainstream British political parties, and particularly to the personas of prime ministers in the period we now consider as neoliberal (since the late 1970s). This chapter therefore investigates how the meaning and genealogy of meritocracy is shaped by political discourse, focusing on the UK and connecting its particularity to wider transnational cultures. In doing so, it explores how what I call 'meritocratic feeling' has been conveyed and encoded in mainstream political discourse, emphasising the cultural rhetoric and emotive appeals that have taken different forms in neoliberal culture. The term 'meritocratic feeling' borrows from Raymond Williams' suggestive idea of 'structures of feeling' alongside the swathe of recent work across the humanities and social sciences which have emphasised the importance of affect (Williams 1977; Gregg and Seigworth 2012). In this chapter, I use it to foreground the tone, mood and appeal made to particular constituencies by different versions of neoliberal meritocracy; how it shapes the appeal made to them; and what promises it makes to extend their 'capacity to act' (Gilbert 2014; Read 2015).

## Thatcherism in Britain

In Britain, neoliberal policies and ideas of meritocracy were profoundly shaped, from the late 1970s, by Thatcherism, the set of meanings and policies coalescing around and promoted by Prime Minister Margaret Thatcher's government between 1979 and 1990 (Hall 1988). Thatcher's actions were not the earliest instances of neoliberal policy in the UK. In 1976, the Labour finance minister Denis Healey struck a contentious deal with the International Monetary Fund (Beckett 2009). The financial arrangement Healey made with the IMF demanded that the government make brutal cuts to UK public spending and services. These cuts in turn spawned a wave of strikes that have become deeply associated with the 1970s in a mediated popular memory of heatwaves and uncollected rubbish (garbage collectors being one of the groups of workers on strike). As John Medhurst puts it

> The IMF's operation was political. It was designed to erase what remained of the socialist aspirations in Labour's 1973 Programme and 1974 Manifestos, to contain [the influential left-wing Labour MP] Tony Benn, and to reassure the City that the nostrums and priorities of the financial sector, not elected politicians, were now setting the economic agenda.
> *(Medhurst 2014: 133)*

This moment, so obscured subsequently in popular memories of the 1970s, is now widely regarded as the formative moment of neoliberalism in the Global North (Harvey 2005; Klein 2008). A set of ideas nurtured by right-wing economists in Chicago and beyond, neoliberalism vigorously promoted corporate power, the marketisation of collective forms of public provision and the idea that competition was a ruling principle for all areas of life. The political test-bed for these ideas had been Chile in 1973, where the democratically elected socialist government of Salvador Allende had been overthrown with US military backing under Richard Nixon, installing the brutal right-wing dictatorship of General Pinochet, a process resulting in thousands of deaths and 'disappeared' citizens (Dorfman 2004). Neoliberalism therefore achieved its power either through direct military intervention or by leveraging local instabilities to gain control. The implementation of neoliberalism's 'shock doctrine', as Naomi Klein memorably put it, involved either persuading the heads of different national governments who were experiencing economic instability to reorganise their nation-states through unrestrained market competition or, as with Chile, doing so through brute force (Klein 2008).

In the case of the UK, an enthusiastic extension of the logic of the IMF's terms, wrapped in a dream of meritocracy, was a hallmark of the Thatcherite government that replaced Labour.[2] Thatcherism made a meritocratic appeal to 'individual choice' whilst dismantling the welfare state's social safety net, crushing union power and initiating a long wave of privatisations through the sale of public utilities like gas, telecommunications and rail (Hall 1988). Thatcher imposed monetarism, normalised the privitisation of public utilities as the only possible response to the supposed malaise of the Keynesian industrial economy (in her famous phrase, 'there is no alternative') and articulated both to an idea of individual freedom. These practices were closely aligned with those introduced by the Republican president, Ronald Reagan, in the US, with whom Thatcher had a close working relationship. The meaning meritocracy was taking at this moment was then clearly being shaped by the broader emergence of neoliberalism from the 1970s.

It is worth revisiting the specific terms in which the Thatcherite mode of meritocratic aspiration was expressed. There was a flexibility and ambiguity to her address which meant it could appeal to both working-class 'grafters' and to middle-class 'yuppies'. The 1979 Conservative Party manifesto for instance linked their pledge to cut income tax with hard work and saving, in effect channelling the Protestant work ethic ('We shall cut income tax at all levels to reward hard work, responsibility and success; tackle the poverty trap; encourage saving and the wider ownership of property'). The 1987 Conservative Party manifesto linked the idea of 'shares for all' in the newly privatised industries to now-normalised forms of hedonistic consumption: 'Just as with cars, television sets, washing machines and foreign holidays, [shares] would no longer be a privilege of the few; it would become the expectation of the many' (Conservative Party 1979, 1987). If Thatcherite discourse initially emphasised the need for stoicism to save the national malaise, it then quickly expanded to include the individual purchase of goods as a barometer of success. As a form of meritocratic discourse, it incrementally linked a notion of achievement and merit with successful consumption and habitually expressed distaste for ingrained privilege, particularly if it was supported by 'the state'. At the same time Thatcherism was typically characterised by social conservatism in its attitudes to sexuality, ethnicity and gender: in particular, by attaching huge rhetorical importance to the heteronormative nuclear family and by repeatedly invoking imperialist white privilege.[3]

Whilst Thatcherism worked in multiple ways to secure consent for its politics, one of its most important aspects was then its meritocratic appeal to consumerism as offering a general mode of participation in public life, inviting people to identify with the notion of themselves as consumers rather than as workers or citizens in a range of public settings (Gamble 1993). The presentation of acquisitive consumerism as the route to empowerment in any social context was closely bound up with the implicit assumption that the accumulation of consumer goods was at once a sign of merit and its tangible reward. One of the most significant moments in Thatcher's first term, for instance, was precisely designed to reposition a population of public-resource users as private owners/consumers: when she gave municipal tenants the right to buy the housing they lived in for prices that were very far below market rates. Crucially this government-subsidised housing stock was not replaced. With the removal of social housing from the market and the dismantling of rent controls and of legal protections for tenants, private landlords were free to raise rents to astronomical levels, in the long term fuelling both the housing boom which has had such deleterious effects on those sectors of the public unable to benefit from it, as well as massively increasing the public cost of subsidising the rents paid by welfare claimants to private landlords (Prynn and Bryant 2013).

Consumption became central to Thatcherism's iconography of 'getting ahead'. The new vanguard of conspicuous consumption were the businessmen and women, the stockbrokers and yuppies whose speedily acquired lavish lifestyles were documented in Sunday supplements and glossy ads. The idea of money pouring through the social body was enshrined in the popular fictional comic TV character played by Harry Enfield called Loadsamoney!: a working-class plasterer from south-east England who had piles of cash and waved it around in a wad, embodying the new class distinctions between those who knew how to dispose of their income and those who did not. At the same time, income in equality rose rapidly, child-poverty doubled, unemployment rocketed and the privatised utilities generated at least as many user complaints as the publicly owned predecessors which they had been expected to outperform (Gamble 1994; Hall 1988).

This, then, was a moment when UK citizens were coming to be imagined by Thatcherite discourse primarily as individual consumers, as wholly bounded entities whose only significant sites of sociality were their families. As Thatcher famously said in an interview for the magazine *Woman's Own*, 'there is no such thing as society. There are men and women and children and there are families.' This phenomenally atomised view of society was made to seem familiar and unthreatening by figuring Britain as a household, with Thatcher in charge, balancing the household budget. As Angela McRobbie has discussed, drawing on Foucault, such figurations of good housekeeping have been a recurring motif of national neoliberal cultures (McRobbie 2013; Foucault 2010). While Thatcher was an arch anti-feminist, portraying the nation as a household with a consumer purse created a gendered appeal (Campbell 1987; Nunn 2001, 2002). Thatcher always had low electoral popularity but she was very successful at winning over women, particularly lower-middle-class and upper-working-class women. These were receptive constituencies both because they had traditionally been denied access to power and because one of the few zones in which traditionally women have had, though in circumscribed fashion, more power than men, is consumption (Bowlby 1985; De Grazia and Furlough 1996; Littler 2009; Nava 2002). The use of consumerism as a means and an apparent visual index of greater social mobility was key to securing consent for Thatcherite neoliberalism, a gendered legacy which chapter 6 scrutinises in more detail (Franklin, Lury and Stacey 1991: 221–304).

Under Thatcherism, then, meritocratic feeling was shaped and encouraged through aspirational femininity in particular and a very bounded, individualised (and/or nuclear-family-based) form of consumerism in general. Popular support for Thatcherism was an expression of some of the most significant iniquities and discontents that the Fordist settlement had generated through its reliance on a hierarchical system of class, race and gender. Resentment at ingrained class hierarchies and gendered subordination were, along with gay rights and anti-racism, what fuelled the fractures in this settlement: the ruptures, rebellions and social movements of the late 1960s that we discussed in the last chapter. Thatcherism's deployment of a meritocratic popular consumerism addressed the gendered and classed components of this disgruntlement in particularly important ways. Its culture and rhetoric persuaded women, and especially lower-middle-class women – the people who voted for her most – that the pursuit of satisfaction as an individualised consumer in the private sphere was the route to empowerment and social mobility. Under Thatcherism neoliberal meritocracy was thereby presented as a pragmatic and emancipatory social solution to the gendered inequalities and industrial strictures of the Fordist welfare settlement.

## Major meritocracy

Thatcher was ousted from power in 1990 by her own MPs who rebelled against her increasingly unpopular policies. Her replacement as leader of the Conservative Party and as prime minister was John Major. With his large square glasses and mild-mannered demeanour, his projected persona appeared in many ways to be the opposite of Margaret Thatcher's haughty bravura and regal posing. He was portrayed in the cartoons and caricatures as a 'grey man'. On the satirical political TV show which used puppets for politicians, *Spitting Image*, the John Major puppet had completely grey skin, as well as clothes. In Steve Bell's widely distributed cartoons he appeared wearing his Y-front underpants outside his suit. This was not a macho masculinity but a weedy company man. If Thatcher had evoked Victorian values, Major evoked early- to mid-twentieth-century surburbanism, his appeal anchored in a reassuringly Fordist image of ordinariness. His vision of Britain was even more nostalgic, as apparent in his much-quoted description of the nation in which he hoped that

> [f]ifty years on from now, Britain will still be the country of long shadows on cricket grounds, warm beer, invincible green suburbs, dog lovers and pools fillers and, as George Orwell said, 'Old maids bicycling to holy communion through the morning mist' and, if we get our way, Shakespeare will still be read even in school.
> *(Major 1993)*

The image was of an everyday small-town company man and 'decent sort'. Major's unvarnished speaking style proved popular with older voters, and his persona played into a longstanding British tradition of anti-intellectualism as well as anti-elitism. His political prop was a soapbox, which he stood on whilst speaking through a loudspeaker, drawing on a longstanding tradition of spontaneous street-corner debates to cultivate an image of himself as an ordinary local man with a passion. Despite these older historical reference points, however, Major also seemed to fulfil the meritocratic dream of social mobility in a way that none of his predecessors or successors did. Significantly, he really did hail from a non-elite background and had not married into money to anywhere near the extent that Margaret Thatcher had. The son of a music-hall performer, he left school at 16 and went to work in a bank, thereby not acquiring the cultural capital of those many MPs attending elite universities. Despite her self-presentation as a greengrocer's daughter and budgeting housewife, Thatcher's cultivated hauteur had a solidly upper-middle-class ring to it; Major's assertion of ordinariness had more credence.

Major's policies largely continued in the vein of those pursued under Thatcher, although they avoided the extreme antagonistic class-based confrontations that his predecessor had pursued through, for example, conflict around the miner's strike and poll tax. (Notably, his government also demonstrated a surprising commitment to democratisation in higher education, allowing polytechnics to convert to universities in 1992.) Like his equivalent in the US at that time, President Bush, part of his image was based on the idea of reigning in the excesses of his predecessor. Major also involved the UK in the formation of the European Union through the Maastricht Treaty in 1992. This action split opinion within the Conservative Party, a schism that was to erupt two decades later in 2016, when 'Brexit' was won by those campaigning in a national referendum to leave the EU (when 'leaving Europe' was a position exploited by racist and xenophobic groups and used as a protest by those who had suffered four decades of neoliberalism). Major's policies therefore pursued the extension of neoliberal marketisation as the key model for the European Union whilst simultaneously re-imaging a selective protectionism for Britain: both by keeping Britain out of the Euro and by foregrounding the version of Britishness outlined above, one evoking the national imaginary of the Fordist family and the suburban 1950s.

Indeed, this image was augmented by the implicit and explicit privileging of whiteness and the patriarchal dynamics of the government. There was only one woman in Major's 1990 cabinet, and all the people in it were white or at least passed as such. In 1990 in Parliament the Labour MP Robert Hughes asked: 'with regard to the Prime Minister's desire for a classless society and social mobility, will he explain why there are no women in his Cabinet?' Major replied:

> In recent years, in all aspects of life in this country, women have been taking a higher profile: in the law, in commerce, in the civil service, in industry and in politics – and that will continue. As those women would wish it to be, they will reach the top on merit.
> (Hansard HC *[series 5], vol. 181, col. 1015 [29 Nov. 1990]*)

Such pronouncements evoked the liberal myth of seamless progress. They also promoted the idea of a level playing field, with merit as the only abstract criterion, part of a longer tradition of blindness and indifference to issues of gender equality in British politics, which the Labour Party was to offer a stark alternative to, through their mid-1990s' use of all-women shortlists for local and parliamentary elections. Despite his personal disapproval of all-women shortlists, Tony Blair benefitted from the progressive image their results gave when the most women in UK history were voted in as Labour MPs. He appointed high numbers of women into prominent cabinet positions, a level of visibility which led to this new group of women being framed by the tabloid press as 'Blair's Babes', which was their jocular and sexist way of signifying New Labour's progressiveness on gender.

One ill-fated part of Major's policy agenda was his attempt to relaunch a moralising social agenda under the slogan of 'Back to Basics'. Probably the single most politically significant dimension of the 'Back to Basics' agenda was a moral panic around single mothers that the media massaged by stigmatising single mothers as feckless and the source of social irresponsibility and moral breakdown (Woodward 1997: 256–260). At this point in the early 1990s in British public life the 'merit' of meritocracy was being profoundly gendered and racialised and was dependent on patriarchal family values for its 'success'. It was wedded to an ideology and aesthetic of conservative Britishness which exacerbated social inequality and promoted marketisation and deregulation at home and in Europe. However, the governing elite's claims to moral merit unravelled as Major's term was rocked by a series of sex and sleaze scandals in the Conservative Party. Numerous grey-suited MPs and cabinet members were revealed to have secret children, to be embroiled in affairs or to have participated in unusual sexual practices inconsistent with the Conservative Party's 'Back to Basics' moral values. Two ministers were caught taking cash for questions by accepting bribes from lobbyists to ask questions in Parliament, and the defence minister, Jonathan Aitken, was convicted for perjury when caught lying under oath in court.

In the Major years, a discourse of meritocracy, in which society was understood as being egalitarian enough and in which getting on was simply framed as a matter of merit, was conveyed through the imagery of early to mid-twentieth-century safe suburbanism. These reference points were to shift under the next prime minister, Tony Blair, whose imagery borrowed from a different historical period: a selective, cleaned-up version of Harold Wilson's 1960s, with its connotations of the 'white heat' of the technological revolution, social liberalism and the idea of a creative, swinging Britain: a set of associations encouraged through such cultural manifestations as Britpop, Young British Artists and Union Jack interior décor (Bewes and Gilbert 1999; McGuigan 2009; Driver and Martell 1998).

## Blairism and beyond

By the late 1990s, meritocracy, understood in these marketised terms, had become a key theme within New Labour policy discourse, which, whilst equally populist, was less anti-intellectual than Thatcherism and, crucially, far more socially liberal than either Thatcher and Major. Blair used the five-syllable term 'meritocracy' more than any other prime minister, used it repeatedly and used it in a wholly favourable way. It was counterposed to the notion of an old elite establishment and signified social liberalism and tolerance. 'The Britain of the elite is over', he pronounced in 1997 when taking office. 'The new Britain is a meritocracy where we break down the barriers of class, religion, race and culture' (*Hansard HL* [series 5], vol. 582, col. 996 [28 Oct. 1997]). Two years later, it was coterminous with an expanding middle class that 'exploited' (note the corporate language) social potential: 'The old establishment is being replaced by a larger, more meritocratic middle-class. ... The meritocratic society is the only society that can exploit its potential to the full for all the people' (BBC 1999).

New Labour's use of meritocratic themes was described (and influenced) by the work of the sociologist Anthony Giddens. In *Where Now for New Labour?* Giddens argued strongly that 'we should want a society that is more egalitarian than it is today, but which is meritocratic ... a meritocratic approach to inequality is inevitable' (Giddens 2002: 38–39). As John Beck argues, when 'meritocracy' was not always explicitly used in New Labour discourse, it was there in its constellation of synonyms: social inclusion, poverty of aspiration, social justice, talent, empowered individuals (Beck 2008: 12–17).

This dual embrace of the idea of retaining some forms of social protection (like the introduction of the minimum wage and paid paternity leave) alongside the erosion of social protection through neoliberal expansion (for example, public–private partnerships, the deregulation of the European labour market and the introduction of academy schools, which were the equivalent of the US's charter schools) structured and guided New Labour's time in power (Finlayson 2003). This back-and-forth movement was memorably termed 'New Labour's double shuffle' by Stuart Hall (Hall 2003: 10–24).

As Jeremy Gilbert pointed out, the forms of protection being promoted were less consistent with social democratic egalitarianism than with neoliberal meritocracy which sought to provide 'equality of opportunity' on marketised and individualised terms (Gilbert 2004). Whilst Thatcherism simply cut back and sold sections of the public sector, Blairism sought to restructure more extensively existing provision in the public sector through the logic of marketisation, for example through the public–private partnerships of the Private Finance Initiative (PFI). Blair's advocacy of neoliberal meritocracy promoted equality of opportunity rather than equality of outcomes. It combined the extension of economic marketisation with selective welfare interventions in the early years (around education and child poverty) and a socially liberal approach.

Blair's agenda was heavily influenced by the success of Democratic President Bill Clinton in the US: Blair was Clinton's UK equivalent. Both were centre-left politicians promoting a socially liberal version of neoliberalism. New Labour famously projected itself as beyond left and right, drawing on Anthony Giddens' conceptualisation of 'the third way' (Giddens 1998); as 'beyond ideology', a project of modernity, its 'latent vanguardism' appealing to reflexive individuals who had transcended class boundaries and other 'restrictive' categories of identity politics (Finlayson 2003: 202). This was a socially liberal version of neoliberal meritocracy. It endorsed feminism and anti-racism only to the extent that they were or could be made compatible with capitalism. For instance, New Labour extended paid parental leave but did not shorten the working week so that men and women could share childcare. It promoted a carefully fashioned image of inclusive national multiculturalism when it suited it and ignored it when it did not. For instance, its cultural policy initiatives often emphasised the importance of organisational diversity, but then it introduced new British cultural citizenship tests based on a very un-diverse understanding of Britishness (see Littler and Naidoo 2005; Byrne 2014).

Blair's socially liberal variant of neoliberal meritocracy therefore tried to not only enable people to rise up the social ladder but also to replace the old guard of the Establishment with new middle-class meritocrats. But simultaneously the Establishment was being protected by the professionalisation of politics. Politics was increasingly seen as the domain of think tanks, political consultants and professional journalists. In the Labour Party in particular Blair initiated a series of reforms severing links between local, or grassroots, constituency Labour Party members and an increasingly professionalised party machine. The Blair project like Clinton's relied on intense media management and messaging and removing many crucial layers of the participation process from ordinary members. MPs were often centrally chosen and parachuted into local constituencies despite having had no previous dealings with the area. Constituency meetings became more of a facade in that they focused on enlisting support for goals that had been predetermined by the central party rather than being representative of localised and grassroots activity. Local parties no longer had a crucial role in debating national policy, and the Party became an aggregation of postal voters getting information not from constituency Labour parties but from the media. As such New Labour constituted a form that the political scientist Peter Mair terms 'partyless democracy' (Mair 2000).

The idea of movement up the social ladder also raises the question of what exactly is being reached for. In Michael Young's book *The Rise of the Meritocracy* what was being reached for was a blend of money and classed prestige. By the late 1990s both were being reconfigured in the wake of the Thatcherite challenge to the social order, New Labour's embrace of the financial sector, and London as a centre for financial transactions and the principal motor of the UK economy (Massey 2007). As New Labour's trade and industry secretary Peter Mandelson famously put it in 1998, 'we are intensely relaxed about people becoming filthy rich' (Keegan 1998). What was being positioned as the top of the ladder was mutating, as CEO pay soared and media's demotic turn popularised 'tempa-celebrities' – or 'celetoids', to borrow Chris Rojek's definition (Rojek 2001). What merit was, and how it was being ranked through status, was therefore changing to reflect New Labour's dual imperatives of corporate growth and populist access – a phenomenon which, as we saw in the last chapter, Anthony Barnett astutely terms 'corporate populism' (Barnett 2003; see also Littler 2000).

As John Beck caustically put it in his perceptive analysis of New Labour's use of the term in relation to education, while even a brief dip into the history serves to highlight how meritocracy and measurement are perennially contested matters, this appears 'to have had remarkably little effect on politicians, particularly those of the centre Left or centre Right, in whose discourse and policies, meritocratic ideas remain persistently prominent' (Beck 2008: 11). The neoliberal meanings of meritocracy, which was now extensively deployed as a prime ministerial keyword, was to be promoted as unproblematically positive from Tony Blair to Theresa May, albeit with different articulations.

## 'Aspiration Nation'

Gordon Brown, Labour's finance minister, took over as prime minister from Tony Blair when he resigned in 2007. Whereas Blair's smart-casual media-friendly metropolitan image and neoliberal agenda won him favourable media coverage, Gordon Brown's dour introverted Puritan persona did not. The trade unions and the social democratic majority in the Labour Party expected Brown to pursue a different, more left-wing and progressive agenda than that of Blair. But they were to be sorely disappointed. Whilst pursuing broadly similar policies to Blair, Brown's team dealt with the financial crash of 2008 by bailing out the banks that caused the crisis, and thus failed to create a coherent left-wing political and media response to it. Three years after he became prime minister, in 2010, New Labour lost their hold on power.

Yet the powerful language of neoliberal meritocracy, connected to aspiration, social mobility and opportunity for all to rise through the social structure, did not become muted in Britain, despite a double-dip recession, growing inequality and a historically unprecedented drop in living standards for the working majority. On the contrary, it escalated under the Conservative–Liberal Democrat coalition government, which came to power in 2010 and whose use of the idea of meritocracy represented a new stage in its development. The language of meritocracy was deployed without the introduction of ameliorating initiatives or forms of collective provision (like the minimum wage), and in conjunction with specific policies directly aimed at cutting the incomes of the poor (like the 'bedroom tax'). The coalition government continued, and sped up, the implementation of neoliberal policies marketising the welfare state – such as the extension of internal markets and corporate involvement in prisons and in the health service – whilst using the alibi of the recession (Hall, Massey and Rustin 2013). Simultaneously, at the 2012 Conservative Party conference, Prime Minister David Cameron declared that under his leadership Britain was now an 'Aspiration Nation': 'we are the party of the want-to-be better-off' (Cameron 2012).

In Cameron's worldview, the ability to 'believe in yourself' and, by extension, your child was primary. This was a psychologising discourse which vested not only power but also moral virtue in the very act of hope, in the mental and emotional capacity to believe and aspire. Hope and promise become more integral in an unequal society in which hard work alone had less and less chance of reaping the prizes. Through such a rhetorical mechanism, the act of addressing inequality became insistently 'responsibilised' as an individual's moral meritocratic task instead of addressing social inequality as a solvable problem. This process devolved onto the individual personal responsibility not just for their success in the meritocratic competition but for the very will to compete and the expectation of victory which were now figured as moral imperatives in themselves. Not investing in aspiration, in expectation, was aggressively positioned as an abdication of responsibility which condemns yourself – and, even worse, your child – to the social scrapheap. To quote Cameron's 2012 Conservative Party conference speech:

> It's that toxic culture of low expectations – that lack of ambition for every child – which has held this country back.
> 
> The Labour party theorists ... stand in the way of aspirational parents by excusing low expectations and blaming social disadvantage.
> 
> *(Cameron 2012)*

Here, aspirational meritocracy works by increasingly aggressively positioning itself against any investment in collective provision, which becomes framed as both a symptom and a cause of low expectation. In his 2013 party conference speech, Cameron reiterated the 'Aspiration Nation' theme, intensifying the rhetoric by describing himself as engaged in a battle against opponents whom he characterised explicitly as not being hard workers – 'smug, self-satisfied socialists'. 'That's who we're fighting against', he asserted, 'and we know who we're fighting for: for all those who work hard and want to get on' (*Huffington Post* 2013).

In this formulation, social disadvantage is only real in that it is an obstacle over which pure mental will and aspiration – if they are expressed correctly by being combined with hard work – can triumph. These tropes and discursive elements help generate the experiential zone that Lauren Berlant aptly identified as 'cruel optimism': the affective state produced under neoliberal culture which is cruel because it encourages an optimistic attachment to the idea of a brighter future whilst such attachments are, at the same time, 'actively impeded' by the harsh precarities and instabilities of neoliberalism (Berlant 2012). If Cameron's 'Aspiration Nation' discourse is one manifestation of such cruel optimism, it also draws on the English trope of 'having a go', which involves a sort of non-competitive competitiveness, of being prepared to compete without any expectation of winning, out of a recognition that sporting competition is a mode of social participation. The difference is that within Cameron's 'Aspiration Nation' you cannot just do your best: you have to want to win (a more familiar sensibility in the US). Cameron, using language borrowed from the Australian right through his advisor Lynton Crosby, distilled this down into a simple binary formulation: you are a 'striver or a skiver'.

But the psychosocial resources required to engage in aspiration are easier for some classes to obtain and deploy than others. There is a rich tradition in the cultural studies of education of analysing how middle-class children are encouraged to aspire while working-class children are instead – to cite the title of Paul Willis's classic book – 'learning to labour' (Willis 1977). Valerie Gilles' analysis of aspirational language used (or not) by parents when talking about their child's behaviour at school is particularly instructive here. Her research showed how for working-class parents, the attributes most likely to be proudly described were children's ability to stay out of trouble, get on with others and work hard, which inculcates the strength to struggle and to defend scant resources; whereas middle-class parents foster 'the right to be bright' and code problematic behaviour in the classroom in terms of intelligence and of needs the classroom should be able to accommodate, which helps reproduce middle-class success. Writing in the Blair years, Gilles criticised New Labour's education policy for encoding middle-class behaviour as morally correct and blaming the poor 'with almost missionary zeal' for their own failure (Gilles 2005: 850). This project was to be extended by Cameron, who was regularly hailed as a prime minister owing much to Blair, and whose accession was made possible by him (Seymour 2010).

Such tendencies have been continued and extended in politics and popular culture in the post-Blair years. From the 2010s, there was a widespread tendency to 'blame the parents' for any problems at the expense of any other social factor such as economic and social impoverishment (extending the early demonisation of single mothers and making it slightly less sexist). This tendency was conveyed, for instance, through the fixation on parenting styles 'over and above all other factors' in relation to children's behaviour and life chances (Jensen 2012). It was foregrounded through the framing of parental responsibility by TV programmes such as *Supernanny*, the reality show where a nanny sorted out parents struggling with their children's behaviour (Jensen 2010; Fisher 2009) and in government and media responses to the 2011 London riots (Allen and Taylor 2012; Couldry and Littler 2011). The tendency to blame the parents is closely bound up with how the family is increasingly figured as a bounded entrepreneurial unit (McRobbie 2013), the ramifications of which I explore in relation to meritocracy, women and work in chapter 5.

## Tragi-comedy: Bojo's 'hard work'

'Aspiration Nation' as a rhetorical strategy and as an expression of meritocratic feeling connected self-belief and aspiration with the trope of hard work. It has been striking how, again and again, hard work combined with self-belief is employed by an unprecedentedly privileged cadre of politicians and millionaire elites to justify their position and success and to prescribe this as the route for others. 'Working hard and wanting to get on' is figured as the way to progress. This trope was repeatedly deployed by former mayor of London and Conservative MP Boris Johnson (later foreign secretary) who, in the words of the *Daily Mail*, 'hailed the Olympics for embodying the "Conservative lesson of life" that hard work leads to reward' (Peev 2012). In 2013 Johnson told Britons that they needed to work much harder, otherwise jobs would go to economic migrants (Johnson 2013).

How does this rhetoric of hard work, such a feature of the contemporary meritocratic deal, work, given that there is a swathe of research proving that inheriting opportunity in the form of finance and social connections is by far more important a factor in the route to riches? (Dorling 2015; Freeland 2012). It is notable that plenty of millionaires who inherited their own wealth, including Boris Johnson and David Cameron, have conveniently promoted hard work as the most influential factor in social mobility. Such discourse simultaneously helps to erase any image of over-privileged indolence from the speaker's persona whilst interpellating the listener as able to achieve a similar social status: a degree of social mobility which is in practice attainable only for a tiny minority. As McNamee and Miller put it, 'meritocracy tends to be believed in more by the privileged' (McNamee and Miller 2009: 3). But the rhetoric of hard work is crucial to today's meritocratic feeling. In research conducted at St Paul's, an elite North American fee-paying school, Khan and Jerolmack noted that typically these students were conscious of the idea of their privilege and replaced a frame of entitlement with one based around merit by continually emphasising how hard they had worked. The researchers argued that 'they generally do not work hard, although they are adept at performing a kind of busyness that looks and feels like hard work'. (Students that did regularly go to the library were conversely positioned as 'freaks'.) As they put it, '"hard work" is mostly a form of talk – but important talk nonetheless. It is a rhetorical strategy deployed by students in a world of "new elites."' These are elites 'saying meritocracy but doing the ease of privilege' (Khan and Jerolmack 2013;

Khan 2010). In the UK, at the opposite end of a similar spectrum, Jessica Abrahams' work on graduates finding employment has shown that whereas middle-class students are far more willing to use their more extensive pre-existing contacts to 'get a foot in the door', working-class students regularly exhibit reluctance to use recent contacts out of a sense that they have to 'prove themselves' through hard work and staying honourable (Abrahams 2016).

Similarly, the UK coalition government's investment in hard work used words with profoundly working-class connotations whilst eliding the dis/advantages of class through their usage. Hard work was coded as 'graft' even when voiced by millionaires or billionaires, celebrities and children at elite private fee-paying schools. This is not completely new: it was a key element in the rhetoric of Thatcherism as well as Blairism. Thatcher notably figured herself as rising up through the classes. As Tom Mills points out, the importance to her success of her husband's considerable wealth was barely acknowledged by Thatcher. She preferred to dwell on her humble roots as a grocer's daughter and to imagine that her achievements were attributable to drudgery and self-discipline (Mills 2013). Cameron and his cabinet, just like Boris Johnson, did not draw on such early moments to calibrate their self-narrative, mainly because they did not have them: their backgrounds are aristocratic or quasi-aristocratic. They did, however, borrow the rhetoric of hard work as graft, just like the privileged children interviewed by Khan and Jerolmack. The very act of saying hard work invites those who do work hard to identify with them and flatters the rest. Then hard work is connected, rather than to a particular lower-class reflexive position, to the necessity of having aspirations: you cannot have one without the other, in this rhetorical strategy, in this worldview: to lack either is a moral failure.

In this way Cameron and Johnson activated a similar discursive frame to Thatcher whilst de-articulating the highly selective, reflexive class biographical detail and replacing it with a generalised notion of aspiration. These actions and tropes were similar to some deployed under Blairism. However, the crucial difference was that the Conservatives' abandonment of the concessions to equality of opportunity that Blair promoted – whilst pushing through neoliberal reforms – in favour of a much more dramatic cutting of the social safety net and a vicious, moralising stigmatisation of the underclass. Cumulatively, the effects of these policies and discourse made the distance aspiration needs to travel that much further and, thus, far less likely to be traversed.

## Blue-collar billionaires: Farage, Trump and the destabilisation of merit

A further way to understand these processes is by pointing, as James Meek does, towards their re-articulation of the Robin Hood myth (Meek 2015, 2016). The people put into the roles of the greedy sheriff and the renegade deliverer of justice have now swapped places. In this version, the traditional poor (such as the unemployed, disabled and refugees) have been placed

> into the conceptual box where the rich used to be. It is they, the social category previously labelled 'poor', who are accused of living in big houses, wallowing in luxury and not needing to work, while those previously considered rich are re-designated as the ones who work terribly hard for fair reward or less. ... In this version the sheriff of Nottingham runs a ruthless realm of plunder and political correctness, ransacking the homesteads of honest peasants for money to finance the conceptual rich – that is, the unemployed, the disabled, refugees, working-class single mothers, dodgers, scroungers, chavs, chisellers and cheats.
>
> *(Meek 2016)*

Nigel Farage, an extremely wealthy former stockbroker and the leader of the UK Independence Party (UKIP) since 2006, with some breaks in service, has operated in exactly this way. Farage has placed himself and his party in the rhetorical position of the exploited, stoking hatred toward elites and immigrants in the process. This rhetorical pattern is similar to that mobilised in the US by right-wing populist billionaires: as Thomas Frank argues, 'the conservative renaissance rewrites history according to the political demands of the moment, generates thick smokescreens of deliberate bewilderment, grabs for itself the nobility of the common toiler, and projects onto its rivals the arrogance of the aristocrat' (Frank 2012: 44).

Likewise, Donald Trump, who was advised by Nigel Farage in his 2016 US presidential campaign, presented himself as a poor, but strong and angry, billionaire, at the mercy of welfare-scroungers and immigrants and as willing to wreak retribution on them by banning Muslims from the US and building a wall on the US–Mexican border. So too, with local and gendered variations, have a range of privileged right-wing populists in Europe including the Netherlands' Geert Wilders and France's Marine Le Pen placed themselves in the rhetorical position of the unjustly exploited.

All these variants of super-rich neoliberal meritocracy exhibit what Thomas Piketty terms 'meritocratic extremism': the 'apparent need of modern society, and especially US society, to designate certain individuals as "winners", and to reward them all the more generously if they seem to have been selected on the basis of their intrinsic merits rather than birth or background' (Piketty 2013: 334). As a broad definition this is useful and accurate. There is also a need to identify both the ideological leanings of such meritocratic extremism and the character it takes, and to emphasise the extent to which a neoliberal plutocratic elite rely on actively constructing such images to maintain their power. This is why this book delineated in chapter 2 a number of different phases of meritocratic meaning, from socialist slander to social democratic meritocracy to neoliberal meritocracy and why it emphasises different versions of neoliberal meritocracy and the range of characteristics it can adopt.

Noticeably in the more right-wing populist examples, the meaning of merit itself also tends to be more profoundly destabilised, and the link between 'merit' and ability attenuated. Anti-intellectualism becomes articulated to anti-elitism. Successfully emoting about your 'passion' and 'drive' starts to replace ability or merit – or to become the new merit. When the MP Andrea Leadsom stood as a potential leader of the Conservative Party in 2016, for example, she repeatedly spoke of her 'passion' for Britain and for justice. Similarly, the US president, Donald Trump, projects a persona embodying passion-based drive, of a 'winner' (Elmer and Todd 2016: 660–662). As Alison Hearn points out, this wild self-promotion itself becomes a sign of merit:

> Against the backdrop of growing economic insecurity, most people must now assiduously self-promote and hustle in order to find or protect their jobs. Trump supporters are not 'dupes' buying the hype then; they recognize that Trump's brand is his skill set, admire it, and see it as all the qualification he needs to become president.
> 
> *(Hearn 2016: 656)*

In the version of neoliberal meritocracy Trump promotes, the notion of merit has shifted markedly away from an association with expert knowledge. It is still a competitive race to the top in which there are most definitely extreme winners and losers – indeed the winners are foregrounded (as Trump would put it, 'bigly'). But in this race previous notions of merit associated with exclusive elites are jettisoned: in the politics of the 2016 presidential campaign, 'post-truth' statements were used with abandon. The affective image of being on the side of ordinary people, of blue-collar labour and the squeezed middle classes, against a corrupt elite that perpetuated the policies producing declining living standards is paramount. Drawing on and stoking xenophobia, racism and sexism, ripping up state spending on climate change, Trump promises a structurally similar formation of competitive meritocracy organised around a refigured notion of merit whose bottom line is unregulated business opportunities for those within its nationalistic borders. Trump, writes Laurie Ouellette, is 'the embodiment of an enterprising subjectivity and a "no nonsense" approach to leadership that draws legitimacy from the market' (Ouellette 2016: 649).

How can such post-truth scapegoating by billionaires pretending to be speaking for the oppressed masses and ordinary people come unstuck? There have been brief examples in the UK. Boris Johnson's abrupt about-turn from campaigning for Britain to remain in the European Union to campaign to leave was widely perceived in the press as a blatant and unprincipled lurch for power, and his departure when the Leave vote won was copiously reported as a cowardly refusal to clean up his mess. Cameron, who called the referendum, was also blamed for Brexit, but he arrived earlier at his personal reputational Armageddon in 'pig gate', the allegations that he had stuck his penis in the mouth of a dead pig during the revelries of a secret society he belonged to during his time as a student at Oxford University.

In an astute piece of writing on the meaning of pig gate, Lawrence Richards argued that why the British were really laughing was because the masochistic/sadistic nature of the secrets kept by the British Establishment as a mechanism for bribery, corruption and control had been spectacularly exposed, in the process viscerally belittling its own myth of meritocracy. Richards drew connections between a series of scandals in recent years – of the widespread establishment silence over the sexual abuse conducted from the 1970s by BBC TV star Jimmy Saville, the ministerial paedophile ring that Margaret Thatcher and Theresa May both refused to investigate, humiliating initiation rituals at Oxbridge societies and the secrets used by Conservative Party whips to bribe their MPs to toe the party line – with the hypocritical nature of narratives of meritocracy.

> The secrets being kept are designed by powerful men to keep other powerful men under control. That kind of arrangement is the antithesis of democracy. And it is also the antithesis to the meritocracy they

proclaim. Not just because it's rich boys getting an easy ride to the top – we already knew that – but because David Cameron's nasty little scandal speaks to a suspicion many people already have: that in British society, you don't get to become Prime Minister because you're talented or because you work hard. You don't even get there just because you're rich. You get there by traumatising the homeless and skull-fucking a dead pig, and that ritual gives you power because you have demonstrated utter, pathetic submission to your fellow oligarchs. *That* is why we're laughing.

(Richards 2015)

Richards' perceptive narrative figured neoliberal meritocracy as not simply involving discrepancies of wealth, but abuse and exploitation that also involves 'pathetic submission' to others who are equally exploitative, lessening their humanity: a process rarely revealed so baldly.

## Theresa May and the Middle England meritocrats

In the wake of the Brexit vote in 2016, David Cameron resigned and Theresa May became the new Conservative prime minister. May's speedy cabinet re-shuffle axed the vast majority of Cameron's expensively educated friends' allies, the upper-class 'Notting Hill set' (or 'chumocracy'). In their wake came a different cohort of conservative MPs: not different in terms of changing the demographic of the Conservative cabinet from being overwhelmingly white and male (a tradition May upheld) but in terms of their privileged class and educational background: 29% of May's cabinet went to private school. Despite only 7% of the UK population going to private school, this figure was, for the Conservative Party – traditionally the party of the Establishment and the rich – something of a departure. Fifty per cent of Cameron's cabinet, for instance, had attended private school (Dominiczak, Hope and Bingham 2016). This 'bold' new government, the British right-wing populist tabloids *The Daily Mail* and *The Sun* announced, was a 'March of the Meritocrats': this was a 'Mayritocracy' (Figure 3.1) (Slack, Groves and Harding 2016; Davidson 2016).

In her first significant speech as prime minster in July 2016, May expanded this newly fashioned idea of the Conservative Party as involving and representing more ordinary and less privileged people than before. Her rhetoric not only included expressions of righteous sympathy for the 'ordinary working class' (a phrase rarely heard spilling from the lips of

| The Sun | HOME | FOOTBALL | SPORT | TV & SHOWBIZ | LIVING | NEWS | VIDEOS |

## MAYRITOCRACY PM makes Sun readers a pledge to build an education system that will work for 'ordinary working-class families'

Theresa May unveiled a vision of meritocracy in which those striving for their kids to get the best chances in life get a leg-up

BY LYNN DAVIDSON WHITEHALL CORRESPONDENT | 9th September 2016, 12:12 pm

10 COMMENTS

THERESA May yesterday made Sun readers a direct pledge as she vowed to transform the education system to benefit "ordinary working-class families".

Revealing the biggest shake-up of schools in 50 years, the PM unveiled a vision of meritocracy in which those striving for their kids to get the best chances in life get a leg-up.

FIGURE 3.1 UK newspaper *The Sun* announces that Prime Minister Theresa May is offering 'Mayritocracy' through a new wave of grammar schools. Photograph by Nick Ansell / PA Wire / PA Images (PA.28579747). Reproduced courtesy of *The Sun* and the Press Association.

Conservative MPs) but also the unequal injustices faced by a variety of constituencies, from black people through women and the youth to the mentally ill. Promising that 'when it comes to taxes we will prioritise not the wealthy, but you', May's new vision of unity now professed that it would be fighting against 'the burning injustice that if you're born poor you will die on average nine years earlier than others' and the fact that 'if you're black you are treated more harshly by the criminal justice system than if you're white'. Somewhat breathtakingly for a Conservative prime minister, then, Theresa May continued to present her public with a list of intersectional injustices:

> If you're a woman you will earn less than a man.
> If you're young you will find it harder than ever before to own your own home. If you're from an ordinary working-class family, life is much harder than many people in Westminster realise.
> *(May 2016)*

Here, May clearly proclaims that she is very aware of social inequalities: of the difficulties people now face, of their unjust unevenness. The Conservative Party, in government, under her, she states, will recognise and redress this injustice. 'When it comes to opportunity we won't entrench the advantages of the fortunate few, we will do everything we can to help anybody, whatever your background, to go as far as your talents will take you.' (May 2016).[4] This is a discourse of neoliberal meritocracy but a different strand to that offered by Cameron. Cameron's discourse was blind to social inequality: this acknowledges it. Whilst May's speech recognises the egalitarian deficit, it reframes this as a deficit not of egalitarianism but of meritocracy. Its solution is yet more privatisation and individualisation, which on the basis of historical evidence works to further entrench, rather than redress, the problems that are rightly identified.

A range of political commentators highlighted the mismatch between Theresa May's new-found identification of social inequality and the fact that her previous voting record as a government minister directly contributed to cause them. May proclaimed she would work for the ordinary workers, help those made poorer off through the recession, would not favour the wealthy, yet she had already voted against protecting tenants in the rental sector, against legislation tightening the capacity of payday loan purveyors (loan sharks), against reforming the banking sector and against investing in affordable housing (Baxter 2016). Theresa May has worn a

T-shirt espousing feminism (she had been photographed in a Fawcett Society T-shirt proclaiming 'this is what a feminist looks like') and yet has made cuts across a range of support and protection affecting women most, from domestic violence centres, rape counselling services, legal aid, health in pregnancy grants, to children's Sure Start centres: a list so long that if it were printed on the back of the T-shirt, pointed out the feminist comedian Bridget Christie, 'it would look like a tailcoat' (Christie 2015). Yet these critical voices had to battle against widespread positive media coverage of Theresa May's statements.

The meritocratic discourse mobilised here, then, is profoundly compatible with the examples of neoliberal feminism and neoliberal anti-racism that we considered in the previous chapter. In different ways and to varying degrees, they all recognise gendered and/or racialised injustice whilst being supportive of neoliberal capitalism and suggesting that these phenomena together are not incompatible. I term these 'neoliberal justice narratives' and 'corporate justice narratives'. They acknowledge social injustice, flag it up, foreground it and yet pronounce that extending neoliberalism is the best way to deal with it. The solution for inequality is better inequality. Commentators are debating whether the advent of Trump and May means the continuation of neoliberalism or not, as Brexit's borders and Trump's nationalism promise to disrupt the flows of international finance capital as well as people's citizenship and personal lives. But at present this formation mainly constitutes a kind of neoliberalism with borders: their policies on target to produce more privatisation, inequality and individualisation, its collectivism not built around sharing the wealth but through capitalism, newly competitive hierarchies, moral distinction and a militarily empowered nationalism.

'I want Britain to be the great meritocracy of the world,' pronounced May several months later, using the word 'meritocracy' with more force and repetition than any prime minister since Tony Blair. This was the title of a speech in which she repeated the word several times, alongside multiple references to the Conservatives being the party of the working classes (May 2016), phrases repeated shortly afterwards by her education secretary Justine Greening (Couglan 2016). The speech outlined her new policy of restarting selective secondary grammar schools – the very type of selective education that spawned Michael Young's book *The Rise of the Meritocracy* and Hannah Arendt's barbed commentary on British education – a policy which had been on ice since the 1970s, with existing schools converting to comprehensives and some remaining in place but no new ones permitted to open. There is widely disseminated proof, including 2016 evidence published by the OECD, that overall grammar schools reduce rather than enable social mobility; that they are disproportionally full of the upper- and middle-class children whose parents can pay for tuition to get them in; and that selecting students to enter on the basis of intellectual ability, whilst the 'failures' went to a secondary modern, has in the past left deep psychologically scarring effects on many of those who took the test (Couglan 2016). If the idea of reintroducing grammar schools is related to longstanding Conservative discourses of worth and achievement, then, it is also related to contemporary post-truth politics.

As with Blair's earlier use of the word, in May's usage there is no recognition of the alternative meaning of meritocracy: it is simply and wholly valorised as positive. But there is a particular layer of irony to its use in this context, given that the word 'meritocracy' is now being used to promote selective education: the very subject which, in the 1950s, meant the word became mobilised as a caustic critique. May's usage of meritocracy built on the meanings given to it through the Thatcher, Major and Blair years in particular. Theresa May's language of meritocracy has been marked to date by three features. First, it is self-consciously presented as inclusive, offering competitive opportunity to all. Second, and intimately connected to this, it recognises, at a rhetorical level, post-recession inequality. Third, it is wrapped in the flag, through the constant reiteration of 'Britain', which serves as a signifier to appease those who voted for Brexit, as part of the reconstructed nationalism and 'a protective state' (Davies 2016). 'Mayritocracy' adopts the neoliberal imperatives of extending competition into all areas of our lives and cutting public provision and services, yet it also focuses incessantly on national sovereignty, policing its own borders, appealing to xenophobic models of belonging and creating a securitised state. It is an extremely nationalistic iteration of meritocracy, acknowledging inequalities, using neoliberal justice narratives to 'solve' the problems they extend and perpetuate.

## 'Aspiration for All'?

To conclude this chapter we should consider what political alternatives to neoliberal meritocracy are being circulated today. In 2015 the socialist MP Jeremy Corbyn, who had been sitting on the backbenches in parliament for over three decades, was the shock winner of the Labour leadership contest. Nominated at the last minute by a group of MPs in response to demands for a less politically narrow, centrist field of candidates, he was not expected to win. Indeed, some of the MPs who nominated him said they regretted having done so: they did not want him to win, just to widen the field. It was a shock to the press and an upheaval for much of the Parliamentary Labour Party, the composition of which had continued to drift rightward since the days of Blair and was dominated by MPs with a 'professional' profile ('moderate' politics, a technocratic approach, and usually educated at Oxford University).[5]

One of Corbyn's key slogans was 'Aspiration for All'. 'The most important message my election offers', he stated

> is that the party is now unequivocally on their side. We understand aspiration and we understand that it is only collectively that our aspirations can be realised.

Arguing that everyone 'aspires to an affordable home, a secure job, better living standards, reliable healthcare and a decent pension', Corbyn criticised the Conservative trade union bill (with customary rhetorical understatement) as a policy which would 'make it harder' for these traditional aspirations to materialise and pledged that Labour would vote against it (Corbyn 2015a). At the Labour Party conference he repeated the phrase slightly differently by focusing on the young: 'We have aspirations for all children, not just a few' (Corbyn 2015b). Through this rhetoric Corbyn was directly challenging the Blairite version of aspiration by pluralising it, disconnecting it from emulation of the rich and reconnecting it to the redistribution of wealth. 'Aspiration' had also been a keyword of his contender for the Labour leadership Liz Kendall, the Blairite candidate who initially expected to win but who came last and whose campaign recurrently reiterated that not only had Labour failed to connect with aspirational voters but that working-class children too often lacked aspiration (Gilbert 2015a). There was thus very little between Conservative and New Labour usage of aspiration, and disillusion with these narrow strata of neoliberal politics propelled Corbyn to victory as a candidate who presented an alternative to the political status quo.

After Corbyn emerged onto the political stage, Conservative discourse attempted to harness the words 'Aspiration for All'. For instance, Cameron argued during the Prime Minister's Questions debate over the dramatic extension of neoliberal policies in schools in the House of Commons: 'That is why we need this reform [making all schools private academies]: to make good schools even better and to help to raise the aspiration of all. That is what it is all about' (*Hansard HC* [series 5], vol. 608, col. 913 [20 Apr. 2016]). But the emphasis between what it is connected or articulated to by these different parties was clearly profoundly different. For Cameron it was private interests, including corporations, being able to run, and profit from running, schools, and the idea of individualised success. For Corbyn, 'Aspiration for All' involved the rights of workers, public ownership of schools, strengthening teachers' trade union representation and collective success (Jones *et al.* 2015).

The task for left politics to actually win electoral victory in the UK is very considerable. This is why Corbyn's initial victory as leader was greeted by an unprecedented level of popular enthusiasm: it suddenly made it seem feasible, with people flocking to local meetings and rejoining the Labour Party at levels unprecedented since the 1970s. The UK media is dominated by a right-wing political–corporate monopoly which was allowed to continue throughout the thirteen years of Labour government (Freeman 2008). Whilst the UK has a multi-party system, political representation in the UK is not proportional but based on 'first past the post', meaning that huge attention is given to 'swing voters' in marginal constituencies and that many parties on both the left and right are not represented in parliament despite the amount of votes they receive. The only ostensibly left-wing government achieving electoral success in Britain in decades, the Blair government, came to power, as we have seen, by adopting a neoliberal agenda and a managerial structure disempowering its local members and branches within the party.

The strength of institutional resistance to an actual left-wing political programme is thus considerable on multiple levels: in the Parliamentary Labour Party, the majority of the mainstream media and amongst Labour Party members wanting to prioritise a tactical appeal to swing voters in Conservative-held seats. In addition, there has been vigorous debate over the precise politics, style and effectiveness of Corbyn's cabinet and approach, both before and after he survived a bitter leadership contest (or attempted coup) and the fallout from the Brexit vote, which he was argued to have not campaigned passionately enough over: both of which considerably damaged his reputation.[6]

Corbyn's platform therefore began to offer an alternative to neoliberal meritocracy that was rooted in a different approach to competitive individualism and consumer success. Yet it has to date not achieved the populism necessary to win. On the one hand, his popularity in the polls is very low, and there is widespread media hostility towards him; on the other hand, despite his personal unpopularity, there is evidence that much of the policy approach, particularly on universal service provision, is popular (Gilbert 2015b).

There are parallels and connections between Corbyn in the UK and Bernie Sanders in the US. Sanders, a longstanding independent senator from Vermont, ran as a Democratic candidate for the presidential nomination during 2015/16, against Hillary Clinton. The popularity of Sanders, who raised more money in the form of small, individual donations than any other candidate in US congressional history, took many by surprise in its extent and reach. Like Corbyn, his political platform offered an alternative to neoliberal meritocracy based around collective provision and the redistribution of wealth. Some aspects of Sanders' and Corbyn's challenges have been different. Sanders was overly slow in connecting with black voters, and he could not be accused of dispassionate public speaking, as Corbyn has been. But other challenges they have faced have been similar, including a backlash from the right of the party; hostile media coverage; and the gaping fact that left-of-centre parties have been historically monumentally slow to elect female leaders (and when women have been put forward they have been to the right of the left, rather than charismatic left populists). In whatever shape it takes, the media, the conservative left and diversity are three core issues that any successful extension of the egalitarian challenge to neoliberal meritocracy has to address.

## Meritocracy versus mutuality

The popularisation of the meritocratic idea of social opportunity and mobility is not new in Britain. In Victorian times, it was palpable in the idea of 'self-help' as the only way to climb the long social ladder up from the street or the workhouse. This discourse was only substantially knocked back, as we saw in the last chapter, by the introduction of collective forms of welfare state provision in the twentieth century. But still, after the forms of collective provision in terms of healthcare, schooling, sick pay, parental leave and pensions were introduced, discrepancies in income combined with class privilege meant that it remained the case that what class you were born into mattered most:

> After 1945, successive governments presented Britain as a meritocracy, in which anyone could climb the ladder with hard work and talent. But only a few could attain 'success'. Far from being a 'meritocracy', in

which anyone could succeed if they worked hard, post-war Britain remained a society where birth mattered more than effort. ... The Labour government maintained private housing, education and healthcare, and the differential wage rates that rewarded salaried professionals and managers more than manual workers. These measures were intended to help create a meritocracy, in which anyone could get on with hard work and talent. But in reality, these policies reinforced existing social divisions, by encouraging middle-class voters to see themselves as a separate interest group from the working class. The 1945 rhetoric of 'the people' against 'vested interests' rang increasingly hollow.

*(Todd 2015: 153)*

As we saw in the last chapter, income inequality has worsened since the mid-century. Neoliberal meritocratic discourse has adapted itself in certain ways to the demands for liberation made on the basis of gender and ethnicity. The dismantling of mechanisms of collective provision has been accompanied by a vigorous discourse of meritocracy in the neoliberal period which has taken various forms under different government regimes, as I have sketched out in this chapter. It is, of course, not the case that a single leader is responsible for these different regimes, despite the strength of our investment in what political theorist Archie Brown has termed, in the title of his book, *The Myth of the Strong Leader* (Brown 2014). Yet it is also precisely the strength of current investment in this notion – both in terms of cultural discourse and political mechanisms – which means that the tone and message set by whoever the prime minister is obviously has great influence in shaping the conjuncture and political mood.

The commitment of the political class to an ideology of neoliberal meritocracy has marked the period I have been discussing in this chapter, which has attempted to trace the different modes such abuse has taken. In Britain, Thatcherism's elision of collective state welfare with the ingrained privileges of 'the great and the good' were mobilised into an anti-intellectual acquisitive, consumerist form of meritocracy. The meritocratic feeling promulgated by the Cameron government perpetuated a possessive individualist, consumerist notion of meritocracy, like the New Labour government before it. Despite these similarities, Cameronism by contrast to Blairism adopted a particularly punitive approach. Its meritocratic feeling placed moral virtue in the affective acts of aspiration and hope, which, when combined with the trope of hard work, is now explicitly pitted against any form of collective provision or mutual forms of social reproduction. 'Aspiration Nation' defined itself against mutuality. You are a striver or a skiver: believing in the necessity of any kind of collective form of social reproduction was demarcated by the Conservatives as simply a lazy excuse for not striving.

This aggressively moralistic dimension of neoliberal meritocracy has become more xenophobic and sadistic in some of its more recent right-wing populist incarnations: in Britain, through some of the rhetoric deployed by UKIP and Nigel Farage as well as Cameron and, in the US, most spectacularly through Donald Trump's election pledges to build a wall to keep Mexicans out of the US and to ban Muslims from entering the country. As we have seen, however, neoliberal meritocracy takes a variety of forms: it mutates (to the extent that there is now debate over whether it is 'ending' in favour of neo-nationalist capitalism [see Jacques 2016]). Theresa May is currently converting demotic populism into a different vein by referring to the difficulties of the working class, of women, of non-white people in order to cultivate an image of a 'stern but fair' version of neoliberal meritocracy. At exactly the same time, vast swathes of the community mechanisms that do most to support people with few resources – childcare centres, benefits to women in crisis, libraries – are being axed, and greater provision benefitting the already wealthy, like grammar schools, are being introduced. Corporate justice narratives claim to address the meritocratic deficit, but capitalism, in both its neoliberal and neo-nationalist variations, structurally perpetuates and extends it.

## Notes

1 Bénabou 1999: 335.
2 In the 1970s capitalism had hit a bust part of its boom–bust cycle, and the Middle East oil embargo had sent oil prices soaring.
3 As Adam Curtis's film *The Attic* shows, the iconography of Victorian Britain was central to her imagery, at the same time as she waged war on the traditional 'great and the good'.
4 May's speech also had some parallels to Cameron's first speech as prime minister in that he highlighted inequality and social mobility and vaunted his solution, his vision of an 'Aspiration Nation'. Along with the suggestions that we should look after the socially excluded ('hug a hoodie'), and the promise, conveyed through Arctic photo-shoots, that he would look after the environment ('hug a husky'), these ambitions disappeared from his agenda not long after being elected leader, in favour of the language of austerity as 'hard medicine' and the moralising stigmatisation of a reconstituted underclass.
5 One of the progressive policies enacted by Corbyn's predecessor Ed Miliband, who had lost the 2015 general election, was to attempt to reinvigorate the Labour Party membership, which had slumped like that of the other parties over

the past few 'post-political' decades. The introduction of a cheap, £3 registered supporter option, combined with the excitement of a candidate who did not occupy or offer a politics of the technocratic centre, meant that the numbers of new registered supporters (who could now vote in leadership elections) and new members swelled. Corbyn was elected as leader with a very large mandate, as he subsequently frequently reminded detractors (Seymour 2016).

6  A bitter leadership contest took place in 2016 after several Labour MPs resigned, citing Corbyn's managerial incompetence and voted a motion of no confidence in him, with the Welsh MP Owen Smith emerged as the key challenger to become the new leader. Whilst he protested he did not want to privatise the NHS, questions were raised as to Smith's background as a PR man for the large pharmaceutical company Pfizer and previous endorsement, in a newspaper interview, of private providers in public services including hospitals and schools (Shipton 2006/16). Smith has been understood by many commentators and much of the Labour membership as part of a 'Blairite coup', like Angela Eagle before him, one which is failing to connect with the membership but has substantial mainstream media allies. The challenge for the leadership election, strung out over months, successfully damaged the image of Corbyn's leadership, a process helped by weaknesses in his inner management team, whilst being unsuccessful in winning widespread support for this alternative.

## References

Abrahams, Jessie (2016) 'Honourable Mobility or Shameless Entitlement? Habitus and Graduate Employment', *British Journal of Sociology of Education*, Online first edition, www.tandfonline.com/doi/abs/10.1080/01425692.2015.1131145?src=recsys&journalCode=cbse20. Accessed 21 March 2017.

Allen, Kim, and Yvette Taylor (2012) 'Placed Parenting, Locating Unrest: Failed Femininities, Troubled Mothers and Rioting Subjects', *MAMSIE: Studies in the Maternal* 4(2), www.mamsie.bbk.ac.uk/back_issues/4_2/index.html. Accessed 1 December 2016.

Barnett, Anthony (2003) 'Corporate Populism and Partyless Democracy', in A. Chadwick and R. Hefferman (eds), *The New Labour Reader*. Oxford: Polity Press, pp. 88–89.

Baxter, Holly (2016) 'When You Cross-Reference Theresa May's Speech with her Voting Record, it's as if She didn't Mean Anything She Said', *The Independent*, 11 July, www.independent.co.uk/voices/theresa-may-prime-minister-andrea-leadsom-policies-voting-record-human-rights-what-did-she-mean-a7130961.html. Accessed 1 December 2016.

BBC (1999) 'UK Politics: Blair Promises Decade of Power', *BBC News*, http://news.bbc.co.uk/1/hi/uk_politics/254931.stm. Accessed 1 December 2016.

Beck, John (2008) *Meritocracy, Citizenship and Education: New Labour's Legacy*. London: Continuum.

Beckett, Andy (2009) *When the Lights Went Out: What Really Happened to Britain in the Seventies*. London: Faber & Faber.

Bénabou, Ronald (1999) 'Meritocracy, Redistribution and the Size of the Pie', in Kenneth Arrow, Samuel Bowles and Steven Durlauf (eds), *Meritocracy and Economic Inequality*. Princeton: Princeton University Press, pp. 317–323.

Berlant, Lauren (2012) *Cruel Optimism*. Durham, NC: Duke University Press.

Bewes, Timothy, and Jeremy Gilbert (1999) (eds) *Cultural Capitalism: Politics after New Labour*. London: Lawrence & Wishart.

Bowlby, Rachel (1985) *Just Looking: Consumer Culture in Gissing, Dreiser and Zola*, London: Methuen.

Brown, Archie (2014) *The Myth of the Strong Leader*. London: Vintage.

Byrne, Bridget (2014) *Making Citizens: Public Rituals and Personal Journeys to Citizenship*. Basingstoke: Palgrave Macmillan.

Cameron, David (2012) 'David Cameron's Conservative Party Conference Speech: In Full', *Daily Telegraph*, 10 October, www.telegraph.co.uk/news/politics/conservative/9598534/David-Camerons-Conservative-Party-Conference-speech-in-full.html. Accessed 1 December 2016.

Campbell, Beatrix (1987) *The Iron Ladies: Why do Women Vote Tory?* London: Virago Press

Christie, Bridget (2015) 'Feminists Never Have Sex and Hate Men Opening Doors for Them, Even into Other Dimensions', *The Guardian*, 22 June, www.theguardian.com/lifeandstyle/2015/jun/22/bridget-christie-feminists-sex-men-book-extract. Accessed 2 March 2017.

Conservative Party (1979) *Conservative Party 1979 Manifesto*. London: Conservative Party Central Office.

Conservative Party (1987) *Conservative Party 1987 Manifesto*. London: Conservative Party Central Office.

Corbyn, Jeremy (2015a) 'Britain Can't Cut its Way to Prosperity: We Have to Build It', *The Guardian*, 13 September, www.theguardian.com/commentisfree/2015/sep/13/jeremy-corbyn-labour-leadership-victory-vision. Accessed 2 March 2017.

Corbyn, Jeremy (2015b) 'Speech to Labour Party Conference', *Labour Press*, http://press.labour.org.uk/post/130135691169/speech-by-jeremy-corbyn-to-labour-party-annual. Accessed 1 December 2016.

Couglan, Sean (2016) 'Greening Pledges Grammar "Meritocracy"', *BBC News*, 12 September, www.bbc.co.uk/news/education-37338601. Accessed 2 March 2017 .

Couldry, Nick, and Jo Littler (2011) 'Work, Power and Performance: Analysing the "Reality" Game of The Apprentice', *Cultural Sociology* 5(2) pp. 263–279.

Davidson, Lyn (2016) 'Mayritocracy: PM Makes Sun Readers a Pledge to Build an Education System that will Work for "Ordinary Working-Class Families"', *The Sun*, 9 September, www.thesun.co.uk/news/1754768/theresa-may-puts-grammar-schools-at-heart-of-radical-plans-to-create-worlds-greatest-meritocracy-in-education-shake-up. Accessed 1 December 2016.

Davies, William (2016) 'Home Office Rules', *London Review of Books* 38(21) pp. 3–6.

De Grazia, Victoria, and Ellen Furlough (eds) (1996) *The Sex of Things: Gender and Consumption in Historical Perspective*. Berkeley: University of California Press.

Dominiczak, Peter, Christopher Hope and John Bingham (2016) 'Theresa May's Cabinet a Triumph for State Education and Women as New Prime Minister Sweeps Away Cameron Favourites in "Day of the Long Knives"', *Daily Telegraph*, 14 July, www.telegraph.co.uk/news/2016/07/14/theresa-mays-cabinet-a-triumph-for-state-education-and-women-as. Accessed 1 December 2016.

Dorfman, Ariel (2004) *Other Septembers, Many Americas: Selected Provocations 1980–2004*. London: Pluto Press.

Dorling, Danny (2015) *Injustice: Why Social Inequality still Persists*, 2nd edn. Bristol: Policy Press.

Driver, Stephen, and Luke Martell (1998) *New Labour: Politics after Thatcherism*. London: Polity Press.

Elmer, Greg, and Paula Todd (2016) 'Don't Be a Loser: Or How Trump Turned the Republican Primaries into an Episode of The Apprentice', *Television and New Media* 17(7) pp. 660–662.

Finlayson, Alan (2003) *Making Sense of New Labour*. London: Lawrence & Wishart.

Fisher, Mark (2009) *Capitalist Realism*. London: Zero Books.

Foucault, Michel (2008) *The Birth of Biopolitics: Lectures at the Collège de France, 1978–1979*, trans. Graham Burchell. Basingstoke: Palgrave Macmillan.

Frank, Thomas (2012) *Pity the Billionaire: The Hard-Times Swindle and the Unlikely Comeback of the Right*. New York: Picador.

Franklin, Sarah, Celia Lury and Jackie Stacey (eds) (1991) *Off-Centre: Feminism and Cultural Studies*. London: Routledge.

Freeland, Chrystia (2012) *Plutocrats: The Rise of the New Global Super-Rich*. London: Allen Lane.

Freeman, Des (2008) *The Politics of Media Policy*. London: Polity Press.

Gamble, Andrew (1993) 'The Entrails of Thatcherism', *New Left Review* 1(138) (March/April) pp. 117–128.

Gamble, Andrew (1994) *The Free Economy and the Strong State: The Politics of Thatcherism*. Basingstoke: Palgrave Macmillan.

Giddens, Anthony (1998) *The Third Way*. London: Polity Press.

Giddens, Anthony (2002) *Where Now for New Labour?* London: Polity Press.

Gilbert, Jeremy (2004) 'The Second Wave: The Specificity of New Labour Neoliberalism', *Soundings* 26 pp. 25–45.

Gilbert, Jeremy (2014) *Common Ground: Democracy and Collectivity in an Age of Individualism*. London: Pluto.

Gilbert, Jeremy (2015a) 'What Hope for Labour and the Left? The Election, the 80s and "Aspiration"', *Open Democracy*, 27 July, www.opendemocracy.net/ourking dom/jeremy-gilbert/what-hope-for-labour-and-left-election-80s-and-%E2%80%98aspiration%E2%80%99. Accessed 1 December 2016.

Gilbert, Jeremy (2015b) 'Corbyn: What's a Leader Really For?', *Open Democracy*, 1 December, www.opendemocracy.net/uk/jeremy-gilbert/corbyn-whats-leader-really-for. Accessed 2 March 2017 .

Gilles, Val (2005) 'Raising the Meritocracy: Parenting and the Individualisation of Social Class', *Sociology* 39(5) pp. 835–853.

Gregg, Melissa, and Greg Seigworth (eds) (2012) *The Affect Reader*. Durham, NC: Duke University Press.
Hall, Stuart (1988) *The Hard Road to Renewal*. London: Verso.
Hall, Stuart (2003) 'New Labour's Double Shuffle', *Soundings* 24 pp. 10–24.
Hall, Stuart, Doreen Massey and Michael Rustin (eds) (2013) *After Neoliberalism: The Kilburn Manifesto*. London: Lawrence & Wishart.
Harvey, David (2005) *A Brief History of Neoliberalism*. Oxford: Oxford University Press.
Hearn, Alison (2016) 'Trump's Reality Hustle', *Television and New Media* 17(7) pp. 656–659.
*Huffington Post* (2013) 'Cameron Spring Conference Speech: A Rousing Battle Cry Against Labour's "Self Satisfied Socialists"', 16 March, www.huffingtonpost.co.uk/2013/03/16/cameron-spring-conference-battle-labour-socialists_n_2890437.html. Accessed 1 December 2016.
Jacques, Martin (2016) 'The Death of Neoliberalism and the Crisis in Western Politics', *The Guardian*, 21 August, www.theguardian.com/commentisfree/2016/aug/21/death-of-neoliberalism-crisis-in-western-politics. Accessed 1 December 2016.
Jensen, Tracy (2010) 'What Kind of Mum are You at the Moment? Supernanny and the Psychologising of Classed Embodiment', *Subjectivity* 3(2) pp. 170–192.
Jensen, Tracey (2012) 'Tough Love in Tough Times', *MAMSIE: Studies in the Maternal* 4(2), www.mamsie.bbk.ac.uk/Jensen_SiM_4_2_2012.html. Accessed 1 December 2016.
Johnson, Boris ( 2013) 'Migrants get Jobs because We're not Prepared to Work as Hard', *Daily Telegraph*, 7 April, www.telegraph.co.uk/news/politics/9977793/Migrants-get-jobs-because-were-not-prepared-to-work-as-hard.html. Accessed 1 December 2016.
Jones, Owen, Christine Blower, Bruce Bennett and Imogen Tyler (2015) *What is Aspiration? How Progressives Should Respond*. London: Centre for Labour and Social Studies.
Keegan, Victor (1998) 'Economics Notebook: Raising the Risk Stakes', *The Guardian*, 26 October, www.guardian.co.uk/Columnists/Column/0,,325036,00.html. Accessed 1 December 2016.
Khan, Shamus (2010) *Privilege: The Making of an Adolescent Elite at St Paul's School*. Princeton: Princeton University Press.
Khan, Shamus, and Colin Jerolmack (2013) 'Saying Meritocracy and Doing Privilege', *Sociological Quarterly* 54(1) pp. 9–19.
Klein, Naomi (2008) *The Shock Doctrine: The Rise of Disaster Capitalism*. Harmondsworth: Penguin.
Littler, Jo (2000) 'Creative Accounting: Consumer Culture, the "Creative Economy" and the Cultural Policies of New Labour', in Tim Bewes and Jeremy Gilbert (eds), *Cultural Capitalism: Politics after New Labour*. London: Lawrence & Wishart.
Littler, Jo (2009) 'Gendering Anti-Consumerism: Consumer Whores and Conservative Consumption', in Kate Soper, Martin Ryle and Lyn Thomas (eds), *Counter-Consumerism and its Pleasures: Better than Shopping*. Basingstoke: Palgrave.

Littler, Jo, and Roshi Naidoo (eds) (2005) *The Politics of Heritage: The Legacies of 'Race'*. London: Routledge.
McGuigan, Jim (2009) *Cool Capitalism*. London: Pluto.
McNamee, Stephen J., and Robert K. Miller (2009) *The Myth of Meritocracy*. Lanham: Rowman & Littlefield.
McRobbie, Angela (2013) 'Feminism, the Family and the New Mediated Maternalism', *New Formations* 80–81 pp. 119–137.
Mair, Peter (2000) 'Partyless Democracy: Solving the Paradox of New Labour', *New Left Review* 2 (March–April) pp. 21–35.
Major, John (1993) 'Speech to the Conservative Group for Europe', 22 April, www.johnmajor.co.uk/page1086.html. Accessed 1 November 2016.
Massey, Doreen (2007) *World City*. Oxford: Polity Press.
May, Theresa (2016) 'Theresa May's First Speech to the Nation as Prime Minister: In Full', *The Independent*, 13 July, www.independent.co.uk/news/uk/politics/theresa-mays-first-speech-to-the-nation-as-prime-minister-in-full-a7135301.html. Accessed 1 August 2016.
Medhurst, John (2014) *That Option No Longer Exists: Britain 1974–76*. London: Zero Books.
Meek, James (2015) *Private Island: Why Britain Now Belongs to Someone Else*. London: Verso.
Meek, James (2016) 'Robin Hood in a Time of Austerity', *London Review of Books* 38(4) pp. 3–8, www.lrb.co.uk/v38/n04/james-meek/robin-hood-in-a-time-of-austerity. Accessed 1 November 2016.
Mills, Tom (2013) 'The Death of a Class Warrior: Margaret Thatcher 1925–2013', *New Left Project*, www.newleftproject.org/index.php/site/article_comments/the_death_of_a_class_warrior_margaret_thatcher_1925_2013. Accessed 1 December 2016.
Nava, Mica (2002) *Changing Cultures: Feminism, Youth and Consumerism*. London: Sage.
Nunn, Heather (2001) 'Running Wild: Fictions of Gender and Childhood in Thatcher's Britain', *EnterText* 1(3), http://arts.brunel.ac.uk/gate/entertext/issue_3.htm. Accessed 1 December 2016.
Nunn, Heather (2002) *Thatcher, Politics and Fantasy: The Political Culture of Gender and Nation*. London: Lawrence & Wishart.
Ouellette, Laurie (2016) 'The Trump Show', *Television and New Media* 17(7) pp. 647–650.
Peev, Geri (2012) 'Games Embody the Tory Ethic of Hard Work that Leads to Reward, Says Boris', *Daily Mail*, 6 August, www.dailymail.co.uk/news/article-2184687/Boris-Johnson-London-2012-Olympics-embody-Tory-ethic-hard-work-leads-reward.html#ixzz2QG4E5oVC. Accessed 1 December 2016.
Piketty, Thomas (2013) *Capital in the Twenty-First Century*. Cambridge, MA: Belknap Press.
Prynn, Jonathan, and Miranda Bryant (2013) 'London Rents at All-Time High as Prices Rocket Eight Times Faster than Wages', *Evening Standard*, 18 April,

www.standard.co.uk/news/london/london-rents-at-alltime-high-as-prices-rocket-eight-times-faster-than-wages-8578230.html. Accessed 1 December 2016.

Read, Jason (2015) *The Politics of Transindividuality*. Chicago: Haymarket.

Richards, Lawrence (2015) 'What the British are Really Laughing About', *The Leveller*, September 21, http://theleveller.org/2015/09/british-really-laughing. Accessed 1 December 2016.

Rojek, Chris (2001) *Celebrity*. London: Reaktion Books.

Seymour, Richard (2010) *The Meaning of David Cameron*. London: Zero Books.

Seymour, Richard (2016) *Corbyn: The Strange Rebirth of Radical Politics*. London: Verso.

Shipton, Martin (2006/16) 'Owen Smith on the Iraq War, Working as a Lobbyist and the Private Sector's Role in the NHS', *Wales Online*, 10 May 2006, updated 13 July 2016, www.walesonline.co.uk/news/politics/owen-smith-iraq-war-working-2338066. Accessed 1 December 2016.

Slack, James, Jason Groves and Eleanor Harding (2016) 'March of the Meritocrats: May Loads New Cabinet with State-Educated Ministers on the Most Brutal Day of Top-Level Sacking in Modern History', *Daily Mail*, 15 July, www.dailymail.co.uk/news/article-3691248/MARCH-MERITOCRATS-loads-new-Cabinet-state- educated-Ministers-brutal-day-level-sacking-modern-history.html. Accessed 1 December 2016.

Todd, Selina (2015) *The People: The Rise and Fall of the Working Class, 1910–2010*. London: John Murray.

Williams, Raymond (1977) *Marxism and Literature*. Oxford: Oxford Paperbacks.

Willis, Paul (1977) *Learning to Labour: How Working-Class Kids get Working-Class Jobs*. Farnham: Ashgate.

Woodward, Kathryn (ed.) (1997) *Identity and Difference*. London: Sage.

# PART II
# Popular parables

# 4

# JUST LIKE US?

## Normcore plutocrats and the popularisation of elitism

> There's class warfare, all right. But it's my class, the rich class, that's making war, and we're winning.
>
> *Warren Buffett*[1]

### Meritocracy and the extension of privilege

How do plutocratic elites use discourses of meritocracy to maintain and reproduce their privilege? Whilst the existence of elites is hardly new, what is to some degree more historically novel is the extent to which large sections of today's plutocracy feels the need to pretend they are not an elite at all. This chapter examines how elites present themselves as ordinary: as 'just like us'. It suggests that we might consider such presentations of the super-rich in relation to a broader palette of social dispositions and a wider differentiated range of mediated cultural tropes. These are: first, the 'normcore plutocrat', when the ultra-wealthy are presented as 'just like us'; second, the 'kind parent', when they look imperiously after the needs of society; and third, the 'luxurious winner', when they flaunt material excess.

This chapter traces such motifs across a range of media, in the process considering a number of examples including the rehabilitation of the UK royal family, changes in CEO culture, the website *Rich Kids of Instagram*, the TV series *Downton Abbey* and the films *Annie* and *The King's Speech*, analysing them in relation to changes in both the demographics of the international super-rich and to the fluctuating meanings of 'meritocracy'. It focuses on how, in such populist modes of presentation, elites are actively mobilising the widely felt injustices of post-democracy and rechannelling these feelings about injustice for their own benefit. Then it analyses the specificity of the normcore plutocrat in a longer historical perspective. For whereas plutocratic excesses were curbed in the post-war period, today they have not been: they have been permitted to flourish, which in turn makes it much more pressing for them to appear 'just like us'.

## The 1%, the new rentiers and transnational asset-stripping

To answer the question of how plutocratic elites negotiate with the idea of meritocracy in public it is useful to consider how elites have changed in recent years. The quantity and demographics of plutocrats have been changing in significant ways in terms of both numbers and composition. The most obvious change is in terms of the sheer amount of money that the ultra-wealthy control: a proportion of global wealth that has simultaneously expanded and received more publicity during the time I have been writing this book. In 2016, the charity Oxfam published the results of research showing that 62 people now own the same amount of money as half the world's population, down from 388 people in 2010; and that the richest 1% now own more wealth than the rest of the world combined (Hardoon, Fuentes-Nieva and Ayele 2016).

The scale of this financial shift from the many to the few is breathtaking in its extremity. As Andrew Sayer puts it: 'in a nutshell, such a transfer of wealth has happened because *changes to institutions and practices have made it possible*' (Sayer 2016; my italics). Neoliberalism – the expansion of marketisation into areas and zones which were previously not for sale, the financialised commodification of debt, the weakening of regulation designed to protect citizens from the extremities of the market, the passing of laws to increase the wealth of the already rich – has made it possible (Sayer 2016; Brown 2015; Klein 2008; Piketty 2013; Foucault 2010). To understand how the changes to such practices, policies and laws have been able to be presented as acceptable, as convincing, is now a relatively sizeable emergent body of analysis to which this book has aimed to make a contribution. In this particular chapter, I consider this issue in terms of how the rich occupy roles which draw on the neoliberal ideology of meritocracy. How have plutocrats made themselves palatable?

The Occupy movement's popularisation of the idea of 'the 1% versus the 99%', and the phrase 'we are the 99%', reverberated way beyond the protest camps asserting the necessity of reclaiming the public sphere and basic amenities for all. As Danny Dorling points out, it is an apt and statistically correct concept, for the 1/99 is the most significant dividing line in terms of wealth in the contemporary era, much more than say, the 80% and the 20%. The bottom 99% are increasingly, as Dorling points out, 'all in this together' as the income and standard of living contracts for the squeezed middle (Dorling 2014) and as what has been termed 'the precariat' expands beyond the working class (Standing 2011). Yet within the 1% itself there is a vast amount of internal differentiation; in particular it is the top 0.1% whose wealth has surged ahead, so much so that in the UK the 0.1% owns four times as much as the average 1 percenter (and the top 0.01% way beyond this; Dorling 2014: 11; see also Freeland 2012: 80–3; Hecht 2014). Inequality is not consistent across countries: in the UK, for example, a 'pre-tax household income for a childless couple of £160,000 puts you among the very poorest of the 1%; in the US you would need $324,000 to be in the same category (Dorling 2014: 10; see also Grsuky and Szelenyi 2011). This is not inevitable: in the far more equitable Japan and the Netherlands the incomes of the 1% have reduced over past decades (Dorling 2014: 10). However, the increasing chasm between the 1% and the 99% is particularly acute in countries where right-wing politicians have implemented 'shock doctrine' neoliberal policies (Piketty 2013; Klein 2008; Dorling 2014).

How has this surge in wealth for the 1% and especially the 0.1% been able to happen? In his insightful book *Why We Can't Afford the Rich*, sociologist Andrew Sayer emphasises the important distinction between earned and unearned income. First, there is money that comes from controlling means of production, which is earned income, producing 'the working rich'. Second, there are those who get most of their income from the fact they already own control of existing assets that yield rent, interest or capital gains. This is unearned income, and these people are 'rentiers' (Sayer 2016; see also Lapavitsas 2013; Valentine 2005). A neoliberal political system supports, above all, rentier interests, in which the 99% become increasingly indebted to the 1%. It is a form of wealth extraction, but it becomes packaged as, and confused with, wealth creation. As Sayer points out, even arch conservative Winston Churchill thought that particular way of earning income was parasitical; today, it is enthusiastically encouraged by neoliberal politicians (Sayer 2016: 49–50).

The super-wealthy now overwhelmingly get their wealth from 'profiting without producing', as Costas Lapavitsas put it, through unearned income from their assets: as interest, rent or profit from selling investments (capital gains) (Lapavitsas 2013). This simple fact is also at the heart of Thomas Piketty's much quoted book *Capital in the Twenty-First Century*, in which he defines the rentier as 'the enemy of democracy' (Piketty 2013: 422). *Capital in the Twenty-First Century* presents as its key finding the formula R > G. In this formula 'G' is economic growth in a national economy in general, and 'R' is the rate of return for capital. Piketty's conclusions are that the economies of the countries he examined grow at 1.0–1.5% per year, but capital at 4.0–5.0% per year, meaning that the wealthy will get vastly more wealthy, unless different political measures are introduced. Piketty's suggested solution is a wealth tax (Piketty 2013).

The neoliberal mantra that the socialised provisions of the welfare state should be gradually sold off to the private sector, piece by piece, has resulted in widespread 'asset stripping' (Meek 2014). Transnational investors buy national assets like housing, trains, telephone, steel or water companies that are being sold off by national governments. This process is of such a magnitude that it is often likened to earlier historical acts of selling off the commons, such as the enclosures, dividing and selling common land which escalated at the beginning of the Industrial Revolution in Europe: it is a similar form of 'primitive accumulation' (Terranova 2015). To say this is not to suggest that history is condemned to repeat itself in some inevitable formula. It does mean that the constant battle over sharing (or not sharing) wealth has taken on very different historical shapes and forms. The most complex of these new forms is the labyrinthine matrix of financialisation, the casino of speculation developed through the commodification of debt (Ross 2013; Massey 2007, 2013).[2]

Today the majority of the profits of the super-rich are made through unearned income on property and through speculation in the financial sector. Politicians have been voted into power who have loosened the constraints on capitalism. They have acted, in one memorable phrase, as 'butlers' to transnational capitalists who have been able to vastly inflate the income they get just by having, or by playing around with, the assets they already have (York 2015; Atkinson, Parker and Burrows 2016).

Alongside this immense hoovering-up of global wealth, the plutocratic elite now have other distinguishing features which have become of interest to the reinvigorated academic field of 'elite studies', which has resuscitated some of the earlier debates on the subject (e.g. Davis 2007, 2015; Williams and Savage 2008; Gilens and Page 2014; Poulantzas 1975; Miliband 1969; Mills 1956). There is a change in the global composition of elites. Chrystia Freeland points out that whilst North Americans are no longer the largest group of millionaires in the world, taken as a group – 37.0% compared to Europeans at 37.2% – they still dominate the 'super-wealthy' (people worth over $50 million). Forty-four per cent of the super-wealthy are in the US, 28.0% in Europe, 19.2% in Asia and the Pacific, and 3.4% in China (Freeland 2012: 35). They are therefore to some extent 'more global, and more diverse geographically and racially' (Khan 2012: 363). In relative terms there are a few more self-made working rich than in the past (Khan 2012). The leveraging of wealth of the working rich through unearned income means that self-made entrepreneurs such as Alan Sugar (businessman and star of UK's *The Apprentice*) are able to easily inflate their assets once they have them. The extensive media presence of such figures exaggerates their numbers and the reasons why they have been able to inflate their assets are frequently translated by the media as simply due to individual 'savvy'.

Whilst social mobility is increasingly difficult for the 99%, there is one place where there is pronounced upward mobility: amongst the upper echelons of the elite. As Seamus Khan puts it of the US:

> Elites have experienced considerable wage movements in the past several decades. A wealthy individual has likely enjoyed income and wealth gains at rates far greater than those immediately below him. Simultaneously, those immediately above him have far outpaced his own considerable gains. Furthermore, there has been a relative increase in self-made elites. Unlike most Americans, elites have experienced considerable wage growth and mobility.
>
> *(Khan 2012: 367)*

In these terms we can see how the ideology of neoliberal meritocracy works for the rich in particular: how supremely easy and how very profitable it is for them to believe it is the best social system. Of course, it is not the case that all the rich are wholly comfortable with this system. The billionaire Warren Buffett for example has regularly called for the rich to be taxed: a minority of the 1% are uncomfortable with the extent of 'the divide' (Hecht 2014). Still, others are profoundly comfortable with it. Indeed, a far larger proportion actively campaign for a continuation of their rights, whether on an overt level (such as the bankers who formed the 'Occupy Occupy Wall Street' protest or Boris Johnson arguing that the rich should be taxed far less as they provide a public service) or on a covert level (through passive acquiescence or the extensive networks of discreet lobbying) (Johnson 2013;

Billera 2011; Monbiot 2016; Stauber and Rampton 1995). Indeed, we can see how very easy it is for the ultra-rich who are the main social group experiencing social mobility to believe, or to try to believe, in the widely peddled idea of neoliberal meritocracy's upward mobility: for it is their own experience as well as suiting their vested financial interests.

The following sections consider how wealthy elites publicly negotiate the ideology of meritocracy in media discourse. Of course, not all wealthy elites are keen to show themselves in public at all: financial elites are less conspicuously or publicly individualised. The sections of the rich that do tend to court and be subject to media representation are framed in a variety of ways to appear egalitarian and, in the process, often draw on meritocratic discourse. In this chapter I identify three forms which do so. First, those sections of the ultra-wealthy who try to appear profoundly ordinary or normal, or what I call 'normcore plutocrats'. Second, the idea that the rich look after us, or are what I term 'kind parents'; and third, the seductive yet potentially more risky position of the 'luxury-flaunter'. These are, of course, not hermetic categories or consistent social types but rather prevalent cultural–political motifs or tropes which gain traction through their seemingly endless media repetition.

## Normcore plutocrats

'Normcore' was the quasi-parodic name given to a fashion trend which junked searching for yet another new clothing style in favour of the everyday: of hoodies and jeans (Farrell 2014). Its gently comic appeal is generated by the word 'normcore' itself, a juxtaposition bolting together the unassuming everyday (the 'norm') with the fierce intensity (the 'core') deriving from its play on the word 'hardcore'. As an expression it is mildly satirical of the insistent search for newness inherent in the profit-driven nature of the fashion cycle and of the idea that 'normal' can fit the usually outlandish category of cool. At the same time, it also suggests – as the work of anthropologists and cultural studies practitioners have taught us for decades – that 'normal' is a set of constructed characteristics.

'Normcore plutocrat' is a phrase indicating how the plutocrat – whose power is gained to an extensive degree through wealth – can attempt to maintain and increase their power and wealth by 'performing ordinariness'. Such discourse expresses the idea that the rich are not that different: they are just like us, everyday, ordinary beings. Whilst it has a long history (Winters 2011), it is not a coincidence that this motif becomes pronounced at moments when the rich are under increased public scrutiny about their increased share of the wealth.

Take, for example, recent CEO culture. Chief executive officers are the most senior figures in charge of managing a corporation.[3] As I have written about elsewhere (Littler 2007), today publicity about CEOs is not restricted to the pages of business publications: on the contrary, many CEOs actively court coverage across the gamut of media, from tabloid newspapers through TV to Twitter (Guthey, Clark and Jackson 2009). And in the process many insistently construct and promote an image of 'extraordinary ordinariness'. The UK businessman Alan Sugar, for example, has become prominent over the past decade by building his persona in the tabloid press and through the TV show *The Apprentice*, the UK version of the transnational reality show discussed in chapter 2.

Sugar's persona has gained popularity through the presentation of a straight-talking working-class cockney who does not mince his words. This, we are told, is an ordinary bloke who did not need any fancy training or cultural capital to rise to the top of the ladder, who treats all his 'apprentices' with equal directness. The titles of his bestselling books graphically indicate this forthrightness: *What You See is What You Get, The Way I See It* and *Unscripted: My Ten Years in Telly* (Sugar 2011, 2012, 2015). 'If I, the barrow boy Sugar can "make it"', is his message, 'so can anybody – as long as you sort yourself out in the way I did'.

Alan Sugar's promotion of his blunt normality has been extremely profitable in securing his rise to elite status. When *The Apprentice* began, he was already 24th in the *Sunday Times Rich List*, and the TV programme did not make him as much money as his 'regular work' (Hutton 2005). But what Sugar's newfound celebrity as gruff TV guru did provide was the opportunity for wider public recognition beyond the business sector: as a basis for columns and interviews, an expansive, proliferating cross-media coverage. As we saw in chapter 2, *The Apprentice* has been vastly influential in promoting cultural norms of entrepreneurialism and competition in the wider culture and has been instrumental in helping extend and embed these norms within state school education.

In delivering a message that no matter where you start off in life, you can, with passion and effort, compete and rise up in business, Sugar is most definitely not alone: it is a recurrent message in contemporary business discourse. *Anyone Can Do It*, for example, is the title of a book by the businessman Duncan Bannatyne (Figure 4.1). Bannatyne accumulated his fortune through a number of routes, including privatised childcare, fitness centres

FIGURE 4.1 Cover of Duncan Bannatyne, *Anyone Can Do It*. Reproduced courtesy of Orion Books.

and nursing homes (in part, then, cashing in on the privatisation of the welfare state), and gained his fame primarily through his appearance as a judge on the reality TV business talent show *Dragon's Den*, in which entrepreneurs have three minutes to pitch a business idea to corporate 'experts' including him. *Anyone Can Do It* is promoted by the publisher through classic neoliberal meritocratic discourse: the blurb on the back cover tells us that this is a book in which our hero 'relives his colourful path to riches, from ice-cream salesman to multi-millionaire, explaining how anyone could take the same route as he did – if they really want to' (Bannatyne 2007).

Today's CEO can occupy their unique cultural location due to a confluence of factors, including and beyond new media platforms and formats. One factor is the image of insistent, 'radical' informality produced by post-Fordist capitalism: where 'dress-down Fridays', shared office space and corporate playtimes encourage ostensibly risk-taking subjects, manifesting what Boltanski and Chiapello identify as 'the new spirit of capitalism' (Boltanski and Chiapello 2005). Another factor is the restructuring of finance capital from the 1980s and 1990s, as discussed above. In business commentary and beyond one expression of this movement and consolidation of money into the hands of a small elite was the widespread cultural lionisation of CEOs. As the business writer Constance L. Hays puts it, during the 1980s an 'information industry burst forth to spread and share information about the business world', and 'CEOs who posted superb results lost their facelessness and became celebrities, their photographs featured on the covers of magazines and their names dropped on talk shows. It was a startling shift' (Hays 2005: 146–147).

As CEOs became celebrities both within and beyond the expanding realm of business media, some took demotic self-presentation beyond the normcore to more flamboyant extremes. The American Apparel CEO Dov Charney liked to appear in his own advertisements with his back to the camera, naked from the waist down; and was happy to talk extensively about his sexual preferences in women's magazines. His sexual harassment of employees eventually landed him with several lawsuits, and he was sacked from his own company (Littler 2007; Moor and Littler 2008).

Business writer James Surowiecki comments that 'one of the deep paradoxes of the 1990s' was that 'even as companies paid greater attention to the virtues of decentralisation and the importance of bottom-up mechanisms, they also treated their CEOs as superheroes' (Surowiecki, 2004: 216). Despite their differences, Sugar, Bannatyne and Charney show how the public figure of the celebrity CEO offered a means of reconciling this paradox: by intertwining the twin imperatives of being a 'corporate superhero' with the new 'bottom-up' ambience symptomatic of the cultural turn. In other words, the persona of many contemporary celebrity CEOs works by trying to turn 'fat cats' into 'cool cats'. They use discourses of bottom-up power and of demotic, normcore ordinariness to do so, and they flaunt such images across an expanded range of media contexts. Cultivating a normcore image means cultivating the appearance of social fluidity, providing the celebrity CEO with a populist reach which is crucial in today's ostensibly meritocratic culture and society.

All these businessmen are plutocrats: their power derives from their wealth. Yet they, as these examples show, are able to attain more wealth, and more power, by extending their celebrity capital and using narratives of neoliberal meritocracy across a range of media. With Alan Sugar, this included becoming an advisor to the government, as we saw in chapter 2, as well as being knighted as Lord Sugar (a non-hereditary life peer). Narratives of neoliberal meritocracy help facilitate mobility within elite circuits of power: being a normcore plutocrat eases access to power as well as to more money.

## Normcore aristocrats

It is worth considering how the normcore plutocrat narrative relates to more established forms of elite wealth. Plutocrats' power derives from their wealth, whereas aristocrats' power technically derives from their title, although, much of the time, considerable associated wealth and land goes with it. Take the particular, yet resonant, example of Britain's royal family. The popularity of the royal family was low in the 1990s, when there was publicity about the Queen's tax-exempt status and just before the death of Diana, Princess of Wales, and it dipped again in the early 2000s (IPSOS-Mori 2012). By this I am not suggesting that republicanism was about to break through – that particular cause did not galvanise any significant numbers – but rather that levels of indifference were, for the modern period, at a record high (IPSOS-Mori 2012).

In recent years, however, the popularity of the British royal family has resurged. A key reason is the popularity of 'Wills and Kate', Prince William and Princess Catherine, the Duke and Duchess of Cambridge. Indeed, most people who want the monarchy to continue want the crown to skip over Prince Charles and for William to be made king instead (Clark 2012). One of the key routes through which they have regained popularity is through their performance of ordinariness. If attempting to present the royals as ordinary is not new, nor has it been consistent or effective (Clancy 2015). Wills, Kate and sympathetic sections of the media have together created an image of everyday normality. Their style and self-presentation is relentlessly at the upper fringes of the middle class: as aspirational yet attainable, respectable yet 'relaxed' (what we might term, after the upper-middle-class clothing company, 'Bodenesque').[4]

Kate Middleton was from the beginning often depicted in the media as a commoner, the elements of her background sounding less immensely privileged (such as her mother being an airline hostess or distant ancestors being coal miners) and being relentlessly dragged into the foreground, as Kim Allen and Laura Clancy have pointed out (Allen et al. 2015; Clancy 2015). She has regularly been described by the press as a modest, humble, austerity-minded, thrift queen who shops at TK Maxx and often wears the same dress twice. Meanwhile, other key information is routinely and conveniently elided, like the fact that Middleton attended a series of private schools, her parents bought her a flat in the extremely affluent London area of Chelsea and her parents' business Party Pieces had an estimated worth of £8 million, even before the royal connection (with the royal connection, it is now worth an estimated £30 million [*This is Money* 2011]).

Images of normality and ordinariness have been carefully cultivated by the royal family through, for example, staged photo opportunities in casual conservative clothing in the Middletons' garden:

> The very image of the couple on the grass with baby George is carefully choreographed to match the middle-class ideal, right down to being taken in the Middleton family garden, and there's certainly no opulent palace towering behind them.
>
> *(Clancy 2015)*

Such insistence on domestic normality was also fully in operation around the Queen's 90th birthday celebrations in April 2016, with the BBC programme *Elizabeth at 90: A Family Tribute* depicting Princes William and Harry and other relatives watching home video footage, *Gogglebox*-style, of their family. These were just like ordinary family members watching films of their nan! Just like us, only richer and tied into the living heritage experience attraction of the UK royal family. Such tropes of the domestic and the technological everyday were extended a few weeks later through a comic viral video sketch promoting the Invictus Games, an athletics competition for US and UK military personnel who have been injured in war, which was circulated to the press and on social media. Whilst Prince Harry is explaining the games to the Queen, his mobile rings with the 'Hail to the Chief' tune. 'It's Michelle [Obama]!' Harry exclaims, and the Obamas challenge Harry to 'Bring it on': 'Boom!' (BBC 2016). If this tightly scripted sketch works through the trusted comic impact of the mock-spar, it also builds its comedy by juxtaposing a degree of American black cool with uptight white aristocratic chintz-laden tradition. In the process, Harry and the royal family become themselves a little cooler and show 'they have a sense of humour'. The edited viral video provides none of the scope for off-message comedy excess that the one-off charity TV gameshow 'It's A Royal Knockout!' – featuring members of the royal family throwing custard pies – did so disastrously in the 1980s (Roseman 1996). As such it also contributes to Prince Harry's recent rehabilitated persona as an ordinary, fun-loving royal – kind-hearted and full of banter – contributing to replacing a previous image of him as a spoilt, lazy, irresponsible prince, who in 2005 thought it funny to wear a Nazi uniform to attend a racist aristocratic 'colonial and natives' party (Tweedie and Kallenbach 2005).

Part of what makes the UK royal family – like other European royals – amenable to being positioned as 'like us' is because they are positioned as having a role ostensibly outside the political sphere. They are outside politics in that they have a largely ceremonial role and no remit to engage directly with political debate (meaning whoever is elected prime minister has a vast degree of unchecked power in comparison with other liberal democracies). Thus royalty operates as a highly paid example of a real, living heritage attraction. Yet the Queen's position is political in that it is fundamental to the constitution: she has to approve bills in parliament before they become law. Operating at the apparent border zone of parliamentary politics, royalty is nonetheless hugely significant in terms of its royal prerogative powers, its role as guarantor of establishment hierarchies and its ambiguous, latent political potential, alongside the fact that the monarch is the recipient of obviously sizeable wealth and privilege (Barnett 1994). The royal family is extremely wealthy and includes some of the richest landlords in the country: the Crown Estate, which includes significant sections of central London and around half the UK shoreline, was in 2016 worth £12 billion (Crown Estate 2016).

In an era when politics has, to a large extent, been colonised by technocrats in suits and is implemented from the top-down, being outside politics is a post-democratic space we have been increasingly encouraged to occupy (Crouch 2004). Such post-democratic culture provides an extremely amenable space for the monarchy to court popularity: it enables them to make a similar linkage – like us, they are outside politics, they are ordinary. This connection is also one of several reasons why Prince Charles, who likes to speak out on selective political matters (particularly environmentalism) whilst retaining a pronounced air of aristocratic formality, is so unpopular (Clark 2012).

The link between monarchy and populace as ostensibly connected through a lack of political power in a post-democracy is also dramatised in the 2010 film *The King's Speech*. This major worldwide box-office critical and commercial success – now regularly pronounced 'the most successful independent British film ever' (Brooks 2011) – shows the trials of a stuttering man who is unexpectedly flung into the role of king after his brother's abdication. He is expected to speak to and for the nation on the daunting new-fangled technology of wireless radio. At one point the new king bursts out in frustration:

> You know, if I'm a king, where's my power? Can I form a government, can I levy a tax, declare a war? No. And yet I'm the seat of all authority. Why? Because the nation believes that when I speak, I speak for them! But I can't speak.
> *(The King's Speech 2010)*

Later, of course, the king learns to speak. The visual backdrop to his successful broadcast is a powerful montage of scenes of people from all backgrounds in Britain whilst the king speaks for them at a time of profound anxiety, the outbreak of the Second World War. Rich and poor are united by their shared lack of political power, but the king has gained a voice, and in the process, the assertive affective implication is, of course, that so have they. The film offers an entertaining conservative narrative in which joy – as a stuttering man overcomes his hardship – becomes fused with the triumphant success of the king speaking for everyone. As such it also links to the category I explore next, paternalism; but in terms of representing the monarchy-as-ordinary, what is particularly interesting about this film is how it dramatises the idea of a shared lack of power between royalty and commoners. George VI and his difficulty in speaking, in having a voice, becomes a metaphor for the nation's people. As Michael Billig pointed out, when people are 'talking of the royal family' they are invariably talking of other things too (Billig 1992). In this case, the film is speaking of the disempowerment of contemporary post-democracy whilst it dramatises the past. Importantly, its filmic power comes from changing this situation, through the powerful concept of gaining a political voice (Couldry 2010), even though this becomes channelled into conservative ends. In this sense it is another, much more covert example of how monarchy has rehabilitated itself in a post-political age – presenting itself as ordinary, with the problem of finding any effective voice.

Clearly, the hereditary privilege that the monarchy possesses, as indicated by the titles of aristocracy, is not a state which applies to all the rich. This is the important distinction between the aristocrat and the plutocrat. However, there is an extremely important unifying narrative between them. The issue of innate privilege and how such assets are then leveraged through vastly inflated returns on unearned income is symptomatic of a wider story about elites in terms of inherited wealth. It also indicates something of the blurred cultural and behavioural boundaries between aristocrats and plutocrats. For instance, until his death in 2016, one of the UK's richest people, and its richest royal, was the sixth Duke of Westminster, Gerald Cavendish Grosvenor. His wealth had been accrued through generations of Grosvenor parents who passed on property-based wealth to their sons and daughters. Originally involving London-based properties – his company, the Grosvenor Group, owns swathes of property in Britain, particularly in ultra-affluent areas of London such as Knightsbridge, Covent Garden, Kensington and Chelsea – in the 1950s and 1960s it expanded into properties worldwide in the US, Canada, Australasia and, in the 1990s, into Asia. The Duke acquired his stratospheric levels of wealth through initial income from inherited wealth in the form of land-based assets which was financialised and commodified through a property empire stretching from Belgravia to Tokyo. Mainly taking the route of plutocratic reticence, when he did appear in rare media interviews his 'normality' was insistently foregrounded, indeed in a not dissimilar vein to that offered by *The King's Speech*: he was the country child who grew up playing in the fields, never expecting to be wealthy, 'the man who wanted to be a beef farmer and ended up the richest man in Britain' (Treneman 1998). Whilst these media representations focus on the normcore plutocrat as profoundly everyday, in 2015 the UK government sought to extend inheritance rights of the wealthy by enabling people to pass on homes worth up to £1 million to their children without being taxed at all: a strategy which extends the wealth of the already wealthy and disadvantages the majority of people, whose parents cannot afford to buy them a house in an overinflated housing market.

As we saw in chapter 3, it is notable that the rich will frequently talk extremely loudly about how hard they work, especially when their money comes from unearned income, trying to offset extensive privilege by framing their activity in terms of manual labour. Seamus Khan's astute study of the US elite fee-paying school St Pauls beautifully traces how hyper-privileged children constantly talk about their hard work whilst usually not working particularly hard at all and indeed simultaneously wearing an air of relaxed, natural learning (Khan 2010). This combination is a necessary mode of self-presentation for contemporary entitled elites. The US Republican president, Donald Trump, the son of a billionaire, regularly uses such a classed language of graft. As we saw in chapter 3, so too does the UK prime minister, David Cameron. The Mayor of London, Boris Johnson, invokes it by castigating Londoners for not working as hard as the Chinese, whilst lobbying for tax breaks for billionaires, all the while foregrounding his jocular 'down to earth' persona.

The urgency with which the ultra-wealthy adopt a range of strategies to appear like normcore plutocrats is remarkable. Whilst the existence of elites is hardly new, then, what is to some degree more historically novel is the extent to which large sections of today's plutocracy feels the need to pretend they are not an elite at all. What is notable is the prominence of a generation of wealthy elites who insistently present themselves as hardworking and meritocratic in order to keep the idea of social mobility churning and to legitimate their own position within this wildly exaggerated schema in order to protect their own interests.

## The kind parent

The second stock character in our tour through personifications of the contemporary rich is that of the kind parent. This figure relates to neoliberal myths of meritocracy somewhat differently but no less insistently works to attempt to reinforce it. The kind parent figure suggests that they look after us: they are paternalistic custodians of society. It is a deeply reassuring motif. Everyone needs a degree of parenting, from some source, even as an adult. The world can in many ways be a scary place, and these people are presented as figures that will look after us. The problem is that they primarily look after themselves and their friends under the guise of looking after others. As with the first stock character, there is interesting traffic between examples in which meritocratic narrative is very palpable and overt and its more selective use by older archetypes which draw on specific elements of contemporary meritocratic discourse in order to justify and bolster their position.

Such narratives have been particularly apparent in the immensely popular TV series *Downton Abbey* which dramatises the range of lives, from cooks to ladies, butlers to lords, in a British stately home in the early decades of the twentieth century. *Downton Abbey*, a joint US/UK production, constructed a slice of British heritage for the domestic and international export market, with extremely and at times unprecedentedly high ratings across a wide range of countries including China, Brazil, Singapore, Denmark, Israel, Belgium and Iceland (Egner 2013). Tightly scripted and plotted, featuring very well-known actors and with a pronounced streak of comedy to its drama, the series presents an account of historical change whilst in the process raising questions about the social and cultural dynamics of class, race and gender (Littler and Naidoo forthcoming).

Part of how and why the drama is so watchable and has achieved such success is precisely because it does explore the idea of different social ranks and privilege. It does raise questions as to whether such social divisions are fair, whilst depicting historical change in such terms as the raising hemlines of fashion, shifting cultural codes of acceptability around relationships, the dwindling numbers of servants in the country house, the arrival of the motor car, the rise of public education for children and the advent of the labour movement. In this respect an important part of its success is undoubtedly produced through its generous provision of multiple narratives about how history altered and changed.

And yet the drama reinvigorates an idea of a deeply divided society, explores its divisions, and then channels them into a profoundly conservative narrative about what is inevitable and pleasing and what is not. Most significantly, it presents an extremely economically unequal social order as ultimately a happy, cheerful community-spirited place. (The ending of the series is particularly symptomatic in this respect, featuring all of the characters in turn – from those who clean the stairs to those who glide down them in luxury eveningwear – toasting everyone 'Happy New Year'). It is highly selective in what it presents as impossible to change – as an interracial relationship, for example, is introduced but it is explicitly presented as just something that could not happen at that time when in reality, the actual historical people whose story it drew on and fictionalised, Edwina Mountbatten and Leslie Hutchinson, had a relationship for over four years (Breese 2012). Yet, and crucially, other kinds of change are embraced and presented as inevitable – such as the aristocrats becoming businessmen and women, through developing enterprise initiatives involving housing, pig-farming and car dealerships.

Within this context *Downton Abbey* figures the rich as complex characters, to be sure, but primarily as benevolent 'mummy and daddy' figures. The earl of Grantham is created as a likeable father-figure, running the whole estate, sympathetic to the needs of his flock and their difficulties: as a thoroughly decent man. His American wife (again reflecting the joint US/UK nature of the production) offers a kind, socially fluid femininity to his occasionally emotionally challenged stiff upper lip masculinity, taking on charitable work and offering leadership to the new hospital. Their daughters, in a stand for liberal feminism, strike out into business: one moving to London to branch out into Bloomsbury-style magazine editing, the other adapting the estate by developing a side-line in pig-farming (when she is not charitably helping her maid with her medical needs). Extreme social privilege is portrayed through such characterisation above all as decent and forward-looking and thus as produced primarily through the savvy of self-governance and wise conduct. And crucially this context is used to valorise enterprise and entrepreneurialism.

It is no accident that such depiction is constructed during a grossly unequal present, a fact which has not gone without media comment. The UK satirical magazine *Private Eye* produced a parodic cover featuring the faces of the millionaire leaders of the UK Conservative Party (David Cameron, Theresa May), members of the Liberal Democrat coalition (Nick Clegg, Vince Cable) and Margaret Thatcher all superimposed onto the costumed bodies of lead characters of the show and standing in front of the building of 'Downturn Abbey' (*Private Eye* 2010). The show was also invoked by the leader of the Trades Union Congress, Frances O'Grady, to argue in 2014 that 'Britain was in danger of becoming a *Downton Abbey* style society … in which social mobility has hit reverse' (Parkinson 2014). The motif of the rich as a 'kind parent' in *Downton Abbey* is packaged for a nostalgic heritage/tourist gaze and works to humanise and justify extreme social inequality. It is presented as simultaneously a natural state of affairs and as a situation which has to adapt to the future. It is no accident that Downton's aristocratic lords and ladies adapt so fluently to multiple forms of entrepreneurialism and 'Big Society'-style patronage.

The rich as kind parents was also, of course, a trope deployed as a justification for imperialism. Britain as 'the mother country' was a motif that was repeated in an attempt to gain deep ideological traction, to legitimise the idea that brutal imperial dominance was not only reasonable but as caring as a parent's love for their offspring. As Catherine Hall writes, it domesticates and naturalises colonial power relations (Hall 1998: 190–191). A related domain where these thematic strands – of the rich as kind parent, imperial parenting and wealthy benevolence – are fused is in 'philanthrocapitalism'. This term describes the fusion of global acts of charity by the super-rich with acts that extend their own corporate business interests (Littler 2015). The Bill and Melinda Gates Foundation, for example, simultaneously performs charitable acts working to disseminate anti-malaria vaccines whilst vigorously promoting private business interests which perpetuate and extend existing inequalities (McGoey 2015). This dual approach, linking philanthropy and capitalism thus solves, or appears to solve, some medical or social problems linked to poverty whilst creating new forms of inequality and poverty (Richey and Ponte 2011).

Philanthrocapitalism has been the subject of stinging critique from the voluntary, or third, sector, particularly in Michael Edwards' broadsides *Just Another Emperor* and *Small Change: Why Business won't Save the World* (Edwards 2008, 2010; see also Hayes and Price 2009) where he argues that these projects serve corporations more than their intended beneficiaries. Citing a survey of 25 joint ventures in the US between charity and business, Edwards points out that in 22 cases there were 'significant conflicts between mission and the demands of corporate stakeholders' (Edwards 2009: 13). Moreover, he writes, on a larger-scale philanthrocapitalism has weakened the third sector and civil society 'through co-optation instead of equal partnership' (Edwards 2009: 15). His argument is therefore to 'reaffirm the importance of a "civil-society-strong" perspective in face of a tsunami of pro-business thinking' (Edwards 2009: 55). For there is, Edwards writes, a fundamental problem with philanthrocapitalism: if it really wanted to achieve its ostensible goals, it would reform its own working practices.

> After all, if business and the super-rich are serious about their social responsibilities there is plenty of work to be done in changing the way that wealth is produced and distributed without the smokescreen of philanthropy. Taking the right steps on wages, working conditions, benefits, consumer standards, tax obligations, political lobbying, monopolies and competition at the heart of business would have a huge social impact. As Daniel Lubetzky (a leading social entrepreneur himself) put it: 'what most resonates with me about the unexamined "noise" surrounding philanthrocapitalism is that it is often used to mask dishonest or noxious behaviour from corporations'.
>
> *(Edwards 2009: 63)*

The idea of the rich as essentially benevolent itself incorporates the fantasy of global trickle-down economics: that 'wealth creation' at the top will gradually flow, like some munificent waterfall, to those on ledges at the sides and those stuck at the bottom of the social valley. Study after study has proven this to be untrue. Yet considerable effort goes into repeating and attempting to perpetuate the idea of wealth creation, a phrase which, as

Andrew Sayer points out, could more aptly be termed 'wealth extraction' (Sayer 2016: 46).

For the stock type of the kind parent, the fantasy of wealth creation, followed by benevolent wealth distribution, is paramount. In the logic of such narratives, it is fine that they rule us: in fact it is better, because, firstly, they have worked hard to activate their talent to achieve individualised greatness, which legitimises their privilege; and, secondly, because emotionally, affectively they are just so kind.

## Luxury-flaunters

A third motif which routinely appears in public mediated discourse is that of the rich as materially superabundant: living lives of outlandish or admirable glamour and luxury. Luxurious excess is flaunted across a range of online and offline spaces: from perfume advertising on gigantic billboards to TV shows like *Lifestyles of the Rich and Famous* and *Made in Chelsea*, from magazines such as *Hello!* to the popular social media site *Rich Kids of Instagram*. The forms such representations of luxury take are not singular. Even on the right-wing of the political spectrum, media sites will present the rich in particular ways depending on what class fractions they are addressing and how they want to engage and position readers as consumers and citizens. For example, on the one hand, UK mid-market tabloid newspaper *The Daily Mail* with its notoriously barbed critical commentary encourages us to be full of envy, desire and resentment, yet not to challenge the position of the rich at the top of the social hierarchy.[5] *Hello!* magazine, with its glossy colour spreads dealing with the lavish celebrations or interior décors of the super-rich and famous, will, on the other hand, encourage us to be cowed yet pointlessly aspirational at the spectacle of their wealth. As readers we are addressed or interpellated in particular ways – encouraged to feel different things, to embrace different affective dispositions: to be intrigued, dazzled or offended.

Spectacles of luxury are often presented in ambiguous ways. The popular Tumblr blog, *Rich Kids of Instagram*,[6] for example, with its arch tagline 'they have more money than you and this is what they do' reposts selfies that the sons and daughters of the international super-rich have shared on the social-media photography site Instagram. Examples include a close-up of seven Rolex-watch-clad hands fist-pumping together (26 April 2016), a photograph of a luxury car parked next to a palatial home with the tagline 'Home at last' (18 April 2016) and numerous photographs of shopping expeditions and young people partying on yachts. *Rich Kids of Instagram*, as Alice Marwick points out, 'functions as both a critique of income inequality and a celebration of it' (Marwick 2015: 154). We are invited to look at the lavish lives of these offspring of the ultra-wealthy like a snake, in fascination; both to gawp and laugh at them. These are the lifestyles that we do not have; they are different from us.

However, spectacles of material superabundance even though (and because) they emanate from extreme privilege are still regularly presented through the mythology of neoliberal meritocracy through the neoliberal meritocratic trope of hard work, as discussed in chapter 3. Marwick discusses how Kane Lim, a 22-year-old Singaporean student studying fashion in California, who regularly posts pictures of his Cartier watches (worth over $10,000) and extensive collection of more than 50 pairs of designer shoes by Louboutin (at least $1,300 each) and who has garnered a degree of micro-celebrity or 'instafame' through social media, regularly invokes in online conversation the idea that he earned it ('we Asians work hard') (Marwick 2015: 155). In addition what can be at play in such particular displays of classed hard work are attempts to make up for the deficits of neoliberal meritocracy: its disempowerments in terms of ethnicity and gender as well as class, as we explored in chapter 2.

In her astute book *Framing Class*, Diana Kendall examines how American media represents wealth and poverty, demonstrating the overwhelming tendency of the majority of mainstream media forms to encourage their audience to identify with the middle class, be awestruck at the elites, and pity or condemn the poor (Kendall 2005). Kendall traces tendencies in media production, such as how the 1980s US TV series *Lifestyles of the Rich and Famous* used framing techniques that became popular with TV networks in the 2000s, and identifies a range of different media frames of the rich, including 'admiration framing' and 'price-tag framing' (Kendall 2005: 29–53).

Where does this interest in the super-rich, that we are invited to join and participate in, come from? In their recent work developing what they term 'critical luxury studies', John Armitage and Joanne Roberts argue that not only is luxury relative but that the desire for it is distinctly modern. Luxury has a distinct status in the modern era in the West which is related to changing Judeo-Christian notions of desire. In the pre-modern era, they write, desire was predominantly thought of as sinful, yet in the modern era, desire came to be a definite element in the modern imagination and thus 'the engine and chief instrument of human morality' (Armitage and Roberts 2016: 4; Berry 1994, 2016). Luxury was to be used as a vitalising, animating force for modern capitalism and as such was also to be condemned for being part of the machinery of such inequality. As they put it, we have seen 'the development of new social graces for the superrich alongside new social disgraces' (Armitage and Roberts 2016: 13).

Intrigue can therefore be generated through difference – 'they have more money than you and this is what they do' – and through desire, along with condemnation. The fact that having a bountiful material life can be very pleasurable and in Armitage and Goodman's words offer 'extreme comfort' will for many sound like a positive and desirable state. Such feelings are not incompatible with anti-capitalism. Kristin Ross's analysis of the demands of the 1871 Paris Commune foregrounds its vision of 'communal luxury' and the elaboration and continuation of the ideas by thinkers and doers like Karl Marx and William Morris – all the way to contemporary protests and campaigns to reclaim privatised public space (Ross 2015). For Jeremy Gilbert, Oscar Wilde's variety of socialism offers an alternative to social conservation or neoliberal individualism, foregrounding aesthetics and advocating socialism 'not just because it is just or good, but because it would make us all freer and our lives more sensuously pleasurable' (Gilbert 2014). The recent popularity on the left of the phrases 'luxury communism for all' and 'fully automated luxury communism' envisages a society that deploys technology to do the most tedious boring work and spreads around the more interesting work and consumer goods with a radical egalitarianism (Merchant 2015; Novara Media 2014; Srnicek and Williams 2015).

The displays of wealth referred to above are, of course, not the fruits of a generous collective welfare state, the consequence of a radical egalitarian use of technology or the result of a venture in co-operative ethical manufacturing. They are the handed-down fruits of late capitalist appropriation and exploitation. Many of the people on *Rich Kids of Instagram* are children of billionaires who gained their wealth through unearned income. Lim, for instance, is widely rumoured to be Singaporean billionaire Peter Lim's son (Marwick 2015).

In addition there is the issue that whilst luxury for all is undoubtedly an enticing prospect, in an era of excessive generation of carbon dioxide, the world pays the environmental price for luxury. As the expression goes, if the whole world bought as many consumer goods as the US, we would need four planets (McDonald 2015). Whilst the production of carbon dioxide is the result of the use of cement in building production, deforestation and the pollution of dirty energy as much as it is from consumer goods, the factor of environmentalism cannot be written out of any study of material excess and indeed needs to be central to discussions of it (Humphrey 2010; Goodman et al. 2016).

## The new rich are different

Some strands of the rich are more prominent than others. Financial elites are often not conspicuously individualised or facialised: they lurk in the shadows, as the title of Janine R. Wedel's book on 'how the world's new power brokers undermine democracy, government and the free market', *Shadow Elite*, puts it (Wedel 2009). The publication in 2016 of the 'Panama papers', the leak of 11.5 million files from Mossack Fonesca, the world's fourth biggest offshore law firm, provided an insight into the faceless rich by showing many of the routes through which they avoid paying tax by exploiting offshore tax havens (Harding 2016). Notably, some of the actual people on *Rich Kids of Instagram* inadvertently landed their parents in hot water when the tax office wanted to know why a particular yacht or car did not feature in their accounts (Marwick 2015).

Whilst these strategies are deployed by the super-rich, more people are becoming poor, and proportionally the poor have been getting poorer. At times unearned income is very obviously directly produced from the poor. As Andrew Ross puts it in his account of contemporary indebtedness, this is epitomised by the high-interest payday loans, their stores now peppering the urban landscape:

> Payday loan stores were virtually unheard of in the 1980s. Now there are more in the US than McDonald's restaurants, and they are concentrated in low-income minority neighborhoods, though, as the economy worsens, they are cropping up on Main Street and in the strip malls of middle-class suburbia.
>
> *(Ross 2013: 88)*

In the US, what is sometimes termed 'the criminalisation of poverty' has expanded as 'a third of US states now jail people for not paying off their debts, even for minor infractions like traffic fines' (Ross 2013: 91–92). Against this backdrop, numerous representations of the rich, as we have seen throughout this chapter, depict them as a very palatable and accessible constituency. Whilst this in itself is not completely new, there are significant historical differences in how the rich tend to be presented now in the Global North from in the past.

Take, for example, the story of *Annie*, a narrative which has had several incarnations over the past century. In 1924, the *New York Daily News* published *Little Orphan Annie*, a comic strip by Harold Gray, which during the 1930s became the most popular comic strip in the US (Gray 2008; Young and Young 2007: 107).[7] Its main characters are Daddy Warbucks, the benevolent, emotionally challenged multi-millionaire; plucky Orphan Annie, the kid he sporadically looks after; and Sandy, her oversized dog; alongside an assorted retinue of women and self-consciously 'Oriental' villains and sidekicks. It has from its beginnings been 'one of the most conservative and topical comic strips ever to grace the pages of American newspapers' (Young and Young 2007: 297; see Schulman 2012; Rothman 2014). Produced in the Great Depression, it is sentimental *noir*, with trouble and danger lurking round every corner, with the curiously blank-eyed Annie (devoid of pupils) showing that 'hard work and self-reliance, or grit, a popular word for the times, provide the keys to happiness' (Young and Young 2007: 297).

*Annie*'s ongoing romanticisation of the rich–poor divide, in all its incarnations, is perhaps epitomised by the theme tune from the late 1970s musical, based on the comic strip, which was popularised by the 1982 film. 'Tomorrow!' is a song about how, as things might well get better tomorrow, we do not really need major social change today. *Annie* the comic strip targeted organised labour, unions and President Roosevelt's New Deal policies with vigour. For instance, 1935 saw 'the demise of a sympathetic kind-hearted inventor, trampled to death by an anti-capitalist mob', and, in the 1940s, Daddy Warbucks was depicted literally dying of disappointment when FDR was elected, although he was later resurrected (much like the character Bobby Ewing in *Dallas*) (Heer 2011: 5)

It is notable that Annie has been most vigorously resurrected and become particularly popular at key times of capitalist crisis: the 1920s/30s (when alongside the comic strip, two films were made and it became a long-running radio show); the late 1970s/80s (when a popular Broadway musical was made and turned into one of the first films I remember being taken to the cinema as a child to see, featuring a red-haired Annie in 1930s context, all puce and grey clothes) and the present, when the musical has again been updated and turned into a film set in present-day New York.[8]

The most recent version, the 2014 film, is set in the present-day US and is telling of the contemporary conjuncture. In this version, neither Annie nor Daddy Warbucks have to be white; instead, they are played by black actors Quvenzhané Wallis and Jamie Foxx. The opening scene has a nice joke about this fact as it pictures kids in school doing their history presentations, and a spoilt, white, redheaded, show-off Annie is shunted out of the way.

At the same time, however, the opening scene also shows the new Annie doing her history presentation: a presentation where she tells her classmates that FDR redistributed wealth to all the poor people. But, she tells the class at the end, he also let the rich get even richer. This is a jaw-dropping piece of conservative revisionism about the New Deal and the man who introduced a piece of legislation in 1935 popularly known as the 'soak the rich tax' (Heale 1999: 32).[9] In this neoliberal meritocratic version of Annie, everyone has opportunity, regardless of their skin colour and getting wildly rich never ever hurts the poor.

As in the other versions, this film works to justify the behaviour of elites and rehumanise the sterile billionaire through his acquisition of a nuclear family. At the same time it is astonishingly revealing of the imaginary of the 1%. What the producers (including Will Smith and Jay-Z) and director (Will Gluck) imagine it is like to be poor is living in a large Brooklyn brownstone, worth millions, with an interior clad with fairy lights and messiness very like a middle-class bohemian house. A key difference from the 1982 version, then, is that they appear no longer able to actually imagine what poverty even looks like.

*Annie*, then, is a story which has been vigorously resurrected at key moments of capitalist crisis, one which offers a very conservative, reassuring narrative about the problems of capitalism and the benevolent super-rich. Yet there are particularly significant features about the present-day version. It has little awareness of actual poverty. It stokes the post-racial myth of it being easy for black citizens to achieve billionaire status, by themselves, eliding the problems of the meritocratic deficit and social poverty. It promotes an abstract idea of equality together with promoting the ability to become super-rich, and separates out these features as being totally unconnected.

These are powerful myths of neoliberal meritocracy; myths which have considerable cultural traction. It is part of a post-crash reaction that needs to be compared to those of the past. As Andrew Sayer writes:

> whereas then the reaction under the US New Deal was to impose high taxes on the rich and tightly regulate finance, this time round neither of these things are happening on either side of the Atlantic. The rich have got away with it and the financial sector is free to do more damage again.
>
> *(Sayer 2016: 5)*

Warren Buffett, the US billionaire, puts it another way: 'there's class warfare, all right. But it's my class, the rich class, that's making war, and we're winning' (Stein 2006). Whereas reaction in the US after the 1930s crash, as Sayer outlines, involved the relief and support systems of the New Deal and curbing the practices of the super-rich, today there has been no significant undermining of the powers of the wealthy. Indeed, the flourishing of the ultra-wealthy has been continually enabled whilst socialised provision continues to come under repeated attack. It is an attack which happens by stealth, and the super-rich continue to promote an idea that we can all get to the top; that society is still equal, even though we have to knuckle down and work even harder to rise; where efforts to appear ordinary, to appear 'one of us', as hardworking and meritocratic are remarkably strenuous.

However, it is interesting that the newer *Annie* film has been widely panned.[10] It does not convince. This is part of a wider formation: as the social ladder lengthens, the top rungs more obviously out of reach, neoliberal meritocracy, and indeed the possibility of meritocracy, is less believable than it used to be. Yet whilst popular parables of neoliberal meritocracy are increasingly framed and perceived as unrealistic and are finding it harder to gain traction, the neoliberal meritocratic narratives of the ultra-rich – the popular parables of normcore plutocrats, benevolent parents and bling kings – are used as a powerful weapon in their arsenal of strategies to maintain and extend their wealth and power.

Given the extent of this expanding inequality alongside the predominance of positive representations of the super-rich, what are the alternatives? Here we might consider the representations of 'fat cats' and 'fat pigs'. These have been widely circulated images in relation to CEOs and bankers in particular (Littler 2007). They have had an important role in popularising the conception that the super-rich can be a negative social force and offset the array of positive images promoted by mainstream media which overwhelmingly tend to be owned by the super-rich or dependent on their advertising money. The array of negative images could be widened; indeed, this is partly why the idea of the 1% was so successful, providing another vivid image and conceptualisation of the problem of the expanding super-rich. Perhaps these images could be expanded further: an array of conceptualisations for an array of contexts. (Where are the images of the rich as a hoover, sucking up collective wealth, for example?) At the same time, demarcating bad behaviour as an abstract evil can only take us so far. Andrew Sayer argues that instead of demonising individuals 'we need a new line of attack, one that focuses on the institutions and practices that allow this to happen'

(Sayer 2016: 19). There is also a need for demarcating and popularising alternatives. I begin to explore both of these themes in the following chapters.

## Notes

1 Stein 2006.
2 Discussing Marx's description of a rentier economy, Jeremy Valentine wryly notes: 'of course Marx missed a dialectical trick by not anticipating the growth of capitalism into a system of finance capital autonomous from industrial production such that money has become a commodity in its own right, or rather, debt has' (Valentine 2007).
3 CEOs are today sometimes known as presidents; indeed, this conflation between the corporation and the nation-state is one of a wide range of reasons why Donald Trump was able to gain the US presidency.
4 After the UK-based upper-middle-class / mid-market clothing company Boden, which often markets itself around a traditional, conservative and fairly white idea of Britishness (www.boden.co.uk. Accessed 2 March 2017).
5 Take for example its reaction to the robbery of Kim Kardashian, when it ran articles including glamourous pictures and suggested Kim was asking to be robbed (*Mail Online* 2016).
6 http://richkidsofinstagram.com. Accessed 3 March 2017. *Rich Kids of Instagram* also has a presence on Facebook, Twitter and Instagram itself.
7 The title was taken from a much more gothic poem, 'Little Orphant Annie', written by James Whitcomb Riley in 1885, in which naughty children are snatched away by goblins. In the 1930s *Little Orphan Annie* became a radio series (1931–1942) and two films were also made, directed by John S. Robertson (1932) and John Speaks (1938).
8 There was also a straight-to-DVD sequel, *Annie: A Royal Adventure*, directed by Ian Toynton (1995) and a Disney made-for-TV movie, *Annie*, directed by Rob Marshall (1999).
9 This was the 1935 Revenue Act which raised tax on higher-income levels and was also known as the 'wealth tax'.
10 For instance, the Rotten Tomatoes website, which collates film reviews and provides aggregate scores of critical and audience approval, scored the 2014 *Annie* film at 29% overall, and counted 104 negative out of the 143 reviews it assessed (Rotten Tomatoes n.d.).

## References

Allen, Kim, Heather Mendick, Laura Harvey and Aisha Ahmad (2015) 'Welfare Queens, Thrifty Housewives, and Do-it-all Mums', *Feminist Media Studies* 15(6) pp. 907–925.
Armitage, John, and Joanne Roberts (2016) 'The Spirit of Luxury', *Cultural Politics* 12(1) pp. 1–22.

Atkinson, Rowland, Simon Parker and Roger Burrows (2016) 'The Plutocratic City: Elite Formation, Power and Space in Contemporary London' (working paper), www.academia.edu/21132863/the_plutocratic_city_elite_formation_power_and_space_in_contemporary_london. Accessed 1 November 2016.
Bannatyne, Duncan (2007) *Anyone Can Do It: My Story*. London: Orion.
Barnett, Anthony (ed.) (1994) *The Power and the Throne: Monarchy Debate*. London: Vintage.
BBC (2016) *Elizabeth at 90: A Family Tribute* (BBC One, 21 April).
Berry, Christopher J. (1994) *The Idea of Luxury: A Conceptual and Historical Investigation*. Cambridge: Cambridge University Press.
Berry, Christopher J. (2016) 'Luxury: A Dialectic of Desire?', in John Armitage and Joanne Roberts (eds), *Critical Luxury Studies: Art, Design, Media*. Edinburgh: Edinburgh University Press, pp. 47–61.
Billera, Michael (2011) 'The Occupy Occupy Wall Street Movement: The 1 Percent Fights Back', *IB Times*, 4 November, www.ibtimes.com/occupy-occupy-wall-street-movement-1-percent-fights-back-tavis-smiley-responds-photos-651088. Accessed 1 November 2016.
Billig, Michael (1992) *Talking of the Royal Family*. London: Routledge.
Boltanski, Luc, and Eve Chiapello (2005) *The New Spirit of Capitalism*. London: Verso.
Breese, Charlotte (2012) *Hutch*. London: Bloomsbury.
Brooks, Xan (2011) 'Never Mind the BAFTAs ... Who will get the King's Speech Riches?', *The Guardian*, 11 February, www.theguardian.com/film/2011/feb/11/baftas-the-kings-speech-riches. Accessed 1 November 2016.
Brown, Wendy (2015) *Undoing the Demos*. Cambridge, MA: MIT Press.
Clancy, Laura (2015) 'Baby's First Photo Call: How the Royals Learned to Act Normal', *The Conversation*, 2 May, http://theconversation.com/babys-first-photo-call-how-the-royals-learned-to-act-normal-40809. Accessed 1 November 2016.
Clark, Tom (2012) 'Queen Enjoys Record Support in Guardian/ICM Poll', *The Guardian*, 24 May, www.theguardian.com/uk/2012/may/24/queen-diamond-jubilee-record-support. Accessed 1 November 2016.
Couldry, Nick (2010) *Why Voice Matters*. London: Sage.
Crouch, Colin (2004) *Post-Democracy*. Oxford: Polity Press.
Crown Estate (2016) *Integrated Annual Report 2015/6*. London: Crown Estate, www.thecrownestate.co.uk/media/761966/annual-report-and-accounts-2016.pdf. Accessed 2 December 2016.
Davis, Aeron (2007) *The Mediation of Power: A Critical Introduction*. London: Routledge.
Davis, Aeron (2015) 'Embedding and Disembedding of Political Elites: A Filter System Approach', *Sociological Review* 63(1) pp. 144–161.
Dorling, Danny (2014) *Inequality and the 1%*. London: Verso.
Edwards, M. (2008) *Just Another Emperor*. London: Demos and the Young Foundation.

Edwards, M. (2009) 'Philanthrocapitalism: After the Gold Rush', in Tony Curzon Price and David Hayes (eds), *The Power of Giving: Philanthrocapitalism Debated*. London: Open Democracy, pp. 11–21.

Edwards, M. (2010) *Small Change: Why Business won't Save the World*. San Fransisco: Berrett-Koehler.

Egner, Jeremy (2013) 'A Bit of Britain where the Sun Never Sets: Downton Abbey Reaches around the World', *New York Times*, 3 January, www.nytimes.com/2013/01/06/arts/television/downton-abbey-reaches-around-the-world.html?_r=2. Accessed 1 November 2016.

Farrell, Aimee (2014) 'Meet Norma Normcore', *Vogue*, 21 March, www.vogue.co.uk/news/2014/03/21/normcore-fashion-vogue—definition. Accessed 1 November 2016.

Foucault, Michel (2010) *The Birth of Biopolitics: Lectures at the Collège de France, 1978–1979*, trans. Graham Burchell. Basingstoke: Palgrave Macmillan.

Freeland, Chrystia (2012) *Plutocrats: The Rise of the New Global Super-Rich*. New York: Penguin.

Gilbert, Jeremy (2014) 'The Soul of Man After Neoliberalism', *New Left Project*, 29 January, www.newleftproject.org/index.php/site/article_comments/the_soul_of_man_after_neoliberalism. Accessed 1 November 2016.

Gilens, Martin, and Benjamin I. Page (2014) 'Testing Theories of American Politics: Elites, Interest Groups, and Average Citizens', *Perspectives on Politics* 12(3), pp. 564–581.

Goodman, Michael K., Jo Littler, Dan Brockington and Maxwell Boykoff (2016) 'Spectacular Environmentalisms', *Environmental Communication* 10(6) pp. 677–688.

Gray, Harold (2008) *The Complete Little Orphan Annie*. San Diego: IDW Publishing.

Grsuky, David, and Szonja Szelenyi (eds) (2011) *The Inequality Reader*. Boulder: Westview Press.

Guthey, Eric, Timothy Clark, Brad Jackson (2009) *Demystifying Business Celebrity*. New York: Routledge.

Hall, Catherine (1998) 'Going A-Trolloping', in Claire Midgley (ed.), *Gender and Imperialism*. Manchester: Manchester University Press, pp. 180–199.

Harding, Luke (2016) 'What are the Panama Papers? A Guide to History's Biggest Data Leak', *The Guardian*, 5 April, www.theguardian.com/news/2016/apr/03/what-you-need-to-know-about-the-panama-papers. Accessed 1 November 2016.

Hardoon, Deborah, Ricardo Fuentes-Nieva and Sophia Ayele (2016) *An Economy for the 1%: How Privilege and Power in the Economy Drive Extreme Inequality and How This can be Stopped*, Oxfam Briefing Paper 210, http://policy-practice.oxfam.org.uk/publications/an-economy-for-the-1-how-privilege-and-power-in-the-economy-drive-extreme-inequ-592643. Accessed 1 November 2016.

Hayes, David, and Tony Curzon Price (eds) (2009) *The Power of Giving: Philanthrocapitalism Debated*. London: Open Democracy.

Hays, Constance L. (2005) *Pop: Truth and Power at the Coca-Cola Company*. London: Arrow.

Heale, Michael J. (1999) *Franklin D. Roosevelt: The New Deal and War*. New York: Routledge.

Hecht, Katharina (2014) 'Why Sociologists Should Research the Increase in Top Income and Wealth Inequality', *Discover Society*, 1 December, http://discoversociety.org/2014/12/01/why-sociologists-should-research-the-increase-in-top-income-and-wealth-inequality. Accessed 1 November 2016.

Heer, Jeet (2011) 'Annie's Violent World', in *Little Orphan Annie*, vol. 7: *The Omnipotent Mr Am!* San Diego: IDW Publishing, pp. 8–19.

Humphrey, Kim. 2010. *Excess: Anti-Consumerism in the West*. Cambridge: Polity Press.

Hutton, Will (2005) 'Firing, But not on all Cylinders', *The Observer*, 8 May, http://media.guardian.co.uk/broadcast/comment/0,,1479026,00.html. Accessed 1 November 2016.

IPSOS-Mori (2012) *Almost all Britons Satisfied with the Queen as Monarch, but Prince William is the Most Popular Royal* (poll), www.ipsos-mori.com/researchpublications/researcharchive/3080/Almost-all-Britons-satisfied-with-the-Queen-as-Monarch-but-Prince-William-is-the-most-popular-Royal.aspx. Accessed 1 November 2016 .

Johnson, Boris (2013) 'We Should be Humbly Thanking the Rich, not Bashing Them', *Daily Telegraph*, 17 November, www.telegraph.co.uk/comment/columnists/borisjohnson/10456202/We-should-be-humbly-thanking-the-super-rich-not- bashing-them.html. Accessed 1 November 2016 .

Kendall, Diana Elizabeth (2005) *Framing Class: Media Representations of Wealth and Poverty in America*. Lanham: Rowman & Littlefield.

Khan, Shamus (2010) *Privilege: The Making of an Adolescent Elite at St Paul's School*. Princeton: Princeton University Press.

Khan, Shamus (2012) 'The Sociology of Elites', *Annual Review of Sociology* 38 pp. 361–377.

Klein, Naomi (2008) *The Shock Doctrine: The Rise of Disaster Capitalism*. London: Penguin.

Lapavitsas, Costas (2013) *Profiting without Producing: How Finance Exploits Us All*. London: Verso.

Littler, Jo (2007) 'Celebrity CEOs and the Cultural Economy of Tabloid Intimacy', in Su Holmes and Sean Redmond (eds), *A Reader in Stardom and Celebrity*, London: Sage, pp. 230–243.

Littler, Jo (2015) 'The New Victorians: Celebrity Charity and the Demise of the Welfare State', *Celebrity Studies* 6(4) pp. 471–485.

Littler, Jo, and Roshi Naidoo (forthcoming) 'All that Jazz: Heritage and Diversity in the Downton Years'.

McDonald, Charlotte (2015) 'How Many Earths Do We Need?', *BBC News*, 16 June, www.bbc.co.uk/news/magazine-33133712. Accessed 1 November 2016.

McGoey, L. (2015) *No Such Thing as a Free Gift: The Gates Foundation and the Price of Philanthropy*. London: Verso.

Mail Online (2016) 'It's no Surprise – with the Way Kim Flaunts Her Riches', 5 October, www.dailymail.co.uk/news/article-3820524/It-s-no-surprise-way-Kim-flaunts-riches-Kim-s-ex-bodyguard-warns-s-time-reality-star-withdraw-social-media-not-skimp-security.html. Accessed 1 December 2016.

Marwick, Alice E. (2015) 'Instafame: Luxury Selfies in the Attention Economy', *Public Culture* 27(1/75) pp. 137–160.
Massey, Doreen (2007) *World City*. Oxford: Polity Press.
Massey, Doreen (2013) 'Vocabularies of the Economy', in Stuart Hall, Doreen Massey and Michael Rustin (eds), *After Neoliberalism: The Kilburn Manifesto*. London: Lawrence & Wishart, pp. 3–17.
Meek, James (2014) *Private Island: Why Britain now Belongs to Someone Else*. London: Verso.
Merchant, Brian (2015) 'Fully Automated Luxury Communism', *The Guardian*, 18 March, www.theguardian.com/sustainable-business/2015/mar/18/fully-automated-luxury-communism-robots-employment. Accessed 1 November 2016.
Miliband, Ralph (1969) *The State in Capitalist Society*. London: Weidenfeld & Nicolson.
Mills, C. Wright (1956) *The Power Elite*. Oxford: Oxford University Press.
Mizruchi, Mark S. (2013) *The Fracturing of the American Corporate Elite*. Cambridge, MA: Harvard University Press.
Monbiot, George (2016) 'Frightened by Donald Trump? You Don't Know the Half of It', *The Guardian*, 30 November, www.theguardian.com/commentisfree/2016/nov/30/donald-trump-george-monbiot-misinformation?CMP=share_btn_tw. Accessed 1 December 2016.
Moor, Liz, and Jo Littler (2008) 'Fourth Worlds and Neo-Fordism: American Apparel and the Cultural Economy of Consumer Anxiety', *Cultural Studies* 22(5) pp. 700–723.
Novara Media (2014) 'Fully Automated Luxury Communism!', www.youtube.com/watch?v=dmQ-BZ3eWxM. Accessed 1 November 2016.
Parkinson, Justin (2014) 'Britain "Becoming like Downton Abbey" says TUC Leader', *BBC News*, 8 September, www.bbc.co.uk/news/uk-politics-29103503. Accessed 1 November 2016,
Piketty, Thomas (2013) *Capital in the Twenty-First Century*. Cambridge, MA: Belknap Press.
Poulantzas, Nicos (1975) *Classes in Contemporary Capitalism*. London: New Left Books.
*Private Eye* (2010) cover: Downturn Abbey (12–25 November).
Richey, Lisa Ann, and Stefano Ponte (2011) *Brand Aid: Shopping Well to Save the World*. Minneapolis: University of Minnesota Press.
Roseman, Andrew (1996) 'Was This the Day when Royalty Lost the Plot?', *The Independent*, 20 April, www.independent.co.uk/news/uk/home-news/was-this-the-day-when-royalty-lost-the-plot-1305932.html. Accessed 1 November 2016.
Ross, Andrew (2013) *Creditocracy and the Case for Debt Refusal*. New York: OR Books.
Ross, Kristin (2015) *Communal Luxury: The Political Imaginary of the Paris Commune*. New York: Verso.
Rothman, Lily (2014) 'The Very Political History of Annie', 19 December, http://time.com/3640455/annie-new-deal-politics. Accessed 1 November 2016.

Rotten Tomatoes (n.d.) 'Annie (2014)', www.rottentomatoes.com/m/annie_2012. Accessed 1 July 2016.
Sayer, Andrew (2016) *Why We Can't Afford the Rich*. Bristol: Policy Press.
Schulman, Michael (2012) 'The Politics of Annie', *New Yorker*, 18 October, www.newyorker.com/culture/culture-desk/the-politics-of-annie. Accessed 1 July 2016.
Srnicek, Nick, and Alex Williams (2015) *Inventing the Future: Postcapitalism and a World without Work*. London: Verso.
Standing, Guy (2011) *The Precariat: The New Dangerous Class*. London: Bloomsbury.
Stauber, John, and Sheldon Rampton (1995) *Toxic Sludge is Good for You! Lies, Damn Lies and the Public Relations Industry*. Monroe, ME: Common Courage Press.
Stein, Ben (2006) 'In Class Warfare, Guess which Class is Winning', *New York Times*, 26 November, www.nytimes.com/2006/11/26/business/yourmoney/26every.html. Accessed 1 July 2016.
Sugar, Alan (2011) *What You See is What You Get: My Autobiography*. London: Pan.
Sugar, Alan (2012) *The Way I See It: Rants, Revelations and Rules for Life*. London: Pan.
Sugar, Alan (2015) *Unscripted: My Ten Years in Telly*. London: Macmillan.
Surowiecki, James (2004) *The Wisdom of Crowds*. London: Little, Brown.
Terranova, Tiziana (2015) 'Introduction to Eurocrisis, Neoliberalism and the Common', *Theory, Culture and Society* 32(7–8) pp. 5–23.
*The King's Speech* (2010) dir. Tom Hooper. Weinstein / Momentum Pictures.
This is Money (2011) 'How the Middleton Family made Their Fortune', 11 November, www.thisismoney.co.uk/money/celebritymoney/article-2067126/How-did-Pippa-Middletons-family-make-money.html. Accessed 1 November 2016.
Treneman, Ann (1998) 'Profile: The Duke of Westminster', *The Independent*, 1 March, www.independent.co.uk/life-style/profile-the-duke-of-westminster-private-property-keep-out-1147573.html. Accessed 1 July 2016.
Tweedie, Neil, and Michael Kallenbach (2005) 'Prince Harry Faces Outcry at Nazi Outfit', *The Telegraph*, 14 January, www.telegraph.co.uk/news/uknews/1481148/Prince-Harry-faces-outcry-at-Nazi-outfit.html. Accessed 1 July 2016.
Valentine, Jeremy (2005) 'Everyone's at It: Regulation and the New Rentier Economy', Signs of the Times Discussion Paper, www.signsofthetimes.org.uk/papers.html. Accessed 1 July 2016.
Valentine, Jeremy (2007) 'Morality of the Culture Industries and The Rentier Economy', Royal Society of Edinburgh lecture.
Wedel, Janine W. (2009) *Shadow Elite: How the World's New Power Brokers Undermine Democracy, Government and the Free Market*. New York: Basic Books.
Williams, Karel, and Mike Savage (2008) *Remembering Elites*. Oxford: Wiley-Blackwell.
Winters, Jeffrey A. (2011) *Oligarchy*. Cambridge: Cambridge University Press.

York, P. (2015) 'The Fall of the Sloane Rangers', *Prospect Magazine*, 19 February, www.prospectmagazine.co.uk/sound-and-vision/the-fall-of-the-sloane-rangers-made-in-chelsea. Accessed 1 July 2016.

Young, William H., and Nancy K. Young (2007) *The Great Depression in America: A Cultural Encyclopedia*. San Francisco: Greenwood Press.

# 5

# #DAMONSPLAINING AND THE UNBEARABLE WHITENESS OF MERIT

> The possessive investment in whiteness [is] a poisonous system of privilege that pits people against each other and prevents the creation of common ground.
>
> *George Lipsitz*[1]

## #Damonsplaining and externalised white male privilege

In September 2015 a scene on the US HBO reality TV show *Project Greenlight,* in which novice filmmakers compete to win the chance to make a feature film, caused a brief social-media storm. In the scene, the judges – a room of white men, plus one white and one black woman – discuss which director should be hired. Effie Brown, award-winning producer of *In the Cut* (2003) and *Dear White People* (2014), gently but firmly raises the issue of diversity. She suggests the people in the room 'need to think, whoever this director is, about how they're going to treat ... the only black person [in the movie] being a prostitute hit by her white pimp. I want to make sure that you're looking at this group, right here [in the room]; at who you're picking, and at the story that you're doing' (HBO 2015: ep. 1). Brown's encouragement to this overwhelmingly white male room to be reflexive about both the racialised dynamics of the script and its production crew is cut short by the white Hollywood actor and producer Matt Damon, who very assertively talks across her so she cannot finish her sentence. Damon tells her why the directorial team she is thinking of – a Vietnamese man and a white woman – is simply not appropriate. Whilst Brown, several times, tries to finish her thread, Damon continues cutting across her speech, telling her:

> When we're talking about diversity, we do it in the casting of the film, not in the casting of the show. Do you *want* the best director?
> *(HBO 2015: ep. 1)*

Accounts of this incident blew up very quickly online and on social media. It provided a graphic and instructive vignette of how white male privilege can be perpetuated by attempting to silence women and people who are not white (combined with a stunning lack of reflexivity about the speaker's own position). It is instructive to pick apart the hypocrisy of Damon's intervention. It involves a white man cutting off a black woman from speaking, in order to lecture her on the 'correct', singular, meaning of diversity in filmmaking practice and to unequivocally assert that diversity in film production does not matter *at all*. 'Ooof!' replied Brown in response, remaining remarkably composed, whilst visibly incredulous, at this verbal and cultural slapdown.

The rise in popular feminist and anti-racist activisms, combined with expanding publicity of the dramatic exclusions of the media industries, provided a very fertile context for the incident to be satirised. The hashtag #Damonsplaining began to trend on Twitter. 'Damonsplaining' was a variant of 'mansplaining', a term originally coined in 2008 after the author Rebecca Solnit wrote a widely shared article discussing how a man at a party repeatedly patronised her by lecturing her on a subject she had written a book on – even continuing at length when he had been told she wrote the book he was telling her about (Solnit 2014: 14).[2] 'Mansplaining', a description resonating with many other women who had similar experiences of being patronised by men explaining things to them that they already knew, gained widespread traction, becoming one of the *New York Times*' 'Words of the Year' in 2010 (Sifton and Barrett 2010).

'Mansplaining' describes how the culturally blind overconfidence of people who tend to have the most social power can translate into patronising, undervaluing and downgrading the intelligence of others in the micro-contexts of everyday life. This meaning, combined with its conjoined nature ('man' + 'explaining'), made it an easily adaptable term to talk about race. Thus 'whitesplaining' was born, a word which fit well in what Solnit termed 'the archipelago of arrogance' (Solnit 2014: 8). The popular online Urban Dictionary defines whitesplaining as

The paternalistic lecture given by Whites toward a person of color defining what should and shouldn't be considered racist, while obliviously exhibiting their own racism.

(*Urban Dictionary* 2010)

Whitesplaining is clearly not a phenomenon confined to the United States. In an article in the UK's *Daily Telegraph* newspaper, for instance, the media producer Ella Achola reflected on her experience of white people explaining racism to her in Britain and Germany in 'a condescending, overconfident, and often inaccurate or oversimplified manner' (Achola 2015).[3]

In this episode of *Project Greenlight* Matt Damon was both 'whitesplaining' and 'mansplaining'. The intersection of unequal racialised and gendered power dynamics was given a further turn of the screw by the fact it was being conducted by a named Hollywood celebrity. There is power in the celebrity name. The elevated status of an 'A-list' star like Damon provides him with extensive reputational capital, even though this exists in a volatile, precarious context: his persona has been expansively validated through the cultural spaces and places of media power (Couldry 2001; Cross and Littler 2010; Van Krieken 2012). In this case, such power was being used to diminish others. Consequently this mansplaining/overweening celebrity/whitesplaining mash-up was ridiculed through a satirical hashtag on Twitter:

> Can Matt Damon tell me why the caged bird sings? #damonsplaining
> *Viktor T. Kerney @wondermann5 14 September*

> Can someone get Matt Damon on the phone? I need him to suggest a good protective style for my hair. #damonsplaining
> *Unapologetic Negro @HollaBlackGirl 14 September*

Damon subsequently issued an apology:

> My comments were part of a much broader conversation about diversity in Hollywood and the fundamental nature of *Project Greenlight* which did not make the show. ... I am sorry that they offended some people, but, at the very least, I am happy that they started a conversation about diversity in Hollywood.

(*Saul 2015*)

That his actions were 'offensive' is registered, but as an apology, this does little to recognise the nature of the issue. As many children are told, only saying you are sorry that you made someone sad is not really a proper apology. Nor does it puncture the hauteur that was part of the problem itself. To claim to have 'started a conversation about diversity' shows little awareness that this conversation had already been started (and not just by Effie Brown); continues the claim of ownership of diversity that was such a large part of the problem in the first place; and demonstrates no awareness of, nor sense of shame about, imperious power dynamics. Apologising for offence taken rather than for causing hurt 'silently displaces the blame for the offense from the offender to those taking offense' (Goldberg 2015: 80). It is a liberal response that is 'happy' to have 'a conversation about diversity' – as opposed to not being happy to talk about it or inhabiting more overt forms of racism that do exist. But it does not address any action that might be taken, nor does it show any sign of even considering the suggestions made by Brown. Similarly Damon does not apologise for dismissing the whole of the production process as having any kind of role in the perpetuation of racialised dynamics: for asserting that the people involved in the production process do not need to be more diverse.

Why this is so is framed and explained in terms of merit. Immediately after the Damonsplaining scene in *Project Greenlight*, the programme cut to a headshot of Matt Damon speaking alone to camera. In this scene he acknowledges that he appreciated Brown raising the issue of diversity; but then comes the 'but':

> Ultimately if you suddenly change the rules of this competition at the 11th hour, it seems like you would undermine what this project is about ... which is about giving someone this job based entirely on merit.
>
> *(HBO 2015: ep. 1)*

'Merit' is mobilised here as a neutral, factually objective term, free from the vagaries of different subjective opinions, of cultural value judgements. For Matt Damon merit is obvious, it is uncontroversial, it is universal: it is simply that some people – like him – can see it more clearly than others. As Brittney Cooper put it in her *Salon* article published soon after the incident:

> Damon plays the *merit* card. The merit card is the white equivalent of a race card – it is the highest trump card, in a game of spades. Merit is

the supposedly race neutral rubric that everyone should *naturally* agree is the best way to judge candidates, all questions of race aside. The myth of meritocracy is one of the foundational and erroneous ideals of white supremacy. Whether we are speaking about increasing racial access to education or jobs, *the term merit is thrown around as though it exists in opposition to diversity.*

*(Cooper 2015; my italics)*

As we have seen in earlier chapters, 'merit' is a profoundly contested term; a loaded, yet unstable, signifier. And as Cooper so cogently writes, it is, in this particular example, and in the contemporary conjuncture, being used as if it is diametrically opposed to diversity. In the following sections I want to unravel something of the history, background and context of this racialised usage of 'merit' to help consider how this construction operates and is being disrupted in the present.

To do this, the chapter considers neoliberal meritocracy's racialisation in a number of ways. First, drawing on David Theo Goldberg's work on the post-racial, it discusses the racialisation of merit as an abstract category; second, it considers these processes in relation to the ascribed merit of cultural products; third, it relates this incident to the racialised exclusions of cultural production in the media industries; and, finally, it analyses the viral status of this event. The chapter reads the Damonsplaining incident as both an arch example of a discourse of neoliberal post-racial meritocracy and also of its rupture. In doing so, then, it explores the question: how is meritocracy racialised in contemporary neoliberal culture, and what are the meanings of its disruption?

## Post-racial meritocracy

That 'race' is a fiction is nicely illustrated by the sheer geographical and historical mobility of racialised stereotypes of merit in terms of intelligence: 'in Japan Koreans are "dull", while in the US Koreans are "bright"; Jews in America were "dull" 75 years ago but are among the cognitive elite today' (Fischer *et al.* 1996: 19–20). Today there is widespread agreement on the lack of validity of race as a key means to classify human differences (Gilroy 1997; Osborne and Sandford 2002; Rattansi 2007). There is also an extensive body of work tracing the geneaologies of 'race' – as an invented category that was primarily used as an instrument of social domination – through various eras including European modernity, scientific Enlightenment rationality, nineteenth-century governmentality and imperial expansion (Bernasconi 2001; Hall 1997; Hannaford 1996).

But whilst race is a fiction, the catastrophic effects of eighteenth- and nineteenth-century concepts of race mean that its legacies are only too palpably felt. In the US, these processes of racialisation structured the violence of slavery and of segregation. In the post-civil-rights era, their legacies persist through savage inequalities and subtle forms of cultural racism. Overt discrimination was outlawed in the 1964 Civil Rights Act and piecemeal legislation has been introduced since attempting to tackle discrimination in a range of other spheres (Goldberg 2009).

Since the 1970s, in the US the appearance of non-whites in professions formerly reserved by whites for whites (including the president) became a media-amplified reality. The idea that we do and should live in a multicultural society gained enough traction to become common sense for vast swathes of the population. At the same time, multiculturalism as an ideal was embraced by neoliberal marketeers as a means to sell goods. Neoliberal capitalism has not been backward in attempting to commodify the impulses and desires of these social movements (Gilroy 2013; Hesse 2000). Some anti-racist demands – like other demands from the 1968 generation around gender and sexuality – have been met. But many others clearly have not. New variants of racism (alongside misogyny and class disparagement) have only too palpably moved into the ascendant.

As in much of Europe, the threat of 'terror' and the neo-imperial wars that stoked it have facilitated the resurgent racist discourse in some conservative and republican quarters that multiculturalism has 'gone too far' (Lentin and Titley 2011). If the widening disparities between rich and poor under the past few decades of neoliberalism have extended racialisation, inequality and racialised inequalities, it has also helped facilitate the emergence of new racisms in which 'certain groups and behaviours ... are pathologised so that they might then be more easily particularised' (Younge 2011: vi). There is what Lentin and Titley term 'the unstated division of subjects into good diversity ... and bad diversity' (Lentin and Titley 2011: 7). Think of how the movements of refugees and migrants are mediated on a daily basis.

In the array of new racist variations that have been produced, those coalescing in the US around 'blackness' have been particularly acute. This is borne out by stark statistics. One in three black males born in the US today 'can expect to go to prison in his lifetime', and there are currently more black men in prison than in college (Goldberg 2015: 43). Almost half of black children in the US live in poverty (Roy 2009; cited in Goldberg 2012:

205). Rumours that President Obama cannot 'really' be American because of his skin colour prompted the release of a copy of his birth certificate. The rates of black Americans being incarcerated and killed by police is widely reported and vigorously campaigned against through Black Lives Matter activism. Neoliberal privatisation and the segregating racial state viciously exacerbated the catastrophic devastation of Hurricane Katrina in New Orleans. To put it in Kanye West's words, 'George Bush doesn't care about black people' (cited in Goldberg 2009: 91).[4]

At the same time, the hegemonic norm of the neoliberal contract in the US, like Europe, has been that everyone should have 'equality of opportunity'. The racialised expression of this contract has been the idea of being post-race: that we have equal opportunities existing for everyone regardless of their skin colour or ethnicity. It is a fragile discourse and one constructed through a selective blindness to inequalities of power in the past and the present. Indeed, an analogous term used in critical race theory is that of 'colourblind racism' (Gallagher 2003; Omi and Winant 1994; Valdez 2015). For Goldberg, post-raciality is a discourse in which racisms have morphed into a new form, one which 'turn[s] the spotlight of attention away from the structural constitution of America made and marked by race' (Goldberg 2012: 205). Arguing that 'the post-racial is a "hyper-condition" of our times, the neo in neo-liberalism' (Goldberg 2012: 203), Goldberg writes that race has become an indication of what cannot be politically dealt with. Key to its functioning is the erasure of the histories 'producing the formations of racial power and privilege, burying them alive but out of recognizable reach' (Goldberg 2015: 101).

The post-racial as theorised by Goldberg fits well with my theorisation of neoliberal meritocracy. Neoliberal meritocracy and post-racialism are both wishful myths denying massive structural inequalities. They are combined, articulated and fused through what might be termed 'post-racial neoliberal meritocracy'. Just as the myth of meritocracy mobilises the idea of a level playing field in terms of class, then, so too does it mobilise the idea of equality of opportunity in terms of race. As the field is nowhere near level – despite the gains since civil rights – these actually existing inequalities are wished away in post-racial discourses. As Goldberg points out, whilst 'it was naïve to think that five hundred years of cemented racisms could be dismantled in the wink of an election or two' it is also 'more revealing to ask: what work is the postracial doing?' (Goldberg 2015: 68). By envisaging racism as 'a stain on the social fabric, to be wished away as quickly as possible', the structural problems and racialised inequalities are not addressed and white privilege is reinforced.

The Damonsplaining incident exemplifies the post-racial, carrying all the ambivalence of the liberal tradition it is part of. Matt Damon did not consciously want to be racist. *Project Greenlight* was full of white men. Effie Brown was included as a judge, both in recognition of her extensive experience and in this particular context as a visible gesture to distance the show and its players from racism. But the incident made it very clear that Brown's presence was as far as the show was prepared to go to address racism in the media industries. It was to be a token gesture: any further racialised inequalities were not up for discussion or debate.

The post-racial condition, in which the category of race and its legacies are erased in favour of a fantasy of equal harmony without addressing the ingrained lingering injustices of the racial, is, as Goldberg argues, now a dominant generalised social logic and one that tends to be extended by default by those inhabiting racialised positions of power – 'whiteness' – unless they are critical and reflexive enough (Goldberg 2015: 160). Matt Damon's forceful interjection to prevent any consideration whatsoever of racialised injustices being addressed during the production process fits only too neatly into this paradigm. Equally tellingly, Damon's co-producer on *Project Greenlight*, the white Hollywood actor Ben Affleck, received publicity in 2015 for an incident shaped by similar post-racial logic. After a 2014 guest appearance on the PBS TV show *Finding Your Roots*, in which celebrity family histories are traced, memos between Sony boss and host of the show Henry Louis Gates Jr. were anonymously published on Wikileaks revealing how Affleck wanted to cover up the fact that one of his ancestors owned slaves. (Notably, at least three other celebrities had already appeared on the show discussing their slave-owning relatives). Instead, Affleck chose to highlight a distant ancestor who was a spiritualist at the time of the Civil War and his mother's work as a 'freedom rider' (civil rights activists who rode non-segregated buses in parts of the south where racist violence was rife and segregation was still being culturally adhered to even after it was illegal).[5] Affleck later published a statement declaring he was 'embarrassed' about the connection (Collins 2015).

With different inflections (Affleck's subsequent apology for suppressing it appeared to acknowledge the importance of engaging with the legacies of the past, which whilst gestural is more than can be said for Damon's non-apology) such behaviour occupies the similar wishful post-racial ground in which a white person both benefits from a racialised legacy of power and wishes to erase any discussion of that racialised benefit (Lipsitz 1998). It is a white liberal position which wants to side against racism – thus appointing Effie Brown, thus feting connections to civil rights activists – but which does not want to interrogate any of its own privilege nor the ugly exploitative constituent context of such privilege. Such whiteness finds not only racism 'unbearable' but also its legacies and its own imbrications in these histories: and in doing so unwittingly extends the logic of racist inequalities. It is this uneven ground from which merit is judged.

## The racialisation of merit: people

How is merit racialised? Merit is both a value judgement and a term that affects who is permitted to act and how. Contemporary narratives of meritocracy, as we have seen, often work through the assumption that talent and intelligence are primarily inborn abilities that are either given the chance to succeed or not. In other words, meritocratic discourse can mobilise a very essentialised conception of ability which ignores or downplays both social context and the role social context has in deciding what merit might be. When Matt Damon says 'Do you *want* the best director?' the argument is that there is to be no argument as to what 'the best' means. But the best is a product of its context, and that context is racialised.

There are numerous examples of how the racialisation of merit has a long and problematic history in the US. One place it is particularly marked is education. Take, for example, Harvard University admissions. At the beginning of the nineteenth century, Harvard's new president Charles William Eliot, increasingly annoyed at getting applications from what he called 'the stupid sons of the rich', abolished the part of the test that was in Greek and tripled the number of locations where it was possible to sit it. The result was many more public-school students, including more Catholics and Jews, applied (Guinier 2015: 14).

In the 1920s, a racist panic over the slight erosion of WASP privilege emerged. Because of the perceived 'Jewish problem' the tests were reformed again under a new president, Lawrence Lowell. Crucially, at this juncture, Harvard insisted on introducing the criteria of having a 'well-rounded character' and of including photos, with all the attached scope for ideologically loaded connotations to play a far greater part in the selection procedure (Guinier 2015: 15). Initially a 'method to limit Jewish enrollment' (Guinier 2015: 15) the amorphous criteria of a 'well-rounded' character and the lack of phenotypical anonymity turned selection into a biopolitical process.

'Well-rounded' is a term similar to 'merit': a big, baggy capacious term with extensive scope for plural definitions. If what is meant by it is not defined and it intersects with racialisation, this capaciousness becomes both a hiding place and a conduit for bias and abuse. In the 1990s, the 'bell curve' thesis of Hernstein and Murray received widespread publicity for appearing to indicate that the jury was out on whether 'ethnic minority' IQs could be lower than those of white. A range of inflammatory media reports seized on their suggestions with barely concealed racist glee. It helped fuel neo-conservative campaigns to dismantle race-based equity programmes (Valdez 2015; Omi and Winant 1994). The collaborative book *Inequality by Design: Cracking the Bell Curve Myth* later exploded such assumptions by exhaustively demonstrating, through its detailed multifaceted analysis, how 'a racial or ethnic group's position in society determines its measured intelligence rather than vice versa' (Fischer *et al.* 1996: 173). Subordination leads to low performance in such tests of merit, Fischer and his colleagues wrote, because there are 'three consequences of caste: deprivation, segregation and stigma'. Socio-economic deprivation results in poor health and educational potential; segregation concentrates disadvantage and accentuates it; the stigma of inferiority based on the wider society's perception of produces cultural and psychological wounds (Fischer *et al.* 1996: 174). *Inequality by Design* also discussed the profound limitations of the IQ test itself (originally designed for army cadets) and its singular version of intelligence, as most psychometric tests use a wide range of conceptions of intelligence (Fischer *et al.* 1996: 174).

The idea of merit is then related to the power dynamics of its context, a context which in the modern era has been racialised in various ways. Whilst the historical prejudices with college admissions tests now take different forms, their legacies linger. Christopher Hayes calls today's American SATS 'affirmative action for the white middle classes' because of the degree of pre-test tuition privileged families can put in to pass this supposedly 'meritocratic' test (Hayes 2012: 58). The lawyer and civil-rights scholar Lani Guinier advocates countering the unevenness both through admissions process and in the structure of teaching and education itself. In her book *The Tyranny of the Meritocracy* she calls for an end to the 'testocracy': for a far less stratified educational system and for the mobilisation of what she calls 'democratic merit', involving more collaborative methods of collective teaching and learning (Guinier 2015).

In the case of Damonsplaining, 'merit' is mobilised as a term which is ostensibly colour-blind and neutral. It fits with the post-racial neoliberal dream which simultaneously uses criteria that privilege white men. As Goldberg remarked in an interview, 'whiteness has continued to define the career of merit and therefore meritocracy' (Searls Giroux 2006: 44). This contemporary formation of post-racial neoliberal meritocracy moulds and is shaped by the liberal belief that racism is in the past at the very same time as merit is once again being re-coded as white. The ostensible neutrality of the term it is mobilised to conceal the morphed racisms that fit into the category of 'the best' and in doing so draws on a long history of racialised merit.

## The racialisation of merit: products

The location of merit, according to Matt Damon, is ostensibly to be found in 'the product itself', which includes the actors but not any earlier or other stage in the production process. This paradoxical statement will be considered in relation to the people involved in production below, but first I want to pause to consider the issue of the racialisation of merit in relation to the status of the product.

In Damon's discourse, things of merit are completely separate from questions of diversity. Indeed, they will be diluted, diminished or polluted, if considerations of diversity are brought into contact with them. This is a logic that has been used for some time in the canon-formation of 'great art': a complex subjective rationale, used in a multitude of conscious and unconscious ways to judge and appreciate, becomes codified and passed on as 'greatness', whilst the criteria being used often remain far less examined and pass as 'natural'. It is also a set of criteria – as decades worth of work by art historians, literary critics and film theorists has shown – which is itself profoundly culturally, historically and socially specific and which has distinct power dynamics (Nochlin 2015). As Griselda Pollock put it (writing about art), 'the canon is political in its patterns of exclusion' (Pollock 1999: 6). These exclusionary politics are racialised and gendered.

The canon of great, universal (and English) literature, for example, was largely invented in the twentieth century by white male literary critics such as F.R. Leavis and favoured elevating a very small group of literary works as offering exquisite insights into the nature of 'universal' human experience, rather than a more inclusive, open approach – thus facilitating a particularly kind of literary snobbery and conservative political outlook (Leavis 2011).[6] 'English literature' developed as an area of study in the nineteenth century as a pursuit with a social mission: one providing a form of soft power that would keep imperial wives busy and attempt to 'civilise the natives' (Baldick 1983). The sheer amount of effort in maintaining a few texts by a few white British upper- and upper-middle-class people as exclusively representing the best is striking. To say this is not to argue that such works do not have merit; rather, it is to highlight what an exclusive and narrow definition of merit was being used.

Canons of great film are more recent than those of literature and are therefore subject to the social mores of their different time and contexts, most having been constructed from the early twentieth century onwards (David Bordwell, cited in Davis *et al.* 2015: 385). Yet here too there is a recurrent pronounced bias towards films with white directors and actors. For example, in the film magazine *Sight and Sound*'s 2012 top 10, the only film with a non-white, non Anglo-US director, or indeed non-white lead actors, was *Tokyo Story* directed by Ozu Yasujiro in 1953. Films like *La Haine* or *The Battle of Algiers* for example – both often regarded as groundbreaking works in terms of aesthetic innovation and cinematic style – could easily fit in the bracket of cinematic 'high culture' that the *Sight and Sound* top 10 was obviously lauding, yet they did not make the cut.

*Project Greenlight* is not a show which aims primarily at producing instantly canonical films. Yet, in mobilising terms of 'worth' and 'merit', it draws on such chains of association, chains of equivalence about what quality in films might be. Its conversation takes place in relation to a filmic landscape of Hollywood cinema which has historically over-privileged whiteness both in terms of production and representation (Bernadi 2007; Hamilton and Block 2003; Negra and Asava 2013). The perpetuation of reductively racialised roles has been the subject of decades worth of scholarly attention (Bogle 2001, 2006; Dyer 1997; Hall 1997; Young 1995). As Donald Bogle's classic work *Toms, Coons, Mulattoes, Mammies and Bucks: An Interpretative History of Blacks in American Films* highlights, this tradition stretches back to the inception of American cinema: in 1903 *Uncle Tom's Cabin* featured a man in blackface; in 1915 D.W Griffith's 'epic' *Birth of a Nation*, one of the highest grossing films of all time, presented black Americans as aliens and the Klu Klux Klan as a heroic force and was widely credited with increasing lynchings in 1915 before it was banned in 19 cities (Bogle 2001: 1, 10–18; Fields and Fields 2012: 1–2). (Bogle writes of watching *The Birth of a Nation* many decades later 'with a black audience that openly cheered for the black villains to defeat the white heroes' [Bogle 2001: xxiv]). It is in relation to this long backdrop that Effie Brown makes her comments in *Project Greenlight* about the need to 'take care' with the figure of the black prostitute.

Definitions of what things – what objects, what creative experiences, what narratives – had merit, were, as a range of historians and sociologists have pointed out, in turn shaped by the wider discourses and formulations of Western modernity from at least the sixteenth century, which were profoundly racialised and gendered in their conceptions of scientific reason and progress (Bhambra 2007, 2014; Hall 1997; Gilroy 1993; Ware 1992). As we will discuss below, this is because of the associations that became connected or articulated to the people who made them. As Ali Rattansi puts it – whilst carefully tracing the evolution of Western modernity – by the mid-nineteenth century,

> women, blacks and the 'lower orders' were all classified together as child-like, overly subject to the 'passions', incapable of rationality and thus requiring strict government by white upper classes.
> 
> *(Rattansi 2007: 38)*

Assessing the work of a film 'entirely on merit' is therefore not a simple objective process but a complex judgement parlaying a number of different criteria. These criteria could be discussed and analysed. In many cases, however – as with Matt Damon's statement – they are not. When they are not, the criteria remain abstract, diffuse, unknown. This is the way pronouncements of greatness can stand, self-importantly, with the racialised codings that implicitly inform them perpetuating themselves. 'Do you *want* the best director?' is a closed question: its terms do not permit debating what the best is, just responding 'Yes' or 'No'. The word 'merit' is, in Cooper's phrase, 'thrown around as if it exists in opposition to diversity' (Cooper 2015) precisely because the question of diversity threatens it. It threatens to expose its neutrality as a fiction. In this construction as neutral, scientific, a construction handed down since the Enlightenment, merit mutates in its actual application whilst remaining hermetically sealed as a term: its very point is to act as a safeguard against a reduction in privilege on the part of those wielding it.

## The racialisation of merit: production

It may seem unfair to submit Matt Damon's comments to such extensive criticism when more obviously racist targets clearly exist. However, I pick apart Damon's responses because of the potential insight this incident offers into the racialisation of merit as a category and its liberal contortions. Damon's closed question/challenge 'Do you *want* the best director?', as we have seen, positions being the most skilled in creating an end product as a neutral, non-racialised and wholly objective issue, a skill some are more equipped to see than others. Having considered something of how merit is racialised in terms of the creative product, we now need to think about how these processes affect the people who are, or are not, permitted to make them: in terms of film production, diversity in the cultural industries more broadly and the wider issue of the racialisation of merit and who is allowed to possess it.

Who is permitted to be a cultural worker is a critical and contradictory issue in Damon's diatribe. It is an issue that is the direct subject of the show itself – it is, after all, a competition in which people compete to have their film made, and in the process to become professional filmmakers. Yet whilst the importance of who is permitted to become a filmmaker is the programme's ostensible concern, Damon's diatribe simultaneously dismisses the work of people behind the scenes as not at all important when it comes to questions of diversity ('when we're talking about diversity, we do it in the casting of the film, not in the casting of the show'). In this logic, reproducing racialised inequalities, not creating racist culture, is something which can only be tackled by which actors play the parts in the film, rather than in terms of the ethnicity of who directs or produces it.

It is notable that *Project Greenlight* broadcast its first three seasons between 2001 and 2005 with a cast of overwhelmingly white male judges and mentors, as well as contestants.[7] Most spectacularly, Season 3 featured a panel of eight white men deciding which white male director to choose from. After a hiatus of a decade, the show returned to the screen and gradually became slightly more visibly diverse, with the inclusion in early episodes of Jennifer Todd (president of Affleck and Damon's production company, Pearl Street Films) and, throughout the series, producer Effie Brown. As *Project Greenlight*'s executive producer Perrin Chiles stated in a media interview, the new diversity of the show was a conscious decision made in the face of criticism about the previous series consisting of 'a bunch of white dudes choosing white dudes' (Easton 2015). Whilst, of course, not providing a level playing field in terms of gender or race, these inclusions were noteworthy in a media climate which was increasingly starting to publicise the exclusions of the media industries and in which those exclusions were in many cases getting worse. Taken together, these contexts had made the white maleness of *Project Greenlight* unbearably visible. Yet still the narrative of the show's leaders that has to be stuck to, which Damon voices, is avowedly post-racial: 'We don't do diversity in production.' No, they clearly do not, despite (and because of) their tokenistic attempts. Whilst the programme makes production its ostensible subject, then, simultaneously an attempt is made to render film production unimportant in terms of the diversity of the workforce. This contradiction is partly what the show cannot contain; it is in part why the incident went viral.

Studies of media production and the conditions and cultures of media work have recently expanded in some innovative academic directions. However, as Hesmondhalgh and Saha put it, there remains an 'alarming' lack of studies of ethnicity and race in relation to cultural production (Hesmondhalgh and Saha 2013: 182; see also Downing and Husband 2005; Thanki and Jeffreys 2007). This is indicative not only of the hegemonic whiteness of the cultural industries but also of those who study it (and the perspectives of those who study it) in academia. As Vicki Mayer argued in *Production Studies*, there need to be more considered analyses of 'the way that power operates locally through media production to reproduce hierarchies and social inequalities at the level of daily interactions' (Mayer, Banks and Thornton Caldwell 2009: 15).

One area which recent academic analysis has been good at highlighting is how the cultural and creative industries cultivate an image of being 'cool, creative and egalitarian' (Gill 2002) whilst in practice, they are anything but. They are bastions of precarity, offering unstable and short-term work, long hours and little social protection, and therefore people who work in cultural industries have been described as 'poster children of the precariat' (Gill and Pratt 2008; Ross 2010; Standing 2014). The cultural industries' myth of egalitarian, meritocratic open access is exactly that: a myth. The precarious conditions, combined with the informal networks of entry, mean that the sons and daughters of people from wealthy and middle-class backgrounds are over-represented. As we have seen in previous chapters, this situation has become amplified over the past few neoliberal decades. Because wealth is unevenly spread in terms of ethnicity – white people comprise a much higher proportion of the wealthy in the US and the UK, for example – this constitutes a major barrier to entry into the cultural industries for many non-white people (Oakley and O'Brien 2015). Another key barrier is the absence of legal or managerial policies on diversity and inclusion (such as equal-opportunities legislation, anti-discrimination policies) which produce what Jones and Pringle call 'unmanageable inequalities' (Jones and Pringle 2015). These go hand in hand with 'relaxed' codes of entry and the creation of 'informal networks of friends who supply each other with tips and introductions and hire people they have worked well with before' (Hesmondhalgh and Saha 2013: 192). The consequence for

> people outside such informal networks – historically and currently typically including people of color and all women – is that access to jobs and the establishment of a career is a great deal more arduous still than for the average White male professional. For whom it is already often remarkably hard.
>
> (Downing and Husband 2005: 163)

This is the process Charles Tilly terms 'opportunity hoarding' (see Rattansi 2007: 143).

Not all sectors of the cultural industries are unequal in the same way. Some are more unequal than others. Film is one of the domains where these inequalities are most apparent.

> Of all the directors of 2012's top 250 grossing Hollywood movies, just 9 per cent were women. You have only to watch the parade of white male figures walking up the steps to collect Academy Awards (save for the female actors' prizes) to realize that the groups of people who make most mainstream films fail to represent the diversity of the world population. Unlike other sectors, the movie business sets up few safeguards to outlaw hiring practices that discriminate against women and people of color.
>
> (Davis et al. 2015: 206)

Despite the reams of writing and publications within film studies, notoriously little analysis of what actually happens in the course of US film production has been generated since Hortense Powdermaker wrote up her behind-the-scenes ethnographic observations made in 1946–7 in her book *Hollywood, the Dream Factory*, published in 1950 (Powdermaker 2012). This is primarily because it is so hard to get access. Sheri Ortner for example wrote a piece analysing how hard she had found it to gain any access to production cultures in Hollywood – either to interview producers or attend meetings – and borrowed the words of one of the producers she did manage to interview to describe Hollywood as 'a culture that thrives on exclusion'. It is structured around exclusion, from the visitor tours round star homes where you only see high walls and mansion gates, to the constant anxiety that people are at better events, parties and productions to which you are not invited (Ortner 2010: 214). Emphasising the tightly bound nature of the community, one screenwriter she interviewed 'likened it to a country club' (Ortner 2010: 214).

Country clubs, of course, are not known for their democratic access, ethnic diversity, progressive gender dynamics or affordable entry and neither is Hollywood. The extensive UCLA *2015 Hollywood Diversity Report: Flipping the Script* makes this abundantly clear, its bald statistics revealing the extent to which white males continued to dominate the positions from which greenlighting and directorial decisions are made in Hollywood:

> Film studio heads were 94 percent white and 100 percent male
> Film studio unit heads were 96 percent white and 61 percent male
> Television network and studio heads were 96 percent white and 71 percent male
> Television unit heads were 86 percent white and 55 percent male.
> *(Hunt and Ramon 2015: 2)*

> Minorities accounted for 37.4 percent of [US] population … and directed 17.8 percent of the films (a slight improvement from previous years). Women directors (from all ethnicities) were an even lower percentage at 6.3%.
> *(Hunt and Ramon 2015: 11–12)*

As Hunt and Ramon highlight, both television and film are vastly unrepresentative of the wider population. The more visible media exclusions have become more widely publically discussed in the media in recent years. This is particularly the case with regard to gender, using handy measurement tools such as the Bechdel Test,[8] newspaper and magazine publicity given to female stars earning less than men, and the publicity given to the Geena Davis Institute, which researches and advocates ways to change gender disparities in the media.[9] Publicity has been given to the dearth of possibilities for black actors, with for example Viola Davis' 2015 speech after winning an Emmy for Best Actress highlighting the lack of roles available for women of colour. The discussion of quotas has re-emerged in media activism and commentary.[10] Such media discussion has helped fuel a more widespread perception that Hollywood privileges white men. It also tends to favour the issue of gender disparity before that of race and to give the most visible issue (acting) most priority. The question of production, and race in production, can tend to fall to the bottom of the inequalities-to-be-addressed list.

Such hierarchies make shows like *Project Greenlight* important as they make the inequalities of cultural production visible, intentionally or not.

Television becomes a powerful tool of media representation. As Mayer, Banks and Thornton Caldwell write, 'we frequently come to know about media producers and their work, ironically, through the representations they make' of themselves as media producers (Mayer, Banks and Thornton Caldwell 2009: 1). The issue of diversity in television as well as film is particularly relevant here given that *Project Greenlight* is a television show about the film industry. Notably the fascination with the workings of the gated communities of media production has spawned a number of TV shows, including *Episodes*, a sitcom in which a British screenwriting couple see their beloved show change beyond recognition when it's remade in Los Angeles and the comedy-drama *Entourage* about an actor 'making it big' in LA and the consequences for him and his group of friends.

*Project Greenlight*, similarly, is 'media telling stories about media', here in the form of a televisual construction of Hollywood which claims to show us something of the real culture through a staged competition. Being a TV show does, of course, provide another layer to its politics of race. Herman Gray has analysed the movement of American TV from the 1960s and 1970s, when he argues that 'television played a major role in circulating and translating the civil rights discourse of equality to the level of everyday life and common sense', to later decades, when 'television played an equally powerful role in deconstructing and rearticulating that political common sense to a neo-conservatism that culturally reinscribed and socially reinstalled white males as the universal subjects' (Gray 2005: 107, see also 2004). Highlighting the 1980s televisual framing of urban blackness and the growth of the vehicle of the black family sitcom (*The Cosby Show*), Gray emphasises how such images were disrupted from the 1990s, as the logic of the neo-network spawned niche marketing and narrowcasting (leading to the proliferation of comedy shows aimed at and featuring white middle-class professionals like *Frasier* and *Friends* [Gray 2005: 83]). By 1999 NAACP were calling for an audience TV network boycott due to a dearth of black actors on TV (Gray 2005: 81).

As a reality TV show, *Project Greenlight* shows 'ordinary' wannabe filmmakers alongside existing film production workers who are not famous, alongside celebrity directors and actors who definitely are. The show has an interestingly complex relationship to the concept of meritocracy, in that it presents itself as a meritocratic rejoinder to the very difficulties of being able to make it in Hollywood. As Ben Affleck and Matt Damon put it in the introductory sequence to Season 4's first episode: 'it's tough to get a directing job … so we held a contest … and we're going to give [the winning] director $3 million to direct a movie for HBO' (HBO 2015: ep. 1). *Project Greenlight* self-consciously seeks to create a mediated meritocratic bubble, a space where the usual entry restrictions to Hollywood's charmed circle are not present, where instead raw talent can be given Affleck, Damon and the show's help to make a film, fast-tracked into a chance it would not normally get. The artificial momentary meritocratic media bubble is, as I explored in chapter 2, a staple of neoliberal contemporary media culture, part of the grammar of banal neoliberal meritocracy. *Project Greenlight* demonstrates with unintentional precision how such bubbles fail to address the wider structural and ingrained issues of inequality, of recognition and representation.

The norms of competitiveness which structure the reality-show format – in which producing creative products becomes an exercise in beating your opponent rather than co-operatively learning from them – are metonymic of wider neoliberal norms, in which brutal competition is positioned as the key driver of everyday life. This is not a particularly productive climate in which to learn how to overcome the legacies of imperialism. It is rather one in which it's only too easy to reinforce the white male privilege which brought the show into being (through Damon and Affleck as producers). Damon's pronouncements that 'doing diversity' only occurs through the visible actors in the product, not in production, contradicts the fact that viewers can see that *Project Greenlight* added in white and black women judges to their own production formula.

Adding in Effie Brown, as the TV producers surely expected, generated further changes to the demographics of the film crew pictured on the TV programme. After the (white, male) Jason Mann won the competition for best director, the rest of this series of *Project Greenlight* depicted Mann's creation of a film (with white actors) about the American aristocracy, *The Leisure Class* (HBO, 2015), including the power struggles on set and the various dramas and challenges of the film-production process. This included a diverse crew, as Effie Brown stated that she largely took the job on *Project Greenlight* in order to help mainstream media diversity:

> I wanted to hire a crew that looked like America so anyone would turn on the TV and see black people, Latino people, Asian people, white people, everybody working together and being like, *It can happen!* I'm kind of a soapbox chick. ... I also wanted to do it a bit because I'm in that world. I feel like I'm the queen of indie movies and I needed to do something where I could break out on a larger level.
>
> *(Effie Brown, cited in Wieselman 2015)*

The contradictions between the self-consciously diverse crew that Effie Brown brought with her into the show and Damon's pronouncements and the all-white cast of Mann's film were therefore stark. The narrative frame of *Project Greenlight* attempted to sporadically showcase this diversity whilst simultaneously exploiting the divisions and tensions between this diverse film crew and producer and its non-diverse film director, cast and TV production team. In particular, this antagonism was focused through the figure of Brown, who was often positioned as a singular problem. For instance, despite Brown having an agreement with her (white) film production partner, Marc Joubert, that they 'were not going to talk bad about each other, [on TV] we were going to have each other's backs', Joubert did throughout (Wieselman 2015). Indeed, Joubert's commentary – and notably Joubert had a simultaneous role as executive producer of the TV show as well as the HBO film – was the most emphatic televisual framing of Effie Brown as a 'hotheaded' problem.

Likewise, Matt Damon's attempts, in his commentaries, to offset the reality of the unequal power dynamics – dynamics that are rightly uncomfortable for white liberals – were made in a partial manner before being negated. Through Damonsplaining and the televisual frame, the merit of meritocracy became mobilised to bolster white male privilege and to attempt to actively push down that of a black female.

## Trying to shut women up

Positioning merit as having nothing to do with gender, race or class has a long history as a construction privileging wealthy white men. As Nirmal Puwar puts it, 'there is an undeclared white masculine body underlying the universal construction of the enlightenment "individual"'(Puwar 2004: 141). The legacies of Enlightenment rationality positioned white masculinity as the site of rational logic and merit, whereas the more volatile state of femininity reproduced nature rather than creating merit-worthy culture:

> This was also the era in which the concept of culture enabled *women* to be positioned as part of *nature*, with important consequences. Being part of nature rather than culture meant that women were regarded as unable to properly self-cultivate, self-actualize, and exercise freedom and rationality.
>
> *(Rattansi 2016: 67)*

The Damonsplaining incident is mansplaining and whitesplaining, a white man talking down to a black woman. Such micro-aggressions, such small gestures of silencing, can and often are cumulative, significant and powerful. Patricia Hill Collins, for instance describes them as

> painful, daily assaults designed to teach me that being an African-American, working-class woman made me lesser than those who were not. And as I felt smaller, I became quieter and eventually was silenced.
>
> *(Hill Collins 2009)*

Effie Brown was brought onto *Project Greenlight* because of her expertise as a film director, as someone who had received many awards and plaudits from the film industry. And yet the logic of the Damonsplaining incident stages this power as merely temporarily granted at the whim of more powerful others. It is a structure where

> those once racially disprivileged but now structurally rendered white by virtue of their class standing nevertheless are offered little or no respite from the bite of failing inevitably to make it quite into the inner sanctum of privilege and power in America. Always on the outside looking in, even when invited in, selected or elected (Balibar 2003). *You* are here at *our* whim, your presence terminable at our discretion, so don't go getting any big ideas now.
>
> *(Goldberg 2012: 203)*

By suggesting that diversity needs to be considered at the level of production, by raising the issue of white privilege and implicit racism, Effie Brown disrupts the myth of post-racial neoliberal meritocracy. In doing so she is 'discussing a taboo subject that is closeted under the veneer of professional neutrality' (Puwar 2004: 155). This is an act which involves a risk to such precariously 'awarded' status:

> Those who choose to come out and speak against racism amongst their ranks risk being seen as engaged in renegade acts. Divulging the secrets of your own occupational tribe is a risky business indeed, especially when your 'space invader' status already marks you out and grants you a tenuous location.
>
> *(Puwar 2004: 155)*

Noticeably, Effie Brown did not provide much media comment on the incident afterwards. She did, however, re-tweet some support provided by other people, including a gif of her saying 'Ooof' to Damon, alongside the descriptor 'when you realize even the most liberal white dudes in Hollywood will mansplain representation to you'.[11]

## Calling out the myth of post-racial meritocracy

I learned of the Damonsplaining incident from Britain through my Twitter feed. *Project Greenlight* was not being broadcast in the UK, though it was publicised to British newspaper readers in *The Daily Mail*, and could be bought here on DVD. The Damonsplaining incident generated media commentary in the UK, positioned as part of a shared transatlantic form of culture and connected social mores.

Racialisation takes different forms – what David Theo Goldberg calls 'racial regionalisations' – but there are shared reference points and co-productions across contemporary black, white and hybrid Atlantics. As UK writer Gary Younge puts it in his book *Stranger in a Strange Land: Encounters in the Disunited States*, 'I've always found America exciting but, for better and worse, never exceptional. Its efforts at global domination seemed like a qualitative and material plot development in the narrative of European empire rather than a break from it' (Younge 2006: x). The contours of US racism clearly take different forms from those 'regional racialisations' which are active where I live in the UK, but they share the legacies of the project of imperial modernity, carried, in this case, across from Europe. American film culture is dominant in the UK: the products of the American cultural industries more broadly have a longstanding, conspicuous place in the cultural landscape. Alongside and throughout all the anxieties about Americanisation and US cultural imperialism, the residual snobberies about US low culture, and the vast quantities of non-US culture that are consumed, products from the US cultural industries remain something that the vast majority of people in the UK grow up with.

Therefore the reach of the post-racial neoliberal imaginary extends beyond the US where the show is screened, connecting with the UK through its mediated post-racial diaspora. In an age when news media providers scour online platforms for hot stories and cheap content the transatlantic currency of the incident was facilitated through online platforms like Twitter and extended through the UK online and offline press. Thus the Damonsplaining incident was covered in much of the UK press such as newspapers *The Daily Mail, The Guardian, The Independent* and *The Telegraph*, and the UK version of online news site *The Huffington Post*.

Matt Damon's performance in the Damonsplaining incident is, as I have attempted to show in this chapter, best understood as a shining example of post-racial neoliberal meritocracy, one which taps into and re-activates longer-standing discourses about racialisation and merit while coding them anew. But if the Damonsplaining incident is an example of neoliberal, misogynistic post-racial meritocracy, it is also at the same time an example of the ideology of neoliberal misogynistic post-racial meritocracy being seen and disrupted, being called out for its racisms.

This calling out, this challenge, this rupture was possible for a number of reasons. To begin with, there is the multifaceted intersectional cauldron of privilege that was being activated. While Damon's performance not only exhibited racism but also misogyny despite his denial of both, this denial resonated in a larger media context where its disingenuousness was for many made clearly visible. The spectacular nature of this contradiction, amplified through overweening celebrity privilege, made Damon's explanations particularly mobile as nuggets of untruth: a spectacular specimen of post-racial, meritocratic contradiction.

This is in part because, as I discuss above, the disruptions afforded by its format enable its contradictions to be apparent and visible. In a media programme about media production, once you start discussing the problems of racism, the sheer whiteness of the producers on screen are hard to hide from, whether or not the incident itself is being used to gain extra viewers though controversy. There were a number of examples indicating that this was so, and that *Project Greenlight*'s production team sought to capitalise on the racialised controversy over Damonsplaining, both by framing Effie Brown as an overly aggressive problem and presenting these tensions as antagonisms to be exploited. One episode, for instance, was entitled 'Hot Ghetto Mess', then hastily retitled after HBO announced that its inflammatory racialised title had been a 'mistake' (*Hollywood Reporter* 2015).

Crucially, the technological means through which Damonsplaining was primarily called out – after the shot of Effie Brown's affective physical response, her raised eyebrow and 'Ooof!' – was through social-media outrage: through the brief media storm of Twitter. The hashtag #Damonsplaining allowed the overweening celebrity, the misogyny and the racism of this event to be exposed and highlighted through satire. The use of hashtags has quite frequently been analysed in social- and digital-media studies in terms of its ability to network and connect otherwise disparate publics, particularly around actualising and nascent political movements and events such as Occupy and the Arab Spring (Gerbaudo 2012; Papachrissi 2015). The use of hashtags in the Damonsplaining case has a less formally coded political affiliation but is nevertheless a very politicised tag which works through comedy and more precisely through sarcasm. The sardonic use of hashtags is a widespread, if interestingly under-discussed, practice. Twitter is notoriously a platform through which people speak to multiple audiences at the same time, a process danah boyd calls 'context collapse' (boyd 2008). You do not need to be 'followed by' or 'following' people on Twitter to view a hashtag: if you click on it, it will take you to a list of tweets by people who are tweeting on that particular topic. Hashtags function as 'an integral part of Twitter's ability to link the conversations of strangers together' (Murthy 2013: 3) through a platform which 'thrives on impromptu form' (Papachrissi 2015: 111).

Zizi Papachrissi terms these impromptu communities 'affective publics', and, whilst it is the case that all publics and all media publics, have some affective dimension, her work is surely right in highlighting how hashtags can often 'combine conversationality and subjectivity in a manner that supports both individually felt affect and collectivity' (Papachrissi 2015: 27) and can produce 'disruptions/interruptions of dominant political narratives by presencing underrepresented viewpoints' (Papachrissi 2015: 130). It can also, of course, provide conservative platforms for the likes of republican presidential candidate and billionaire Donald Trump and facilitate the strategies of micro-celebrity (Senft 2012) through the processes by which ordinary people amplify their possessive individualism through self-framing on social media. Yet this Twitterstorm did indeed work by at least briefly disrupting a dominant political narrative, using an informal sarcastic register to register the transindividual slights experienced and/or understood as metonymic component of vast social injustice. Its danger is that its response itself could recode its exposure of the post-racial problem in post-racial form, by making it about only a problem with the racism of one very prominent Hollywood man. #Damonsplaining became a popular, 'trending' hashtag; a viral event spread through a social media structure of speedy contagion and replication. As Nahon and Hemsley put it in their work on viral media, 'viral information is one indicator of what is important to a particular society at a given moment' (Nahon and Hemsley 2013: xii).

#Damonsplaining was not alone as a hashtag using comedy to foreground racism; it might be situated in the broader context of what has variously been called 'Black Twitter' or 'blacktags': the 'ambient affiliations' of racialised aggregations which as Sanjay Sharma expertly points out frequently mobilises 'humour-laden provocation and social critique', a trend encouraged by Twitter, which, as a company, 'has shrewdly positioned itself as concerned with social justice' (Sharma 2012; Brock 2012). As Sharma highlights, there are a high proportion of black tweeters in relation to Twitter's wider demographic, but we have to understand these tweets not simply as reflecting a preconceived group of actors but as a wider racial aggregation and assemblage.

The comedy of Damonsplaining interrupted post-racial, misogynistic neoliberal meritocratic discourse. It had a brief life as an incident, but its existence and the extent to which it spread shows something of how this post-racial meritocratic dream is in crisis. It is not believed. It is ruptured, exposed, caught in the act of being a lie. If the post-racial meritocracy is potent, so too, increasingly, is its opposite. The whiteness of neoliberal post-racial meritocracy was, through the Damonsplaining controversy, exposed: it was widely perceived, in that moment, to be unbearable.

The potential of this assemblage was substantially extended in one direction in 2016 when #OscarsSoWhite went viral. The New York-based journalist April Reign had coined this hashtag a year previously and it was resuscitated when not a single person of colour was included in the Oscar list of acting nominees (Kirst 2016).[12] The trending of #OscarsSoWhite helped facilitate offline action and media coverage, as celebrities including Jada Pinkett Smith, Spike Lee and Michael Moore announced they would boycott the 2016 Oscars ceremony. Shortly afterwards Cheryl Boone Issacs, the only black person amongst 51 Academy governors, released a statement on behalf of the Academy Awards. It stated that they would immediately add three non-white governors and pledged to double the number of women and non-white members of the Academy by 2020, so they would comprise 48% and 14% respectively of those casting the votes. Debate is currently still raging over the extent and pace of these changes (Feinberg 2016). A less widely reported fact is that, as part of these changes, a handful of non-white members have also been added to the six committees working on the Academy Awards: one of these people was Effie Brown.[13]

## Externalised and internalised neoliberal meritocracy

Damonsplaining is an example of a discourse of neoliberal meritocratic power on display: what we might call 'externalised meritocratic privilege'. However, meritocratic narratives are not only external 'injuries', laid on women or non-white people (for example) by white men. They are also discourses and narratives which are internalised and inhabited by less socially privileged groups of people.

In the following chapter I consider how neoliberal meritocracy is particularly vigorously incited as an internalised state of being to constituencies with less social power than that most often occupied and wielded by rich white men. Indeed, notably it is often people who face significant disempowerment in terms of their resources and available choices who are most intensely incited to construct a neoliberal meritocratic self. Whether through corporate populism, black entrepreneurialism and/or marketised feminism, the meritocratic deficit has continued to affect particular groups more than others. In considering how particular constituencies have been positioned as particularly amenable to a meritocratic discourse of 'empowerment', I want to focus on another case study where the incitement to internalised meritocratic subjects is or has been taking place: the emergent social figure of the 'mumpreneur'.

## Notes

1 Lipsitz 1998: xix.
2 Solnit states that she did not coin the term, but she was told it was inspired by her essay. Her article 'The Archipelago of Arrogance' was originally published online and she later wrote a book about it, *Men Explain Things to Me* (Solnit 2014).
3 My thanks to Roshi Naidoo for this reference.
4 Christopher Hayes writes on how New Orleans' tragedy during Hurricane Katrina was in part 'a planning failure enabled by social distance', with Newt Gingrich for example complaining about the uneducated who did not get out, when those people simply did not have any means to leave and escape the floods (Hayes 2012: 198).
5 George Lipsitz wrote: 'Too many of us continue to imagine that we would have supported the civil rights struggle of thirty years ago, when our actions and opinions today conform more closely to the record of that struggle's opponents. We have so demonised the white racists of 1960s Mississippi that we fail to see the ways in which so many of their most heinous practices and policies have triumphed in our own day' (Lipsitz 1998: xv).
6 Although the groundwork for this formulation had been set the century before. Literature as 'the best that has been thought and said', in Matthew Arnold's influential formulation, also happened to be work tending to maintain the bourgeois public sphere, rather than supporting the lower orders with their pesky demands for full representation (Arnold 2009).
7 For instance, in Season 1, the longlisting was carried out by white men and the shortlisting by six white men and one white woman. In Season 1 only one female potential director appeared in the initial top ten list; the rest were white

men. In Season 2, the shortlisting of scripts from top 50 to top 10 was carried out by five white male judges.
8  The Bechdel Test asks whether a fictional work features at least two women who talk about something other than a man. It has been used to draw attention to inequality in film (roughly, only half of US films meet this criteria) and fiction. It is named after the graphic artist Alison Bechdel who credits her friend Wallace (as well as Virgina Woolf) with the idea, and thus it is sometimes known as the Bechdel-Wallace Test. Sometimes further criteria, such as the characters being named, are added.
9  https://seejane.org. Accessed 1 December 2016.
10 Alongside a backlash against discussion of quotas (see Julious 2015). A UK example of activism around racialised quotas in acting is Act for Change (www.act-for-change.com. Accessed 1 December 2016).
11 Another re-tweet included one from Ava DuVernay, the director of civil-rights film *Selma*, sharing a gif of a 1980s sitcom clip of three people doing a black power salute.
12 Kirst's recommendations include the DuVernay test: 'It operates like the Bechdel test, which checks a film's feminist credentials. But its benchmark is low, requiring simply that "African Americans and other minorities have fully realised lives rather than serve as scenery in white stories"' (Kirst 2016).
13 This includes areas such as education and outreach, membership and finance. Effie Brown was appointed to the museum committee in 2016 (Academy of Motion Picture Arts and Sciences 2016).

## References

Academy of Motion Picture Arts and Sciences (2016) 'The Academy Adds Diverse Voices to Its Leadership', www.oscars.org/news/academy-adds-diverse-voices-its-leadership. Accessed 1 December 2016.
Achola, Ella (2015) 'Whitesplaining: It's not Just Matt Damon: Why I Set Up a Black Women's Blog', *Daily Telegraph*, 25 September, www.telegraph.co.uk/women/womens-life/11890566/Whitesplaining-not-just-Matt-Damon-Why-I-set-up-a-black-womens-blog.html. Accessed 1 December 2016.
Arnold, Matthew (2009) *Culture and Anarchy* [1869]. Oxford: Oxford University Press.
Baldick, Chris (1983) *The Social Mission of English Criticism, 1848–1932*. Oxford: Clarendon Press.
Balibar, E. (2003). 'Election Selection'. Keynote address, 'tRACEs: Race, Deconstruction and Critical Theory', University of California Humanities Research Institute, 10 April. Available at https://vimeo.com/album/1631670/video/25691025. Accessed 21 March 2017.
Bernardi, Daniel (ed.) (2007) *The Persistence of Whiteness: Race and Contemporary Hollywood Cinema*. London: Routledge.
Bernasconi, Robert (2001) *Race*. Oxford: Blackwell.
Bhambra, Gurminder (2007) *Rethinking Modernity: Postcolonialism and the Sociological Imagination*. Basingstoke: Palgrave Macmillan.

Bhambra, Gurminder (2014) *Connected Sociologies*. London: Bloomsbury.
Bogle, Donald (2001) *Toms, Coons, Mulattoes, Mammies and Bucks: An Interpretative History of Blacks in American Films*, 4th edn. New York: Bloomsbury Academic.
Bogle, Donald (2006) *Bright Boulevards, Bold Dreams: The Story of Black Hollywood*. New York: One World and Ballantine.
boyd, danah (2008) *Taken Out of Context: American Teen Sociality in Networked Publics*, PhD dissertation. University of California.
Brock, André (2012) 'From the Blackhand Side: Twitter as a Cultural Conversation', *Journal of Broadcasting and Electronic Media* 56(4), pp. 529–549.
Collins, Scott (2015) 'Ben Affleck Sorry He had "Finding your Roots" Conceal Slave-Owning Ancestor', *LA Times*, 22 April, www.latimes.com/entertainment/tv/la-et-st-affleck-slaves-20150423-story.html. Accessed 1 December 2016.
Cooper, Brittney (2015) 'Matt Damon's Staggering Meritocracy Lie: What his "Project Greenlight" Blow-Up with Effie Brown Really Shows', *Salon*, 16 November, www.salon.com/2015/09/16/matt_damons_staggering_meritocracy_lie_what_his_project_greenlight_blow_up_with_effie_brown_really_shows. Accessed 1 December 2016.
Couldry, Nick (2001) 'The Hidden Injuries of Media Power', *Journal of Consumer Culture* 1(2) pp. 155–177.
Cross, Steve, and Jo Littler (2010) 'Celebrity and Schadenfreude: The Cultural Economy of Fame in Freefall', *Cultural Studies* 24(3) pp. 395–417.
Davis, Glyn, Kay Dickinson, Lisa Patti and Amy Villarejo (2015) *Film Studies: A Global Introduction*. New York: Routledge.
Downing, John D. H., and Charles Husband (2005) *Representing Race: Racisms, Ethnicity and the Media*. London: Sage.
Dyer, Richard (1997) *White*. London: Routledge.
Easton, Anne (2015) 'Project Greenlight EP on Racial Controversy: We Welcome Discussions like This', *Observer Culture*, 16 October, http://observer.com/2015/10/project-greenlight-ep-on-diversity-controversy-we-welcome-discussions-like-this. Accessed 1 December 2016.
Feinberg, Scott (2016) 'After #OscarsSoWhite, the Academy Struggles with Diversity, Age and "Relevance"', *Hollywood Reporter*, 27 April, www.hollywoodreporter.com/features/oscarssowhite-academy-struggles-diversity-age-885633. Accessed 1 December 2016.
Fields, Karen E., and Barbara J. Fields (2012) *Racecraft: The Soul of Inequality in American Life*. New York: Verso.
Fischer, Claude S., Michael Hout, Martín Sánchez Jankowski, Samuel R. Lucas, Ann Swidler and Kim Voss (1996) *Inequality by Design: Cracking the Bell Curve Myth*. Princeton: Princeton University Press.
Gallagher, Charles A. (2003) 'Color-Blind Privilege: The Social and Political Functions of Erasing the Color Line in Post Race America', *Race, Gender and Class* 10(4) pp. 22–37.
Gerbaudo, Paolo (2012) *Tweets and the Streets*. London: Pluto Press.

Gill, Rosalind (2002) 'Cool, Creative and Egalitarian? Exploring Gender in Project-Based New Media Work in Europe', *Information, Communication and Society* 5(1) pp. 70–89.

Gill, Rosalind, and Andy Pratt (2008) 'In the Social Factory? Immaterial Labour, Precariousness and Cultural Work', *Theory, Culture and Society* 25(7–8) pp. 1–30.

Gilroy, Paul (1993) *The Black Atlantic: Modernity and Double-Consciousness*. Cambridge, MA: Harvard University Press.

Gilroy, Paul (1997) *Between Camps: Nature, Cultures and the Allure of 'Race'*. London: Routledge.

Gilroy, Paul (2013) 'We Got to Get Over before We Go Under': Fragments for a History of Black Vernacular Neoliberalism', *New Formations* 80–81 pp. 23–38.

Goldberg, David Theo (2009) *The Threat of Race: Reflections on Racial Neoliberalism*. Oxford: Wiley Blackwell.

Goldberg, David Theo (2012) 'A Tale of Two Obamas', *Qualitative Sociology* 35(2) pp. 201–212.

Goldberg, David Theo (2015) *Are We All Postracial Yet?* Oxford: Polity Press.

Gray, Herman (2004) *Watching Race: Television and the Struggle for Blackness*, 2nd edn. Minneapolis: University of Minnesota Press.

Gray, Herman (2005) *Cultural Moves: African Americans and the Politics of Representation*. Berkley: University of California Press.

Guinier, Lani (2015) *The Tyranny of the Meritocracy: Democratising Higher Education in America*. Boston: Beacon Press.

Hall, Stuart (1997) 'The Spectacle of the Other', in Stuart Hall, Jessica Evans and Sean Nixon (eds), *Representation: Cultural Representations and Signifying Practices*. London: Sage, pp. 13–74.

Hamilton, Marsha J., and Eleanor S. Block ( 2003) *Projecting Ethnicity and Race: An Annotated Bibliography of Studies on Imagery in American Film*. Westport, CT: Praeger.

Hannaford, Ivan (1996) *Race: The History of an Idea in the West*. Baltimore: Johns Hopkins University Press.

Hayes, Christopher (2012) *Twilight of the Elites*. New York: Crown Publishing Group.

HBO (2015) *Project Greenlight*, Season 4.

Hesmondhalgh, David, and Anamik Saha (2013) 'Race, Ethnicity, and Cultural Production', *Popular Communication* 11(3) pp. 179–195.

Hesse, Barnor (ed.) (2000) *Un/settled Multiculturalisms: Diasporas, Entanglements, Transruptions*. London: Zed Books.

Hill Collins, Patricia (2009) *Black Feminist Thought*. London: Routledge.

*Hollywood Reporter* (2015) 'HBO "Project Greenlight" Episode was Titled "Hot Ghetto Mess" by Mistake', 19 October, www.hollywoodreporter.com/news/hbo-project-greenlight-episode-was-833132. Accessed 1 December 2016.

Hunt, Darnell, and Ana-Christina Ramon (2015) *2015 Hollywood Diversity Report: Flipping the Script*. Los Angeles: UCLA.

Jones, Deborah, and Judith K. Pringle (2015) 'Unmanageable Inequalities: Sexism in the Film Industry', *Sociological Review*, 26 May, http://journals.sagepub.com/doi/10.1111/1467-954X.12239. Accessed 21 March 2017.

Julious, Britt (2015) 'Hollywood Race Casting: What the Industry is Getting Wrong about Diversity', *The Guardian*, 25 March, www.theguardian.com/tv-and-radio/tvandradioblog/2015/mar/25/deadlines-race-casting-article-tvs-diversity-wrong. Accessed 1 December 2016.

Kirst, Seamus (2016) '#OscarsSoWhite: A 10-Point Plan for Change by the Hashtag's Creator', *The Guardian*, 25 February, www.theguardian.com/film/2016/feb/25/oscarssowhite-10-point-plan-hashtag-academy-awards-april-reign. Accessed 3 March 2017.

Leavis, F.R. (2011) *The Great Tradition* [1948]. London: Faber & Faber.

Lentin, Alana, and Gavin Titley (eds) (2011) *The Crises of Multiculturalism*. London: Zed Books.

Lipsitz, George (1998) *The Possessive Investment in Whiteness: How White People Profit from Identity Politics*. Philadelphia: Temple University Press.

Mayer, Vicki, Miranda Banks and John Thornton Caldwell (eds) (2009) *Production Studies: Cultural Studies of Media Industries*. New York: Routledge.

Murthy, Dhiraj (2013) *Twitter*. Oxford: Polity Press.

Nahon, Karine, and Jeff Hemsley (2013) *Going Viral*. Oxford: Polity Press.

Negra, Diane, and Zelie Asava (2013) 'Race and Cinema', in Krin Gabbard (ed.), *Oxford Bibliographies Online: Cinema and Media Studies*, www.oxfordbibliographies.com/view/document/obo-9780199791286/obo-9780199791286-0127.xml?rskey=Sz9bYY&result=181. Accessed 18 March 2017.

Nochlin, Linda (2015) 'From 1971: Why Have there Been no Great Women Artists?', *Art News*, 30 May, www.artnews.com/2015/05/30/why-have-there-been-no-great-women-artists. Accessed 1 December 2016.

Oakley, Kate, and Dave O'Brien (2015) *Cultural Value and Inequality: A Critical Literature Review*. London: AHRC.

Omi, Michael, and Howard Winant (1994) *Racial Formations in the United States: From the 1960s to the 1990s*. New York: Routledge.

Ortner, Sherri (2010) 'Access: Reflections on Studying Up in Hollywood', *Ethnography* 11(2) pp. 211–233.

Osborne, Peter, and Stella Sandford (2002) 'Introduction: Philosophies of Race and Ethnicity', in Peter Osborne and Stella Sandford (eds), *Philosophies of Race and Ethnicity*. London: Continuum, pp. 1–12.

Papachrissi, Zizi (2015) *Affective Publics*. Oxford: Oxford University Press.

Pollock, Griselda (1999) *Differencing the Canon: Feminist Desire and the Writing of Art's Histories*. London: Routledge.

Powdermaker, Hortense (2012) *Hollywood, the Dream Factory: An Anthropologist Looks at the Movie-Makers* Eastford: Martino Fine Books.

Puwar, Nirmal (2004) *Space Invaders: Race, Gender and Bodies out of Place*. Oxford: Berg.

Rattansi, Ali (2007): *Racism: A Very Short Introduction*. Oxford: Oxford University Press.

Rattansi, Ali (2016) 'Race, Imperialism and Gender: Partial Absences, Serious Consequences for Zygmunt Bauman's Sociology', in Michael Hiviid Jacobson (ed.), *Beyond Bauman: Critical Engagements and Creative Excursions*. London: Routledge, pp. 65–85.

Ross, Andrew (2010) *Nice Work if You Can Get It: Life and Labor in Precarious Times*. New York: NYU Press.

Roy, Joydeep (2009). 'Most Black Children Grow Up in Neighborhoods with Significant Poverty', *Economic Policy Institute*, 7 October, www.epi.org/publication/most_black_children_grow_up_in_neighborhoods_with_significant_poverty. Accessed 21 March 2017.

Saul, Heather (2015) 'Matt Damon Apologies for Offending People with Comments about Diversity', *The Independent*, 17 September, www.independent.co.uk/news/people/matt-damon-apologises-for-offending-people-with-comments-about-diversity-10505036.html?icn=puff-6. Accessed 1 December 2016.

Searls Giroux, Susan (2006) 'On the State of Race Theory: A Conversation with David Theo Goldberg', *JAC* 26(1–2) pp. 11–66.

Senft, Terri (2012) 'Microcelebrity and the Branded Self', in John Hartley, Jean Burgess and Axel Bruns (eds), *The Blackwell Companion to New Media Dynamics*. Hoboken: Wiley-Blackwell.

Sharma, Sanjay (2012) 'Black Twitter? Racial Hashtags, Networks and Contagion', *New Formations* 78 pp. 46–64.

Sifton, Sam, and Grant Barrett (2010) 'Words of the Year', *New York Times*, 18 December, www.nytimes.com/2010/12/19/weekinreview/19sifton.html?_r=0. Accessed 1 December 2016.

Solnit, Rebecca (2012) 'The Archipelago of Arrogance', *Tom's Dispatch*, 19 August. www.tomdispatch.com/blog/175584. Accessed 1 March 2016.

Solnit, Rebecca (2014) *Men Explain Things to Me*. New York: Haymarket.

Standing, Guy (2014) *The Precariat: The New Dangerous Class*. London: Bloomsbury Academic.

Thanki, A., and S. Jeffreys (2007), 'Who are the Fairest? Ethnic Segmentation in London's Media Production', *Work Organisation, Labour and Globalisation* 1(1) pp. 108–118.

Urban Dictionary (2010) 'White splaining', www.urbandictionary.com/define.php?term=White-%27splaining. Accessed 1 December 2016.

Valdez, Zulema (2015) 'The Abandoned Promise of Civil Rights', *Sociological Forum* 30 pp. 612–626.

Van Krieken, Robert (2012), *Celebrity Society*. New York: Routledge.

Ware, Vron (1992) *Beyond the Pale: White Women, Racism and History*. London: Verso.

Wieselman, Jarett (2015) 'Everything You Wanted to Know about "Project Greenlight" from Effie Brown', *BuzzFeed*, 2 November, www.buzzfeed.com/jarettwieselman/effie-brown-project-greenlight-interview#.aejpkqp9K. Accessed 1 December 2016.

Young, Lola (1995) *Fear of the Dark: 'Race', Gender and Sexuality at the Cinema*. London: Routledge.
Younge, Gary (2006) *Stranger in a Strange Land*. New York: New Press.
Younge, Gary (2011) 'Preface', in Alana Lentin and Gavin Titley (eds), *The Crises of Multiculturalism*. London: Zed Books, pp. vi–ix.

# 6
# DESPERATE SUCCESS
## Managing the mumpreneur

> Social mobility [is] a politically driven distraction that diverts our attention from the real problems that need to be addressed: problems of increasing social and economic inequalities that require redistribution not social mobility.
>
> *Diane Reay*[1]

> What is required, above all, is to overcome financialised capitalism's rapacious subjugation of reproduction to production – but this time without sacrificing either emancipation or social protection.
>
> *Nancy Fraser*[2]

### Doing it all

'Mumpreneur', 'mompreneur' or 'mumtrepreneur' depending on your geographical location and preference is a relatively recent term.[3] It has been regularly used over the past decade to signify a mother who establishes her own business from the kitchen table whilst her children crawl beneath it. There have been many articles discussing the rise and expansion of this new social type in the press (e.g. Morrison 2013; Smith 2011), sometimes featuring startling statistics such as '65% of mothers want to launch their own businesses from home' (Russell 2014). Established prizes for outstanding examples of mumpreneurialism now include the yearly 'Mumtrepreneur Awards' in New Zealand[4] and the 'Mumpreneur Awards'[5] and the *Daily*

*Mail* 'Mumpreneur of the Year' Awards[6] in the UK. Online and offline services and networking events are directly marketed by and to them, such as the *M:UK* and *CEO Mums* website magazines (Ekinsmyth 2014). A plethora of guidebooks have emerged to show their readers how to become a mumpreneur, such as *Mum Ultrapreneur* (Odev and Weeks 2010), *Kitchen Table Tycoon* (Naik 2008), *Just Do It: Rules to Go from the School Run to the Boardroom*; (Rigney 2014) and *Mumpreneur* (Karmel 2015; Figure 6.1). Ranging from cute, infantilising pink, through butch-femme corporate balancing of shoulderpads, phone and buggy, to holistic earthtones, the bookcovers of mumpreneurialism signal that the phenomenon is not confined to one singular socio-aesthetic genre. The enterprising maternal also surfaces in popular women's fiction: in 'henlit' novels, that branch of women's popular fiction aimed at the chicks of 'chicklit' who have now grown into 'mother hens' (Sanders 2004; Littler 2013), in 'memoirs' like *The Mumpreneur Diaries* (Jones 2009), and across an array of glossy women's magazines, in articles showcasing the tribulations of mumpreneurs and offering up their stories as examples to emulate (Eikhof, Carter and Summers 2013).

Whilst what mumpreneurs produce is varied, there is an overwhelming emphasis in media profiles on their role in generating lifestyle products and services that are consumed by women and parents, such as skin cream, cupcakes, wedding services, children's clothes and potties. Mumpreneurs do, of course, have predecessors and earlier incarnations. Their representation in popular culture includes Allison Pearson's 2002 novel about work-life balance, *I Don't Know How She Does It*, and the film *Baby Boom* (1987) both of whose heroines downsize from corporate jobs to home enterprises making dolls houses and apple sauce, respectively (see Littler 2013). It is, nonetheless, a term that has had a noticeable surge in use since the 2008 financial crash. As Diane Negra and Yvonne Tasker astutely highlight, the gendering of the post-2008 recession, at this time of 'tough measures', is both significant and overlooked (Negra and Tasker 2014), and indeed as a variety of reports have shown, it is women who have been hit hardest financially (Pearson and Elson 2015). Negra and Tasker discuss the emergence in women's magazines of the figure of the 'recessionista', the savvy female consumer who knows how to be thrifty yet stylish (Negra and Tasker 2014: 4). The mumpreneur has a family resemblance to the recessionista, and her contemporary popularity clearly owes something to the same context the recessionista has emerged from. Yet there is also an obvious core difference in that one key theme which surfaces again and again across the array of mumpreneur articles, how-to guides and memoirs is the idea of

**FIGURE 6.1** Cover of Annabel Karmel, *Mumpreneur*. Reproduced courtesy of the Random House Group Ltd.

mumpreneurialism as a solution to the problems of combining work and childcare. As the back cover blurb from Anita Naik's *Kitchen Table Tycoon* asserts: 'Many mothers are quitting their day jobs and starting up on their own, eager to cut out the nursery fees and see more of their kids.' The mumpreneur is presented as a meritocratic means of solving an array of problems, problems exacerbated by the recession: of the expense of childcare and of the gendered inequalities and inflexibilities of much paid work. It promises even more freedom to climb the ladder of meritocracy as long as you put up with the substantial difficulties. 'Now you are the boss', says *Supermummy: The Ultimate Guide to Business Success*, 'you can promote yourself straight to the top of the ladder' (McGee 2009: 35).

This chapter analyses the figure of the mumpreneur to focus a discussion of the role of gender and entrepreneurialism in neoliberal meritocracy. The chapter has three interlinked sections. To begin, it considers representations of the mumpreneur in relation to the wider context of social reproduction, particularly in terms of how the relationship between gender, work and childcare remains dramatically inequitable. It discusses the attempted temporary crystalisation of gendered drives for self-realisation through entrepreneurial discourses of work and their pressured articulation to coping strategies which bypass the potential for collective co-operation raised by second-wave feminism. It argues that neoliberal meritocratic discourse has been extended through the contemporary moment of capitalist crisis using a trope I term 'desperate success'. Secondly, the chapter considers what mumpreneurialism reveals about the gendering of entrepreneurialism (as a category theorised in academia as well as a lived gendered reality). To do this it discusses recent work on neoliberalism which it relates to what is now often marginalised work on gender and enterprise coming out of cultural studies in the 1980s and 1990s. Thirdly, the chapter considers the specificity of the contemporary 'post-post-Fordist' conjunction between gender and enterprise by following the mumpreneur online and discussing its relationship to self-branding. The chapter ends by considering what discourses and alternatives might prove useful resources for finding routes out of the mumpreneur's pragmatic yet constrained worldview.

## Child labour

The dynamics of social reproduction, or the question of how a society reproduces itself and patterns of in/equality, was a problem repeatedly analysed by second-wave feminism, a movement which regularly treated the issues of paid and unpaid labour as questions to be considered together, as pieces of a social puzzle which would need some substantial reorganisation in order to be in any way fair (James 2012; Oakley 1974). Particularly central was the issue of childcare: the question of who should look after the children and what the dynamics of this care and unpaid labour were to look like in relation to paid work in the public sphere (McRobbie 2013). Yet almost half a century later, this central problem of childcare – the issue that second-wave feminists were so active in highlighting as perhaps the major obstacle to gender equality – remains, as Beatrix Campbell put it, 'dramatically unresolved' (Campbell 2008).

Nancy Fraser's classic essay 'After the Family Wage' (Fraser 1994) supplies some useful tools for disaggregating the charged dynamics around this issue. This article considered the implications of 'the crumbling of the old gender order', centred as it had been on the normative idea of a family wage during the Fordist welfare state, in which the dominant model was men earning a stable income whilst women undertook unpaid labour looking after children and the home. Fraser's aim was to consider what gender justice might look like in a new post-industrial age of unstable employment, family diversity and women in the public workplace in increasing numbers. She argued that two main models exist which attempt to redress the problematic relationship between gender, childcare and employment. The first is the 'universal breadwinner' model, in which working mothers strive to emulate male employment patterns. The second is the 'caregiver parity' model, in which women are remunerated for being full-time stay-at-home mothers. 'After the Family Wage' surveys the strengths and weaknesses of each type by breaking their components down into a range of categories and analysing the extent of their 'gender justice': poverty, exploitation, income, leisure-time, respect, marginalisation, and androcentrism or gender norms (Fraser 1994).

Fraser concluded that neither model is ultimately very satisfactory. So instead she proposed the universal caregiver model – in which both men and women are structurally enabled to share the load – as a fairer solution. A contemporary example of this paradigm would involve both parents being able to work part-time, spreading the load of work more thinly, without being discriminated against in terms of career advancement and being able to afford housing. Its emphasis on sharing work throughout the wider society resonates with Ulrich Beck's idea of solving unemployment and overwork by spreading work around more equitably and combining social protection with diverse working patterns (Beck 2000) as well as with recent initiatives in Sweden to introduce a six-hour working day (Matharu 2015).

However, as Fraser has argued more recently, progress towards the gendered equitability of the universal caregiver model is not much in evidence in the Global North (Fraser 2013, 2015, 2016). Instead, even wealthier women are incited to copy the universal breadwinner model and offload domestic tasks onto the less wealthy:

I don't see any progress at all really. And in fact this idea of universal care-giver is really a kind of socialist feminism that requires re-thinking the whole split between production and reproduction – which in my view is absolutely definitive of capitalist societies. So it'd take a very profound structural change to begin that. Instead we have the hegemony of a liberal feminist model, which doesn't grapple with this issue at all: and in effect just tries to make privileged women lead lives that are socially male, while abandoning other women.

(Fraser 2013: 21–22)

The now notorious example of such a liberal feminist model is Facebook COO Sheryl Sandberg's book, *Lean In*, in which she encourages women to deal with this complex of issues by embracing corporate working culture and succeeding in the workplace rather than leaving it and returning to the home (Sandberg 2013). The critical opposition to such liberal feminist corporate norms is pithily encapsulated in the title of UK writer Dawn Foster's book, *Lean Out* (Foster 2016). As Angela McRobbie argues, such discourse overwhelmingly operates to extend the inequalities of corporate culture rather than rein them in (McRobbie 2013). To translate this opposition into Fraser's terms, liberal feminist discourse, like Sandberg's, merely extends the universal breadwinner model to an elite group of financially advantaged women – a constituency known in Norway as 'golden skirts' – leaving domestic household labour as a feminised role for poorer women (James 2015).

Interestingly, the discourse of the mumpreneur tries to reconfigure production and reproduction differently from that promoted by universal breadwinners like Sandberg. It attempts to meld work from both the private and public spheres into a new configuration. Work from the (masculinised) public sphere is brought into the space of the home. Yet there are a range of problems here, and they include the notion that self-employment is an automatically empowering, meritocratic alternative, which in the majority of instances is far from the case.

## Desperate success

The mumpreneur is symptomatic of the contemporary world of work and its increasing number of self-employed workers. In the UK at present, self-employment rates are higher than at any time over the past forty years, comprising 15% of the workforce; in the US three out of ten jobs are held by the self-employed and the workers they hire (Office for National Statistics 2014; Pew Research Centre 2015). Both figures have risen since the 2008 recession, along with growth in 'forced' or 'sham' self-employment and an expansion of precarious labour through companies subcontracting out, offering previously permanent staff positions on a temporary basis, sometimes on zero-hour contracts, a practice rife in creative industries such as publishing.[7] Since 2011, the UK government has encouraged the growth in 'individual entrepreneurship' though the New Enterprise Allowance (NEA) available to unemployed people who become self-employed.[8] Meanwhile the glamorisation of 'the independents' of the creative industries, and of the 'industrialisation of bohemia' (Leadbeater and Oakley 1999) has continued alongside revelations of precarious working conditions (Ross 2003; Gill and Pratt 2008; McRobbie 2015).

Self-employment offers the promise of breaking from the Fordist 9–5 working day. It offers flexible hours, portfolio working and the idea of control and agency over working lives, over both the means of production and of self-realisation. But notoriously the ascendancy of right-wing neoliberal governments in post-Fordist times and beyond has meant that these more fragmented modes of work have frequently been accompanied by an erosion and loss of the forms of security won during the high point of the social democratic welfare state, including pensions, sick pay and holiday pay (Adkins 1995; Beck 2000; Bauman 1998). Subcontracted employees are no longer required to receive the same employee benefits and protections as permanent employees. Self-employment has therefore also come to be associated with the rise of 'the precariat'. As Guy Standing argues the precariat is not simply composed of the working classes but has expanded to include middle-class workers (Standing 2011), the growth in temporary lecturers in academia being one example (Chakrabortty 2016). This uncertainty has even affected the very legal status of work: the binary divide in labour law between the image of the subordinate employee and the dynamic entrepreneur has now become blurred and manipulated with the growth of highly precarious employment, as the idea of entrepreneurialism has been manipulated in ways that lead to deeper cracks in the very idea of standard employment relationships (Bogg 2015). To use those two ugly but highly useful neologisms, self-employment – including mumpreneurs – is a phenomenon now more often shaped by 'flexploitation' rather than the 'flexicurity' it ostensibly offers (Ross 2010). Nevertheless, through this blend of government policy and cultural and media discourse, glossy media features, workplace subcontracting and incentivisation to those with limited possibilities, individuals are increasingly encouraged to become entrepreneurs.

Alongside the cost of childcare, flexibility is repeatedly invoked as a core incentive for becoming a mumpreneur:

> Many mums leave those successful careers behind to have children and then struggle to return to the workplace – due to high childcare costs and the incompatibility between their new life as a mum and the inflexible long hours often expected as an employee.
>
> *(Karmel 2015: 2)*

The issue of flexible working hours, so often cited by mumpreneurs as a reason for embracing self-employment, is produced by the inflexibilities of much permanent and/or full-time employment. In the UK, for example, employees have the right to request flexible work but not to get it. There is no legal onus on a company to provide a percentage of jobs on a flexible or part-time basis. Furthermore, many professions, particularly those in the creative industries – such as film and TV work – expect employees to work lengthy shifts as a matter of course, leading to an exodus of women of childbearing age in particular (Wing-Fai, Gill and Randle 2015).

High childcare costs have been a key issue for parents and carers outside the Nordic countries (where the strong tradition of socialised childcare makes it both well paid and relatively inexpensive). In the UK, the expansion of free provision for two-year-olds has been increasingly subsidised by the parents paying nursery fees rather than the government as nurseries have had to put up fees to cover their post-recession high costs (Rutter 2015). As Angela McRobbie writes, the long social-democratic tradition of public nursery provision as a key feature of feminist discourse and as a wider social good – a benefit that improves the health and well-being of children from poorer families whilst enabling women to work – has been attacked since the Blair years, when 'banal phrases like work-life balance' were bandied around, replacing an emphasis on state funding and thus 'opening the pathway for the present day demonization of welfare' (McRobbie 2013: 127–128; see also Riley 1983; Littler and Winch 2016). In the US, since the 1980s, a renewed cultural emphasis on intensive mothering has been accompanied by an astonishing demonisation of collective day care provision, surveyed in fascinating detail in *The Mommy Myth* where Susan J. Douglas and Meredith Michaels pick apart sensationalist media reports lambasting the 'dangers' of putting children in day care (Douglas and Michaels 2004). The stay-at-home and downscaling mom has achieved a new idealised prominence in the past two decades at exactly the same time as neoliberal policies have sought to cut back on state day care provision. Such analysis is illustrated by Diane Negra's persuasive account of the glorification of feminine domesticity over the last few decades as a form of retreatism from the problems of the public sphere (Negra 2009: 130).

Within this context, the mumpreneur, who is predominantly assumed to be a figure doing her own childcare or reproductive labour, is frequently packaged as an enticing meritocratic solution which offers a promise of resolving problems of restrictive work and expensive childcare whilst also providing glamour and personal fulfilment. ('Are you ready to carve out that new and rewarding life as a mum in business?' asks Annabel Karmel [Karmel 2015: 9].) Nonetheless, it does similarly reinforce the traditionally gendered role of the woman as the primary domestic carer. We do not hear of 'dadpreneurs' mixing their family life with domestic-based entrepreneurial activity. The masculinity of the entrepreneur is the unnamed norm. The twee address of the mumpreneur thus works to reinforce the role of woman as what Rebecca Asher in her book *Shattered* calls the 'foundation parent' – of how, even in most nominally equal arrangements, women are usually the first point of contact for schools, those addressed by food manufacturers, those doing more housework (Asher 2011). Mumpreneurialism rarely disrupts the conventional nature of such androcentrism by encouraging men to get more involved with childcare (as explored in Burrows 2013). Instead it reinforces the pattern that women should somehow manage both spheres. It continues to position mothers as the primary childcarers, who are home-based, but also seeks to render that state economically productive. As Emma Dowling has discussed, there is a systematic imperative to extend markets into previously unremunerated zones of social reproduction in the pursuit of neoliberal profitability (Dowling 2016), and the mumpreneur fits neatly into this model.

In this combined context, with women often bearing the burden of childcare responsibilities alongside precarious economic security and what Hochschild termed the 'third shift' of domestic administration in the home (Hochschild 2001) – those who are incited to become mumpreneurs face a meritocratic deficit in terms of both recognition and redistribution. In real life, mumpreneurs often report difficulties in balancing home/work life and overworking at home (Ekinsmyth 2013: 533–538). In mumpreneur guidebooks the sheer difficulty of being encouraged to strive individually to offset these structural inequalities when the odds are stacked heavily against you is palpable. For instance in the guidebook *Kitchen Table Tycoon* there is a whole chapter devoted to how women simply must accept that they are going to be very stressed and very overworked:

> If you're going to work from home you need to be prepared to be stressed most of the time, because running a successful business out of your home and scheduling your work around your kids is difficult, and there's no getting away from that.
>
> (Naik 2008: 200)

The attempt is to encourage the reader to 'conduct their conduct' by managing these massive forms of overwork, treating it as a necessary sacrifice to the gains of individualised achievement and flexibility-to-come. The problem of managing childcare and work is to be absorbed by the individual: and the individual mother even more than the individual family.

Working hard to activate your talent is positioned as the only route to mumpreneurial success. For instance, Annabel Karmel – who has a substantial following amongst UK parents due to her popular recipes for children and babies beginning to eat – recently published a guidebook simply and authoritatively entitled *Mumpreneur*. This book repeatedly uses the neoliberal meritocratic discourse of there being 'no barrier' to opportunity:

> Whatever background you come from, however little money you start off with, there is no getting away from the value of talent, hard work and vision. If you have passion for something and plenty of entrepreneurial spirit, you can do it.
>
> (Karmel 2015: 15)

However, the vast majority of women Annabel Karmel interviews in her book, when closely examined, tend to already have sizeable amounts of private capital with very privileged backgrounds (and are often white). Thomasina Miers, for instance, the founder of Wahaca, a chain of Mexican restaurants in Europe, attended the very expensive private girls' school St Pauls (and is listed in Debretts, the guide to the UK aristocratic establishment). Liz Earle, who co-founded a skincare company bearing her name, had a father who was an admiral. Both are feted in *Mumpreneur* as members of a range of celebrity members of 'Annabel's Kitchen Cabinet', a motif through which public sphere government is transposed into a cutely re-feminised private sphere, of 'domestic battle stations' (Karmel 2015: 23, 179). Likewise, Carol

Ekinsmyth's empirical research with UK-based mumpreneurs notes that 87% of her respondents had relied on personal wealth or savings in order to self-fund their start-ups (Ekinsmyth 2011: 109).

The types of work foregrounded as mumpreneurial often involves producing consumer goods conventionally targeted at women, whether body lotion or baby clothes, thereby linking together discourses of feminised pleasure in consumption and pleasure in production. Mumpreneurial production is made possible through women's knowledge and work as consumers (see Pettinger 2015). Fulfilling, enjoyable work is to be found by generating consumer lifestyle products: to be 'closer' to the imagined centre of that milieu. In the henlit novel *Goodbye Jimmy Choo*, for example, two newly countryside-based mumpreneurs set up a business selling a rural wonder skin cream based on one of their distant French relatives' recipes, calling their company Paysage Enchanté and selling their product for a large profit in upscale metropolitan skincare emporiums (Sanders 2004). For these henlit characters, just like the women portrayed in lifestyle magazines like *Eve*, the synchronicity and congruence between the branded producer and the consumer products they produce and/or sell is crucial. (In the novel this is played out through comic scenes about excessive image management, as the mumpreneurs dress up as 'rustic peasants' in a way far removed from their everyday lifestyle). The vast majority of businesses run by mumpreneurs featured in magazines tend to be home-oriented, caring-related or directed at a female consumer (Lewis 2010; Eikhof, Carter and Summers 2013). For Patricia Lewis, such reportage both reduces business potential and is a regressive discourse as it endorses or assumes women adopting full domestic responsibility within the household (Lewis 2010). Indeed, in 1963, for Betty Friedan, small-scale home-based entrepreneurial projects like crafting was part of the 'feminine mystique', 'small businesses which open and close with sad regularity' and which, as Stephanie Taylor points out, have a continuity with much 'mumpreneurial' activity today (Taylor 2015: 184). The domestic-oriented nature of these enterprises are not without contestation: Mumpreneur UK, for example, has recently argued that the term should not be pigeonholed as restricted to baby and child-related businesses (Farren 2014). Yet the highly pronounced nature of the association remains, indeed is built into the phrase itself.

Success in mumpreneurialism is mainly striven for in a tenor of liberatory desperation. In the 2000s the glossy women's magazine *Eve* sold the mumpreneur as an aspirational and liberated position in its regular monthly feature, 'Women doing their Own Thing' (Eikhof, Carter and Summers 2013).

Being a mumpreneur was framed as a potential pursuit that was for any woman a realistic and accessible option, one requiring little training apart from 'personality and passion' (Eikhof, Carter and Summers 2013). For Eikhof, Carter and Summers, such framing endorses a bypassing of business skills which is problematic both in terms of gendered routes into mumpreneurialism and in general.[9] (Indeed, the magazine *Eve* itself folded shortly after this run of mumpreneurial articles). In her book *The New Entrepreneurs: How Race, Class and Gender Shape American Enterprise*, an ethnographic project based on interviews with a range of US-based cafe owners, Zulema Valdez notes the extent to which all her interviewees continually emphasised their success, even in businesses that closed shortly after the interviews (Valdez 2015). A similar tenor of desperate insistence on entrepreneurial success is detectable in the Facebook self-employment descriptor (offered by a drop-down box) to describe work status: 'Self-employed and loving it!' Such an affect is shared by mumpreneurial discourse, in which the possibility of solving the combined problem of childcare and inflexible work will be resolved through her individualised acumen. There is frequently an insistence that it has to, it will, it must all work out perfectly, for there are precious few other solutions to the childcare/work problem presented by the current context. The tenor of mumpreneurialism is often one that could be characterised as an insistent form of desperate success. That this form of neoliberal meritocratic struggle takes place against a more than difficult backdrop is indicated by how, in Karmel's guidebook, a lengthy section is called 'How to Persist against All Odds' (Karmel 2015: 250).

Such desperation in the narratives of mumpreneurialism indicate, despite themselves, the weight of responsibility and lack of options in an increasingly shrivelled social context. In 2015 *The Daily Mail* launched its 'Mumpreneur of the Year' search by profiling four women. Alongside mumpreneurs who had created wedding furnishing accessories, cleaning fluid and zippered babygros, was 'Mona Shah, 45, founder of Harry Specters chocolate' (Sturgis 2015). The article outlines how Harry Specters chocolate company was largely set up by Mona and her husband to provide employment and work experience for people with autism, after they worried about the employment prospects for their autistic son. In the UK, only 16% of people diagnosed as being on the autistic spectrum and of working age are employed; only 32% do any kind of paid work (NAS 2016). Harry Specters chocolate company employs six people part-time who are on the autistic spectrum, and 'provides work experience opportunities for 40 young people with autism' (Sturgis 2015).

This business is laudable in providing opportunities for some young people with autism (a lifelong learning condition) who want to engage with potentially interesting work (NAS 2016). At the same time its status is clearly a small-scale survival strategy. There is no regulatory onus on employers to have any kind of quota system, to take a proportion of their staff who are differently abled: such policies were abandoned in the UK in the 1995 (Innesti, Radevich-Katsaroumpa and Sargeant 2016). Support and day-care services up and down the UK for the differently abled and disabled have faced severe cuts as local councils with reduced budgets have been forced to slash expenditure (Hedley 2010). In this highly precarious context of reduced provision, people are forced to adopt individualised solutions.

As we have seen, the role of individualised entrepreneurs in actuality is predominantly a role occupied by the white upper-middle classes, which is presented to the middle, lower-middle and, at times, working classes for emulation. Desperate success is augmented by class. Susan Luckman notes how mothers partaking in what she terms 'home-based micro enterprise' are positioned as middle-class, white heterosexual women who are 'simultaneously of the home and of the global marketplace' (the case she writes about, 'crafting', often figures 'an unrealistic image of seemingly blissful hipster domestic perfection' [Luckman 2015]). Yet despite this upper-middle-class focus, its logic resonates throughout the class spectrum. Julie Ann Wilson and Emily Chivers Yochim have incisively analysed how mothers in the US post-industrial rust-belt engage with consumer thrift and flexible enterprise (Wilson and Yochim 2015, 2017). Here the enterprise spans the intensive clipping out of coupons for money-off products and participating in a franchise scheme to promote products at the school gates and on social media. These activities are not the same as inventing and establishing a new business and connect to much longer histories of housewives working with commercial franchises like Tupperware and Avon, and yet their work of managing activity in the home (what Arlie Hochschild calls a 'third shift') in order to engage in what Yochim and Wilson term 'mamapreneurialism' or 'mothering through precarity' have obvious resonances with the examples I have been discussing here (Hocshchild and Manchung 2012; Wilson and Yochim 2015).

Entrepreneurialism is deeply and extensively problematic: it channels all life activity into a mode of competition, extending inequality and validating the environmentally destructive model of economic growth. But it also needs further picking apart. Whilst in some ways it is easy for academics to carp from the side-lines about people colluding in their own oppression, we also need to think hard about mechanisms, modes and strategies of disentanglement as well as entanglement, processes of construction alongside excavatory analysis. It is also therefore useful to dwell a little on what is meant by 'entrepreneurialism' and to move a step beyond some of the more asphyxiating accounts of neoliberal governmentality. This is not to say we should not understand the extent or depth of its savagely atomising, viciously impoverishing effects: to understand its depths, how low it can go, to stare it in the face. But treating it as an unrolling logic of inevitability gives it more power. It is salutary to remind ourselves that these are unrolling logics which have become powerful but which are not inevitable. The need to simultaneously understand its depths and identify some of its moments of instability: to consider its appeal and how its appeals might be redirected.

In this case I suggest one means of doing this is to consider what entrepreneurialism has become 'articulated to' (in the Laclau and Mouffe sense of 'connecting to and with') and how this articulation is gendered (Laclau and Mouffe 1985; Hall 1987; Slack 1996). The following sections therefore consider the gendering of the entrepreneur within the gendered rationalities of neoliberalism, in order to try to extend and to help open up alternative directions for this figure we call the mumpreneur and all those connected to her.

## Entrepreneurial man

Clearly we can understand the mumpreneur in terms of the percolation of neoliberalism into the domestic sphere. This after all is one of neoliberalism's key features: extending the ethic of competition into the nooks and crannies of everyday life or what Foucault describes as the extension of marketised dynamics throughout the social body (Foucault 2010; see Brown 2015). It is, however, particularly important to consider what is meant by 'entrepreneurialism' as entrepreneurialism has historically functioned as a potent and double-edged drive, one both facilitating creative energies and their capitalist capture. It is useful to consider these trajectories alongside the gendering of entrepreneurs and the gendering of neoliberal theory. One suggestive source here is Dardot and Laval's Foucauldian account of neoliberalism's intellectual and political genealogies, *The New Way of the World* (2013). Much like Wendy Brown's *Undoing the Demos*, it takes inspiration from and is a lengthy exegesis of Foucault's *Birth of Biopolitics* lectures. Delivered in France in 1978–1979 but only translated into English in 2010, these are the lectures (despite the somewhat misleading title of the book) in which Foucault analyses the origins of neoliberalism.

*The New Way of the World* foregrounds the centrality of the entrepreneur, enterprise and competition to everyday life and the role of entrepreneurialism as a guiding principle of neoliberalism. As Foucault, who they are elaborating upon, argued, this is what makes neoliberalism different from classical liberal thought: competition is not natural, it needs to be worked at. Dardot and Laval trace how these ideas percolated from Austrian economists and sociologists Ludwig von Mises and Frederick Hayek through to their synthesisation in the UK and US by both them and their students, including Israel Kirzner, and the subsequent adoption of their ideas by management gurus including Peter Drucker. These writers

> aim to show how a certain dimension of humanity – entrepreneurship – is constructed in competition, which is the potentially universal principle of conduct most essential to the capitalist order.
> (Dardot and Laval 2013: 102)

Dardot and Laval highlight this genealogy of neoliberal entrepreneurialism in a chapter titled 'Entrepreneurial Man', which analyses the formulations and centrality of the figure of the entrepreneur for neoliberal theory and neoliberalism. (For von Mises, for instance, 'in any real and living economy every actor is always an entrepreneur' [Dardot and Laval 2013: loc. 2570]). It is, however, unclear as to whether Dardot and Laval's chapter title is also a reflexive commentary on how man stands for all the genders. Given that it does not explicitly foreground or discuss this issue or the question of gender at all, it seems to indicate not. But such lack of clarity also leaves the issue of the gendering of the political rationality of neoliberalism a somewhat glaring undiscussed absence.

Dardot and Laval's gendered formulation of entrepreneurial man is also interesting for other reasons. The authors pick apart key characteristics of entrepreneurialism, such as how it entails being a vigilant, alert, self-constructing subject:

> [For Kirzner,] the entrepreneurial element in the behaviour of market participants consists ... in their alertness to previously unnoticed changes in circumstances which may make it possible to get far more in exchange for whatever they have to offer than was hitherto possible. ... For von Mises, as for Kirzner, entrepreneurship is not only an 'economizing' behaviour – that is, geared to profit maximisation. It also

contains an extra-economising dimension of the activity of discovery, of detecting 'good opportunities'.

(Dardot and Laval 2013: 111)

Dardot and Laval foreground the years of theorisation, argument and percolation which were involved in creating the entrepreneurial rationality of neoliberalism. They lay bare the idea that, through competition, you might be able to get more, which is the basis of the marketised mantra of meritocracy and paves the way for our contemporary moralising neoliberal discourse that it is your own fault if you do not. And they foreground how the characteristics of discovery, being alert and being resourceful become channelled into a logic of competition.

We can I think note that these characteristics are also important to co-operation (Sennett 2013). They are attributes that people want to have to extend their capabilities, to realise their potential, or what Marx called their 'species-being': to flourish (Marx and Engels 1976; Wright 2010; Hesmondhalgh 2016). These characteristics are connected to corporate entrepreneurialism through this chain of equivalence, formulated in entrepreneurial man's economic laboratory. But they do not have to be taken this way.

## Magical femininity

Where can we find 'entrepreneurial woman' in theoretical literature? Problems caused by sexism and neoliberalism are not just a problem in everyday life but also in academia and political theory, where texts that are often presented as being particularly significant, weighty analyses of neoliberalism also often happen to be ones with no or little reference to gender. In this context it is both important and useful to refer to suggestive earlier work on entrepreneurial culture, to connect these to key works on post-feminism and to more recent work on gender and entrepreneurialism from a range of disciplines including organisation and gender studies. This can help a consideration of just how new the meritocratic mumpreneur is: both to historicise her as a social type and to help track the changing nature of the formation of gender and entrepreneurialism of which she is a significant part.

In 1986, Swasti Mitter noted that women working at home were on the rise. Mitter focused on Bangladeshi women in London sewing and doing piecework at home as post-Fordism took hold and the garment industry shut many of its factories, laying off men and white women and subcontracting the labour to cheaper exploited zones overseas and the fourth-world zones in Europe (Mitter 1986).[10] The rise in what became termed 'flexible managing' and the creation of pools of domestic-based insecure and disposable labour was the early stages of a longer process in which, as Lisa Adkins more recently put it, 'the subcontracting associated with post-welfare states is a strategy via which women's work is actively being transformed into precarious work' (Adkins and Dever 2015). On the one hand, these tendencies can be understood as both being part of the long post-Fordist moment: the patterns developing in the 1980s are recognisably of the same epoch. On the other hand, there are now different intensities and modulations which I want to discuss here in relation to earlier examinations of the cultural relationship between gender and enterprise.

To do this we can turn to cultural studies. Whilst it is often the male-authored or edited collections on Thatcherism that receive the most prominence in discussions of cultural studies work on the political conjuncture or conjunctural analysis (e.g. Hall *et al.* 1978; Hall 1988), important feminist work has notoriously challenged and extended it. For instance, the 1991 edited collection *Off-Centre: Feminism and Cultural Studies* contained a sizeable amount of work explicitly concerned with the gendering of enterprise. It is useful to consider these pieces, now often occluded, in some depth here, both because some of the tools they offer are useful and because of the continuities and breaks with this earlier stage in post-Fordist culture.

For example, Janet Newman's incisive chapter 'Enterprising Women' in *Off-Centre* followed the emergent figure of the entrepreneurial woman across the pages of advice manuals from the 1980s. This figure, writes Newman, is part of the ideological onslaught of Thatcherism, constituted through endorsing the qualities of free market enterprise and standing against collective provision. The chapter tracks the appeal of these manuals to someone who does not want to follow tradition but could succeed and find their own niche 'in the marketplace of the world of work ... if you have enough self reliance, financial nous, competitive spirit and the determination to overcome the barriers you might find on the way' (Newman 1991: 241). 'Enterprising Women' foregrounds how these ideas become trenchant by offering such sheer galvanising potential, noting that they speak to a missing dimension often ignored in feminist analysis of work – 'women's experience of the structures and cultures of the workplace and business world' (Newman 1991: 242). Predating the slew of Foucauldian-inspired work on the management of the self within neoliberalism by well over a decade, Newman argued that the ideology on offer is one in which clever managing and purchasing will bypass structural social inequalities, and

> [t]he whole of life is thus constructed within the discursive practices of managerialism; and the potential contradictions between different elements of women's lives and identities can be resolved – if only women work hard enough and manage well enough they can have it all (or nearly).
> *(Newman 1991: 250)*

Estella Tincknell's chapter in the collection considers the same issue of how entrepreneurialism and femininity were being fused. 'Enterprise Fictions' examines the popularity in the 1980s of entrepreneurial heroines who make it from 'rags to riches', focusing on the heroine of Barbara Taylor Bradford's bestselling novel turned hugely popular TV series, *A Woman of Substance*, who starts out as a servant and ends up as the wealthy owner of a department store. Tincknell reads this narrative as an aspirational fantasy actively working to popularise the ideology of the individual bourgeois woman who can 'make a space for herself within capitalism', one which 'recognises class conflict but not class struggle' and bypasses the mutual help of the second-wave feminist movement, evading 'any sort of discussion of the obstacles in the way of aspiring female entrepreneurs'. What such fictions offer instead is 'the assurance that magical femininity will be the key to individual success in a world which demands that only one woman at a time can sit at the boardroom table' (Tincknell 1991: 272). The analysis of the novel is therefore read in terms of a Thatcherite vision for women which does not trouble the sexism of existing social structures but makes success a matter of what Tincknell usefully terms 'magical femininity'. This is a matter of dressing well, using the right attitude and feminine authority, and in the process reinvigorating 'the mythology of the unique individual and its promise of self-fulfilment' (Tincknell 1991: 262).[11]

Both chapters examine the uses and attitudes toward consumer goods (in the form of media artefacts and business books as well as their representation of the landscapes of consumption) to explore how the highly individualised, right-wing figure of the enterprising, consuming female was gaining cultural and political currency at this time at the expense of a more collective feminist vision of the social order. They indicate the importance of the discourse of the consuming woman who manages her way out of her class position and social difficulties to the neoliberal ideological project from the 1970s.

Despite some hugely imaginative and important work (e.g. Rowbotham, Segal and Wainwright 2012), it also indicates the wider failure of the political left to offer a popular mainstream version of social democratic feminism in relation to this vision of liberation through individual hedonistic consumerism and a managerial, entrepreneurial self.

How such formations spoke to younger women pursuing careers in the cultural industries has been extensively analysed by Angela McRobbie in a series of multifaceted pieces since the 1990s, writing which also drew on her earlier influential work on gender, consumption and individualisation (e.g. McRobbie 1978, 1991). McRobbie foregrounds how creative workplaces often present themselves as more like clubs than companies, are organised through 'network sociality' and incite self-exploitation through their appeals to passion for work. She traces how the insistence of the labour market on flexible, entrepreneurial subjects has meshed with a wider gender settlement, producing an array of gendered types ranging from the phallic 'top girls' disavowing feminism and adopting aspects of 'masculine' behaviour, through to the more recent strand of corporate liberal feminism that ostensibly takes 'feminism into account', offered by the likes of Sheryl Sandberg and her acolytes (such as the chicklit author, UK Conservative MP and US media commentator Louise Mensch) (McRobbie 1999, 2000, 2008, 2009, 2015).

In part what characterises all these writings is their close attention to the congruence between work and consumption for the success of entrepreneurial discourse. Magical femininity is an affective property built through a constellation of desires: it is repeatedly presented as easily obtainable if the individual simply puts her energies in the right direction. This is also the promise offered to the mumpreneur, in terms of how entrepreneurial working from home becomes offered as a magical solution to the problems of post-Fordist work (Luckman 2015) and as a feminised affect which downplays skill and accentuates passion. For instance, in the *Daily Mail* profile mentioned earlier, Mona Shah is presented as the woman behind the chocolate-production. However, articles in the business press see the company positioned somewhat differently, as a more equal partnership between Shah and her husband, combining her experience in making chocolates and the knowledge he gained doing an MBA (Moules 2015). Ostensibly offering an empowering feminist image by virtue of Shah's singular efforts, the *Daily Mail*'s type of mumpreneur media profiling therefore underplays the material and business skills needed to launch enterprises (Eikhof, Carter and Summers 2013), whilst the magical femininity of the mumpreneur continues to be framed as simply produced by the activation of her affective passion. Indeed, such a sizeable lacuna between affective empowerment (as the singular virtue) and the acquisition of the necessary skills to carry it through is a slippage deeply characteristic of liberal, neo-conservative feminism more broadly. In addition, a key difference between these 1980s and 2010s moments is the extent to which the individual women are now incited to be self-branding microcelebrities.

## The mumpreneur and the branded self

'Self-branding' has become a generalisable cultural imperative that extends way beyond those setting up businesses. As Alison Hearn argues, today most teenagers are encouraged, particularly through social-media activity, to establish an 'improved self'. Online self-representation becomes a promotional vehicle designed to sell you as an active agent (Hearn 2008: 205): 'The branded self is a commodity-sign: it is an entity that works and, at the same time, *points to itself working, striving to embody the values of its environment*' (Hearn 2008: 201; my italics). Striving, rather than skiving, has also, as we have seen in previous chapters, become a contemporary keyword, one often imbued with a moral charge and a glow of righteousness. Alison Winch notes that striving is also a charge created between women, through what she terms the 'gynopticon', or 'girlfriend gaze', under which 'what is rewarded and acclaimed is striving for perfection. Indeed those who are effortlessly perfect are bitchily vilified in the mainstream media as they do not evidence the success and necessity of the neoliberal work ethic' (Winch 2015: 234). This formulation also draws from Ros Gill's extensive work on the sensibility of post-feminism 'in which notions of autonomy, choice and self-improvement sit side-by-side with surveillance, discipline and the vilification of those who make the "wrong" choices' (Gill 2007: 163). The intensity through which women are incited into this subject position (in contradistinction to a masculinity which is constructed as not needing to be constructed) leads Gill to pose the question:

> To a much greater extent than men women are required to work on and transform the self, to regulate every aspect of their conduct, and to present all their actions as freely chosen. Could it be that neoliberalism is always already gendered, and that women are constructed as its ideal subjects?
>
> *(Gill 2007: 164)*

Sarah Banet-Weiser persuasively makes the case for such neoliberal selfhood marking a shift from post-Fordism and vividly illustrates this transition by tracing the historical strategies the cleansing product brand Dove has used to sell its products to women. In 1957, Dove privileged white femininity and addressed a 'unified' Fordist subject through advertisements featuring a white model posing in the bath. After the emergence of post-Fordist niche marketing, in the 1980s, Dove developed ads in which different 'ordinary' women addressed the camera as 'themselves'. Today this empowerment agenda has mutated into Dove's 'Self-Esteem Project', which involves consumers engaging by, for instance, voting, uploading videos to YouTube, and participating in 'activist' outreach work by encouraging teens to use online Dove workbooks to create their own 'healthy self-esteem' (Banet-Weiser 2012). Through such activity, which is heavily dependent on 'prosumption' and immaterial labour, corporations strive to extend the reach and depth of their brand and become social actors. Women are positioned as the ideal neoliberal subjects to be enlisted into such activity.

Such a diagnosis of the contemporary promotional use of social media as marking a break from post-Fordism finds a further reverberation in recent statements by the industrial economist and influential early theorist of post-Fordism Robin Murray (Murray 1989).[12] Murray makes the case that there has been a major shift to 'post-post-Fordism' (Murray 2015) marked by the emergence of the platform economy and the dominance of digital platforms alongside – and in many cases over – content. In an attention economy, he argues, capital needs to control platforms, and thus capitalism's main work becomes focused on attempting to capture them; but not everything can be captured and codified, and 'in one sense the means of production have been internalised within labour and cannot be entirely appropriated from labour' (Murray 2015: 195). This reading therefore foregrounds the political potentiality of the worker/prosumer alongside the wider extension of corporate power facilitated by a digital platform economy.

The shift to the platform economy of post-post-Fordism is apparent in how forms of mumpreneurial self-branding have mushroomed in the blogosphere, with some estimating the existence of 4 million 'mommy bloggers' in the US. As Jessica Taylor cogently argues, mommy blogging, often specifically a pursuit of white middle-class women, simultaneously involves capitalism attempting to harness maternal sociality as it moves online, women trying to extend their sociality and generate income; and 'reproductive labour becom[ing] a site for potential investment not just in children or in members of the household but in a creative self' (Taylor 2015: 115). The US 'queen of the mommy bloggers' Heather Armstrong (who has 1.53 million followers and the profile description 'I exploit my children for millions and millions of dollars on my mommyblog' on Twitter) announced in 2015 that she was stopping her blog, *Dooce*, because of the pressure from advertisers to brand her family:

> At the beginning, it was, 'We're just gonna put the logo at the end of the post. Write something around this.' … And then it was, 'Well, actually, we need you to show pictures of the product'. And then it was, 'We need you to show the product.' And then it was, 'We need your kids involved in the post.'
>
> *(Dean 2015)*

Armstrong posted images to Instagram with the hashtag #NotAnAd to indicate her rebellion against corporate control. (Later, she partly resumed her blog, branched out into podcasts, and now marks advertisements on Twitter more clearly, with the hashtag #Ad). Such actions were reminiscent of the actions of Essena O'Neill, the Australian teenager with 612,000 Instagram followers, who, in 2015, spectacularly dethroned her own social media construction. O'Neill replaced her previous photo captions with revelatory phrases documenting the banality and effort involved in staging apparently spontaneous and carefree glamour, such as 'Not real life. Only reason we went to the beach this morning was to shoot these bikinis' (Speed 2015). The examples of both O'Neill and Armstrong do undoubtedly indicate how public acts of breaking with 'Brand Me' can paradoxically garner more publicity. They follow, to some extent, the journalistic structure Richard Dyer discusses in relation to celebrity as the staged exposure of a 'real' persona (Dyer 1980). At the same time they also reveal the pressures to create a congruent brand which is inhabited by the self and the faultlines, the splinterings, breaks and moments of profound resistance, whether micro or macro, to such corporate-sanctioned versions of selfhood.[13]

Similar fissures are also apparent in the chicklit mumpreneur novel *Goodbye Jimmy Choo*. Here, the mumpreneur heroines launch skincare product Paysage Enchanté and on the advice of their PR friend extend the brand to themselves and their home in Provençal/Amish fashion, adopting a rustic look, altering their interior to remove gadgets, dressing their children in breeches and themselves in white blouses and flouncy skirts and altering their conduct by giving up smoking and drinking. The novel's denouement happens when a photographer captures images of one of the mumpreneurs in her garden smoking, drinking alcohol and dancing with her daughter wearing a post-feminist pink t-shirt with 'FCUK' on it whilst her son plays a GameBoy.[14] Mumpreneurial activity is depicted as necessarily being heavily imbricated with self-branding and self-presentation: she has to not only sell the product but represent it, embody it, live its brand in her daily life. In the novel, this is depicted as a false presentation, the exposure of which means the end of the business. It is also necessary: at the end, the main characters retain the pots of money that they have made – it was all 'worth it'. However, despite this, the contradictions and psychological expense of manufacturing such entrepreneurial, meritocratic selves seep through and become foregrounded.

## Disaggregation and alternatives

The mumpreneur promises a meritocratic solution to the overwork culture, the inflexibility of institutionalised labour, inadequately funded and socialised childcare, and the costs of recession within neoliberalism, all wrapped up in a package of glamour and self-realisation. The problems of overwork and potential failure that come with being a mumpreneur are often mediated as enjoyable chaos, part of a frenetic journey towards difficult but very probable triumph. Yet the mumpreneur primarily operates through a register of desperate success. The guidebooks urge the potential mumpreneur toward complete affective and psychological commitment: 'The best (and only) way to sustain yourself over all the obstacles is to feel passionate and fanatical about what you are doing', writes Annabel Karmel (Karmel 2015: 6). Wannabe mumpreneurs are regularly prepared for the losses, loneliness and exhaustion that lie ahead. 'I don't think anything of going to bed at 2 or 3 am and then getting up again and doing the school run, trying to grab a nap in the day, sleeping in cars', says Myleene Klass (Karmel 2015: 6). Mumpreneurs are incited to offset such desperation, and to propel themselves up the ladder of success, through passion. 'Are you on the passion ladder?' asks the mumpreneur website, *CEO Mums* ([Huelin] 2014; Figure 6.2).

The solution and terms of reference offered by the mumpreneur are neoliberal: they are organised around marketing an entrepreneurial branded self and generating profit. They perpetuate the patriarchal model of woman as primary carer who is primarily in the domestic sphere whilst making her 'productive' in a capitalist sense.

How could we imagine these varying neoliberal corporate imperatives being reconfigured differently, more progressively, around motherhood and

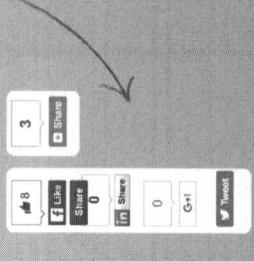

FIGURE 6.2 'Are You on the Passion Ladder?', *CEO Mums*. Reproduced courtesy of Nicola Huelin and *CEO Mums*.

work? There are always many ways into an issue. To conclude here I will consider some potential points of leverage.

The mumpreneur's relationship to capitalist discourse often stands on something of a faultline. It can consist of interesting creative activity that is attempted to be captured, scaled up and funnelled into a capitalist mould. These small enterprises often take an anti-monopoly, anti-corporate stance. Such points of self-identification are often strong and clear, if also fleeting, in the guidebooks and memoirs. At the end of the memoir, *The Mumpreneur Diaires,* for instance, Mosey Jones proudly reflects: 'six months down the line and I still haven't taken back the corporate shilling' (Jones 2009: 307). One route beyond neoliberal meritocracy in this case, then, is by orienting such activity further away from corporate discourse, against becoming exploitative organisations based on a corporate model. Here opening up the possibilities for and desirability of mumpreneurial activity forming co-operatives instead becomes an interesting area of potential. A lot of the current vibrant discussion of co-operatives (Murray 2010; Sandoval 2016a, 2016b) is focused around the young, but it has great potential to connect more extensively to this constituency. In addition it is important to emphasise the distinctions between the smaller organisation and the monopolistic, predatory exploitations and corporate tax-avoidance of the large corporation (Gilbert 2015).[15]

Another crucial faultline is between childcare and work, and here there is ample potential to move closer to Fraser's 'universal caregiver' model and share the load of both. As mentioned before, there are very different childcare patterns according to country.[16] Maternity pay should be paid and extended so that parents aren't pressured back into work; paid paternity/partner leave needs to be expected to be taken; the right to ask to work flexibly or part-time needs to become the right to work flexibly or part-time; and tighter legislation needs to exist to stop employers demoting staff when they become parents. The cultural conversation around differently gendered multi-tasking needs to be enlarged and institutionally embedded. Rebecca Asher's book *Shattered* includes a raft of practical policy suggestions on this front, including ensuring partners attend meetings during pregnancy with midwives so their role as a caring parent is embedded early on in the process. Gideon Burrows' book *Men can do It!* proposes a range of solutions for tackling the reasons why men do not do enough childcare, including changing masculinities and arguing that 'men should not only get the good stuff out of childcare; they also need to take the hit for equality to really be achieved' (Gideon Burrows in Littler and Winch 2016; Burrows 2013).

This debate also connects to the rich history of socialised co-operative childcare (McRobbie 2015; Riley 1983), the importance of which, for so many children and parents, is hard to over-estimate.

None of these issues are isolated but are part of a wider social tapestry. For instance, parents overwork not only because of a lack of employer flexibility – although this is obviously a crucial factor – but also because of the associated issues of the cost of living. (In metropolitan centres this is often, crucially, the cost of housing). This is why 'social reproduction' is such a useful term, because it enables these issues, which are joined up in everyday life, to also be joined up in theory. Social reproduction, at its best, involves forms of co-production which are open, egalitarian and creative. As such it connects to wider debates on 'post-work', which suggest reconsidering the primacy we give to paid employment relationships and reconceptualising what human productivity and creativity means, as well as prioritising social care rather than the exploitations of financialised capitalism (Fraser 2016; Weeks 2011; Srnicek and Williams 2015). The crisis of care, as Nancy Fraser puts it, involves reinventing the distinction between reproduction and production without sacrificing liberation or social protection (Fraser 2016).

These suggestions are ways into reconfiguring the zones, the discourses and components which together form the assemblage of and around the mumpreneur. The means of making these changes is, of course, highly debatable and contextually specific, and the way these issues are connected together into chains of equivalence – and how and by whom – depends on context, will and available resources. But these better solutions at micro and macro levels both have generalisable elements and contextual specificities. In terms of the specificity of this chapter's example, the key task here is to reorient the mumpreneur and the relationship between gender and the corporation: not to 'lean in' to neoliberal meritocratic discourse so that we are pushed into its contours, but to lean on it so hard it is flattened, so its implicit resources can be reorganised around our collective needs.

## Notes

1 Reay forthcoming.
2 N. Fraser 2016: 117.
3 'Mumpreneur' is most commonly used in the UK, 'Mompreneur' in the US and 'mumtrepreneur' in New Zealand.
4 www.mumtrepreneurawards.co.nz. Accessed 1 December 2016.

5 www.mumpreneuruk.com/awards/mumpreneur-awards. Accessed 1 December 2016.
6 www.dailymail.co.uk/femail/article-3040629/Wholl-Mumpreneur-year-major-new-trend-women-juggling-motherhood-setting-businesses-like-four-looking-inspiring-stories.html. Accessed 1 December 2016.
7 'Everyday Self-Employment', day event, City, University of London, 30 October 2015. Particular thanks to Rachel Cohen for pointing me towards the appropriate statistics.
8 The scheme was a revival of an earlier scheme developed in the 1980s under the Thatcher government.
9 Eikhof, Carter and Summers noted that whilst mumpreneur activity was very much portrayed as an aspirational fantasy, its protagonists tended to 'transition into sectors with typically high levels of occupational segregation across all forms of employment, lower prestige and earnings' (Eikhof, Carter and Summers 2013: 558). Promoting such domestically centred, under-capitalised forms of entrepreneurship, they argued, was activity that 'could be expected to entrench and increase existing gender inequalities in entrepreneurship' (Eikhof, Carter and Summers 2013: 558–559).
10 The piece work seamstress has a longer history, and was a powerful symbol of economic exploitation in the nineteenth century, as represented in Thomas Hood's famous poem 'The Song of the Shirt'.
11 This also resonates with Phil Cohen's work on 'magical solutions' which Susan Luckman refers to in her article on entrepreneurial home-working as offering a 'magical solution' to the problems of the post-Fordist sexual contract (Luckman 2015).
12 Murray's influential 1989 article 'Benetton Britain' sketched the nature of post-Fordist production/consumption patterns. It outlines the movement, from the 1970s, toward a multiplicity of intersecting practices by manufacturers – of which Benetton was paradigmatic, just as Ford was for Gramsci in 'Americanism and Fordism' – such as the use of consumer-led focus groups, computerised orders and shifts towards the production of small batches of consumer goods that could be made quickly using ultra-cheap, contracted-out, exploited labour far away from corporate HQ and retail sites ('just-in-time production' or 'flexible specialisation') (Murray 1989).
13 Afterwards, Armstrong said she missed producing her blog, as it provided her with a relief and it was something she was proud of ('I made this. I'm proud of it' [Dean 2015]). She re-activated the blog on a part-time basis.
14 On post-feminist aesthetics, including pink FCUK t-shirts, see Gill 2007.
15 In the UK, for example, in 2016, the opposition leader Jeremy Corbyn stood on a platform for 'small businesses, co-operatives and social enterprises' (Corbyn n.d.).
16 The US, for example, has no paid parental/partner leave, whereas the UK has two weeks which can be shared with a mother's maternity leave.

# References

Adkins, Lisa (1995) *Gendered Work: Sexuality, Family and the Labour Market*. Maidenhead: Open University Press.

Adkins, Lisa, and Maryanne Dever (eds) (2015) *The Post-Fordist Sexual Contract: Living and Working in Contingency*. London: Palgrave.

Asher, R. (2011) *Shattered: Modern Motherhood and the Illusion of Equality*. London: Harvill Secker.

Banet-Weiser, Sarah (2013) *Authentic TM: The Politics of Ambivalence in a Brand Culture*. New York: NYU Press.

Bauman, Zygmunt (1998) *Work, Consumerism and the New Poor*. Maidenhead: Open University Press.

Beck, Ulrich (2000) *The Brave New World of Work*. Cambridge: Polity Press.

Bogg, Alan (2015) contribution to 'Dependency and the Social Relations of Self-Employment' panel at 'Everyday Self-Employment', day event, City, University of London, 30 October.

Brown, Wendy (2015) *Undoing the Demos*. Cambridge, MA: MIT Press.

Burrows, Gideon (2013) *Men can do It! The Real Reason Dads don't do Childcare, and What Men and Women can do About It*. London: NGO Media.

Campbell, Bea (2008) 'Understanding Society and Remaking Politics', Soundings: 'Cultures of Capitalism' seminar, London, 18 January.

Chakrabortty, Aditya (2016) 'Nottingham Academic on Casual Contract: I had more Rights as a Binman', *The Guardian*, 16 November, www.theguardian.com/uk-news/2016/nov/16/nottingham-academic-on-casual-contract-i-had-more-rights-as-a-binman. Accessed 1 December 2016.

Corbyn, Jeremy (n.d.) *Better Business*, http://corbynforbusiness.com. Accessed 1 December 2016.

Dardot, Pierre, and Christian Laval (2013) *The New Way of the World: On Neoliberal Society*, Kindle edn. London: Verso.

Dean, Michelle (2015) '"I cannot be that person": Why the "Queen of the Mommy Bloggers" had to Quit', *The Guardian*, 23 September, www.theguardian.com/media/2015/sep/23/heather-armstrong-leaving-dooce-mommy-blog-advertisers. Accessed 1 December 2016.

Douglas, Susan J., and Meredith W. Michaels (2004) *The Mommy Myth: The Idealisation of Motherhood and How it has Undermined all Women*. New York: Free Press.

Dowling, Emma (2016) 'Valorised but not Valued? Affective Remuneration, Social Reproduction and Feminist Politics beyond the Recovery', *British Politics* 11(4) pp. 452–468.

Dyer, Richard (1980) *Stars*. London: British Film Institute.

Eikhof, D.R., S. Carter and J. Summers (2013) '"Women doing their Own Thing": Media Representations of Female Entrepreneurship', *International Journal of Entrepreneurship Behaviour and Research* 19(5), pp. 547–564.

Ekinsmyth, Carol (2011) 'Challenging the Boundaries of Entrepreneurship: The Spatialities and Practices of UK "Mumpreneurs"', *Geoforum* 41(1) pp. 104–114.

Ekinsmyth, Carol (2013) 'Managing the Business of Everyday Life: The Roles of Space and Place in "Mumpreneurship"', *International Journal of Entrepreneurial Behaviour and Research* 19(5) pp. 525–546.

Ekinsmyth, Carol (2014) 'Mothers' Business, Work/Life and the Politics of "Mumpreneurship"', *Gender, Place and Culture* 21(10) pp. 1230–1248.
Farren, Amanda (2014) 'The Mumprenuer Debate', *Mumpreneur UK*, February, www.mumpreneuruk.com/the-mumpreneur-debate. Accessed 1 December 2016.
Foster, Dawn (2016) *Lean Out*. London: Banner Repeater Books.
Foucault, Michel (2008) *The Birth of Biopolitics: Lectures at the Collège de France, 1978–1979*, trans. Graham Burchell. London: Palgrave Macmillan.
Fraser, Nancy (1994) 'After the Family Wage: Gender Equality and the Welfare State', *Political Theory* 22(4) pp. 591–698.
Fraser, Nancy (2013) *Fortunes of Feminism*. London: Verso
Fraser, Nancy (2015) 'The Fortunes of Socialist Feminism: Jo Littler interviews Nancy Fraser', *Soundings* 58 (January) pp. 21–33.
Fraser, Nancy (2016) 'Contradictions of Capital and Care', *New Left Review* 100 (July–August) pp. 99–117.
Gilbert, Jeremy (2015) *Common Ground: Democracy and Collectivity in an Age of Individualism*. London: Pluto Press.
Gill, Rosalind (2007) 'Postfeminist Media Culture: Elements of a Sensibility', *European Journal of Cultural Studies* 10(2) pp. 147–166.
Gill, Rosalind, and Andy Pratt (2008) 'In the Social Factory? Immaterial Labour, Precariousness and Cultural Work', *Theory, Culture and Society* 25(7–8) pp. 1–30.
Hall, Stuart (1987) 'Gramsci and Us', *Marxism Today*, June, pp. 16–21.
Hall, Stuart (1988) *The Hard Road to Renewal: Thatcherism and the Crisis of the Left*. London: Verso.
Hall, Stuart, Chas Critcher, Tony Jefferson, John Clarke and Brian Roberts (eds) (1978) *Policing the Crisis: Mugging, the State and Law and Order*. London: Macmillan.
Hearn, Alison (2008) 'Meat, Mask, Burden: Probing the Contours of the Branded Self', *Journal of Consumer Culture* 8(2) pp. 197–217.
Hedley, Sarah (2010) 'Funding Cuts will Affect Autism Charities', *The Guardian*, 15 December, www.theguardian.com/voluntary-sector-network/2010/dec/15/funding-cuts-autism-charities. Accessed 1 December 2016.
Hesmondhalgh, David (2016) 'Capitalism and the Media: Moral Economy, Well-Being and Capabilities', *Media, Culture and Society* 39(2) pp. 202–218.
Hochschild, Arlie Russell (2001) *The Time Bind: When Work Becomes Home and Home Becomes Work*. New York: Holt Paperbacks.
Hochschild, Arlie Russell, and Anne Manchung (2012) *The Second Shift: Working Families and the Revolution at Home*, 2nd edn. London: Penguin.
[Huelin], Nicola (2014) 'Are You on the Passion Ladder?', *CEO Mums*, 15 March, http://ceomums.co.uk/are-you-on-the-passion-ladder. Accessed 1 December 2016.
Innesti, Alessandra, Elena Radevich-Katsaroumpa and Malcolm Sargeant (2016) 'Disability Quotas: Past or Future Policy?', *Economic and Industrial Democracy*, http://journals.sagepub.com/doi/abs/10.1177/0143831X16639655?journalCode=eida. Accessed 21 March 2017.

James, Selma (2012) *Sex, Race and Class: The Perspective of Winning: A Selection of Writings 1952–2011*. New York: Common Notions.
James, Selma (2015) 'Carers of the World Unite', *Open Democracy*, 17 December, www.opendemocracy.net/transformation/selma-james/carers-against-market. Accessed 1 December 2016.
Jones, Mosey (2009) *The Mumpreneur Diaries*. London: Harper Collins.
Karmel, Annabel (2015) *Mumpreneur: The Complete Guide to Starting and Running a Successful Business*. London: Vermillion.
Laclau, Ernesto, and Chantal Mouffe (1985) *Hegemony and Socialist Strategy*. London: Verso.
Leadbeater, Charles, and Kate Oakley (1999) *The New Independents: Britain's New Cultural Entrepreneurs*. London: Demos.
Lewis, Patricia (2010) 'Mumpreneurs: Revealing the Post-Feminist Entrepreneur', in Patricia Lewis and Ruth Simpson (eds), *Revealing and Concealing Gender: Issues of Visibility in Organisations*. London: Palgrave.
Littler, Jo (2013) 'The Rise of the "Yummy Mummy": Popular Conservatism and the Neoliberal Maternal in Contemporary British Culture', *Communication, Culture and Critique* 6(2) pp. 227–243.
Littler, Jo, and Alison Winch (2016) 'Feminism and Childcare: A Roundtable Discussion with Sara de Benedictis, Gideon Burrows, Tracey Jensen, Jill Rutter and Victoria Showunmi', *MAMSIE: Studies in the Maternal* 8(1), www.mamsie.bbk.ac.uk/articles/10.16995/sim.212. Accessed 4 March 2017.
Luckman, Susan (2015) 'Women's Micro-Entrepreneurial Home-Working as a Post-Fordist "Magical Solution" to the Work-Life Relationship', in Lisa Adkins and Maryanne Dever (eds), *The Post-Fordist Sexual Contract: Living and Working in Contingency*. London: Palgrave.
McGee, Mel (2009) *Supermummy: The Ultimate Mumpreneur's Guide to Online Business Success*. Great Yarmouth: Bookshaker.
McRobbie, Angela (1978) 'Jackie: An Ideology of Adolescent Femininity'. CCCS Stencilled Occasional Paper, University of Birmingham, http://epapers.bham.ac.uk/1808. Accessed 1 December 2016.
McRobbie, Angela (1991) *Feminism and Youth Culture: From Jackie to Just Seventeen*. London: Macmillan.
McRobbie, Angela (1999) *In the Culture Society: Art, Fashion and Popular Music*. London: Routledge.
McRobbie, Angela (2000) 'Clubs to Companies', *Cultural Studies* 16(4) pp. 516–532.
McRobbie, Angela (2008) 'Young Women and Consumer Culture: An Intervention', *Cultural Studies* 22(5) pp. 531–550.
McRobbie, Angela (2009) *The Aftermath of Feminism: Gender, Culture and Social Change*. London: Sage.
McRobbie, Angela (2013) 'Feminism, the Family and the New Mediated Maternalism', *New Formations* 80–81 pp. 119–137.
McRobbie, Angela (2015) *Be Creative*. Cambridge: Polity Press.
Marx, Karl, and Friedrich Engels (1976) *Marx and Engels Collected Works*, vol. 5: *1845–1847*. London: Lawrence & Wishart.

Matharu, Hardeep (2015) 'Sweden Introduces 6 Hour Work Day', *The Independent*, 1 October, www.independent.co.uk/news/world/europe/sweden-introduces-six-hour-work-day-a6674646.html. Accessed 1 December 2016.

Mitter, Swasti (1986) *Common Fate, Common Bond: Women in the Global Economy*. London: Pluto Press.

Morrison, Sarah (2013) 'Mums do the Business: The Number of Female Entrepreneurs who Juggle Work and Looking after their Children is Growing Fast', *The Independent*, 29 September, www.independent.co.uk/life-style/health-and-families/health-news/mums-do-the-business-the-number-of-female-entrepreneurs-who-juggle-work-and-looking-after-their-8846577.html. Accessed 1 December 2016.

Moules, Jonathan (2015) 'Chocolate Entrepreneurs with a Social Aim', *Financial Times*, 1 February, www.ft.com/cms/s/2/f87ff902-81f1-11e4-a9bb-00144feabdc0.html#slide0. Accessed 1 December 2016.

Murray, Robin (1989) 'Benetton Britain: The New Economic Order', in Stuart Hall and Martin Jacques (eds), *New Times*. London: Lawrence & Wishart, pp. 54–64.

Murray, Robin (2010) *Co-Operation in the Age of Google*. London: Co-Operatives UK.

Murray, Robin (2015) 'Post-Post-Fordism in the Era of Platforms: Robin Murray talks to Andrew Goffey and Jeremy Gilbert', *New Formations* 84(5) pp. 184–208.

Naik, Anita (2008) *Kitchen Table Tycoon: How to Make it Work as a Mother and an Entrepreneur*. London: Piaktus.

NAS (2016) *The Autism Employment Gap: Too Much Information in the Workplace*. London: National Autistic Society.

Negra, Diane (2009) *What a Girl Wants? Reclamation of the Self in Postfeminism*. New York: Routledge.

Negra, Diane, and Yvonne Tasker (eds) (2014) *Gendering the Recession*. Durham, NC: Duke University Press.

Newman, Janet (1991) 'Enterprising Women', in Sarah Franklin, Celia Lury and Jackie Stacey (eds), *Off-Centre: Feminism and Cultural Studies*. London: Routledge, pp. 241–259.

Oakley, A. (1974) *Housewife*. London: Penguin.

Odev, Susan, and Mark Weeks (2010) *Mum Ultrapreneur*. Great Yarmouth: Bookshaker.

Office for National Statistics (2014) *Self-Employed Workers in the UK: 2014*. London: ONS, http://webarchive.nationalarchives.gov.uk/20160105160709/http://www.ons.gov.uk/ons/dcp171776_374941.pdf. Accessed 1 December 2016.

Pearson, Allison (2002) *I Don't Know How She Does It*. London: Vintage.

Pearson, Ruth, and Diane Elson (2015) 'Transcending the Impact of the Financial Crisis in the United Kingdom: Towards Plan F, a Feminist Economic Strategy', *Feminist Review* 109(1) pp. 8–30.

Pettinger, Lynne (2015) *Work, Consumption and Capitalism*. London: Palgrave Macmillan.

Pew Research Centre (2015) 'Three in Ten US Jobs are Held by the Self-Employed and the Workers they Hire', www.pewsocialtrends.org/2015/10/22/three-in-ten-u-s-jobs-are-held-by-the-self-employed-and-the-workers-they-hire. Accessed 1 December 2016.

Reay, Diane (forthcoming) 'The Cruelty of Social Mobility: Individual Success at the Cost of Collective Failure', in Steph Lawler and Geoff Payne (eds), *Everyone a Winner?* Abingdon: Taylor & Francis.

Rigney, Laura (2014) *Just do It: Rules to go from the School Run to the Boardroom*. London: CreateSpace.

Riley, Denise (1983) *War in the Nursery: Theories of the Child and Mother*. London: Virago.

Ross, Andrew (2010) *Nice Work if You can Get It: Life and Labor in Precarious Times*. New York: NYU Press.

Rowbotham, Sheila, Lynne Segal and Hilary Wainwright (2012) *Beyond the Fragments: Feminism and the Making of Socialism*. 3rd revd edn. London: Merlin Press.

Russell, Scarlett (2014) 'Rise of the "Mumpreneur": As Price of Childcare Soars by 20% in a Year, 65% of Mothers Want to Launch Own Businesses from Home', *Daily Mail*, 21 April, www.dailymail.co.uk/femail/article-2609339/Rise-mumpreneur-As-price-childcare-soars-20-YEAR-65-mothers-want-launch-businesses-home.html. Accessed 24 September 2015.

Rutter, Jill (2015) *Childcare Costs Survey 2015*. London: Family and Childcare Trust.

Sandberg, Sheryl (2013) *Lean In: Women, Work and the Will to Lead*. London: W.H. Allen.

Sanders, Annie (2004) *Goodbye, Jimmy Choo*. London: Orion.

Sandoval, Marisol (2016a) 'Fighting Precarity with Co-Operation? Worker Co-Operatives in the Cultural Sector', *New Formations* 88 pp. 51–68.

Sandoval, Marisol (2016b) 'What would Rosa do? Co-Operatives and Radical Politics' *Soundings* 63 pp. 98–111.

Sennett, Richard (2013) *Together: The Rituals, Pleasures and Politics of Co-Operation*. London: Penguin.

Slack, Jennifer Daryl (1996) 'The Theory and Method of Articulation in Cultural Studies', in David Morley and Kuang-Sin Chen (eds), *Stuart Hall: Critical Dialogues in Cultural Studies*. London: Routledge.

Smith, S. (2011) 'Ask the Experts: Becoming a Mumtrepreneur', 26 September, *Financial Times*, www.ft.com/cms/s/0/42773e2e-debe-11e0-a228-00144feabdc0.html#axzz214h7EgzN. Accessed 1 December 2016.

Speed, Barbara (2015) 'The Lies of Instagram: How the Cult of Authenticity Spun Out of Control', *New Statesman*, 13 November.

Srnicek, Nick, and Alex Williams (2015) *Inventing the Future: Postcapitalism and a World without Work*. London: Verso.

Standing, Guy (2011) *The Precariat: The New Dangerous Class*. London: Bloomsbury.

Sturgis, India (2015) 'Who'll be Our Mumpreneur of the Year?', *Mail Online*, 15 April, www.dailymail.co.uk/femail/article-3040629/Wholl-Mumpreneur-year-major-new-trend-women-juggling-motherhood-setting-businesses-like-four-looking-inspiring-stories.html. Accessed 1 December 2016.

Taylor, Jessica (2015) 'Laptops and Playpens: "Mommy Bloggers" and Visions of Household Work', in Lisa Adkins and Maryanne Dever (eds) *The Post-Fordist Sexual Contract: Living and Working in Contingency*. London: Palgrave.

Taylor, Stephanie (2015) 'A New Mystique? Working for Yourself in the Neoliberal Economy', *Sociological Review* 63(S1) pp. 174–187.

Tincknell, Estella (1991) 'Enterprise Fictions: Women of Substance', in Sarah Franklin, Celia Lury and Jackie Stacey (eds), *Off-Centre: Feminism and Cultural Studies*. London: Routledge, pp. 260–273.

Valdez, Zulema (2015) *The New Entrepreneurs: How Race, Class and Gender Shape American Enterprise*. Redwood City, CA: Stanford University Press.

Weeks, Kathi (2011) *The Problem with Work: Feminism, Marxism, Antiwork Politics and Postwork Imaginaries*. Durham, NC: Duke University Press.

Wilson, Julie Ann, and Emily Chivers Yochim (2015) 'Mothering through Precarity', *Cultural Studies* 29(5–6) pp. 669–686.

Wilson, Julie Ann, and Emily Chivers Yochim (2017) *Mothering through Precarity: Women's Work and Digital Media*. Durham, NC: Duke University Press.

Winch, Alison (2015) 'Brand Intimacy, Female Friendship and Digital Surveillance Networks', *New Formations* 84(5) pp. 228–245.

Wing-Fai, Leung, Rosalind Gill and Keith Randle (2015) 'Getting In, Getting On, Getting Out: Women as Career Scramblers in the UK Film and Television Industries', in Briget Conor, Rosalind Gill and Stephanie Taylor (eds), *Gender and Creative Labour*. London: Wiley Blackwell.

Wright, Erik Olin (2010) *Envisaging Real Utopias*. London: Verso.

# CONCLUSION

## Beyond neoliberal meritocracy

> Many people question the notion that individual interests reign supreme; that anyone can get on with hard work and effort; and that this society is as good as it gets. Those who won wars, who got an education against the odds, who fought for better rights at work, and who worked hard to give their children the best possible start only to see them joining dole queues emphasise that life has not always been thus, and that it can change again.
>
> Selina Todd[1]

### Failing to convince

As we have seen throughout this book, discourses of meritocracy are relatively mobile and capable of being articulated in different directions. We are currently living in an interesting moment because there are more narratives in circulation indicating in various ways that there are problems with contemporary neoliberal meritocratic discourse. Simply put, this is primarily because since the financial crash of 2008, and the political use of the recession to extend the rights and wealth of the 1% rather than rein them in, the social ladder between rich and poor has become conspicuously longer, and the distance to traverse it increasingly difficult, or impossible, for the majority who do not have considerable structural privilege. Consequently, as we saw at the beginning of this book, there are now more articles and books in circulation questioning the very concept of meritocracy

(Bloodworth 2016; Frank 2016; Hayes 2012; McNamee and Miller 2009). There are also more dramatic narratives implicitly questioning the idea that working hard is enough to activate talent and propel it to the top.

Take, for example, how the so-called new 'golden age of television' has thrown up some flamboyant examples of narratives that show that working hard and having talent just is not enough. In the popular cult TV series *Breaking Bad*, being brilliant and diligent at chemistry is clearly depicted as simply not enough to enable career success or even survival in a cruel atomised neoliberal world of over-privileged elites and a lack of social safety nets. *Breaking Bad*'s anti-hero Walter White, a brilliant chemistry teacher who cannot afford to pay for his cancer treatment, slides into becoming a crystal-meth dealer. In *Breaking Bad*'s spin-off drama, *Better Call Saul*, there are powerful depictions of lawyers and shopkeepers who are stymied by a lack of money and the vested interests of the rich. Effort and talent simply not being sufficient in a social structure undergoing evisceration was also the critical context of the highly acclaimed Baltimore-based US drama series *The Wire*. Each of its five seasons focused on the manifestation of this problem within a different zone: education, drugs, transport, media and law. The language of career opportunities is now often presented as more fraught with difficulty and drudgery than in the 1990s. The precarious creative labour depicted by Lena Dunham's *Girls*, in which the protagonists struggle with unfulfilling menial positions, is noticeably different from that in the 1990s show *Sex in the City*, in which labouring in the cultural industries is overwhelmingly glamourous and fulfilling (Fisher 2014). In film, one of the main reasons the dystopian drama of *The Hunger Games* has been wildly popular is because it expertly foregrounds the sadistically uneven power dynamics of reality TV's competitive individualism.

In short, then, there are more narratives in popular circulation which are exposing the meritocratic myth as being in crisis, and there are some which challenge it. But this destabilisation of a 'secure' neoliberal narrative of meritocracy has not simply involved progressive movement towards a more egalitarian future. On the contrary, it has been seized upon by new variants of neoliberal and neo-national discourse. The most graphic example here is the billionaire Donald Trump purporting to speak for oppressed masses let down by a meritocratic dream that failed to materialise.[2] Trump offers a corporate justice narrative of meritocracy. He loudly voices his recognition of increased difficulties faced by the working and middle classes, for which he promises anti-elitist nationalism ('Make America Great Again'), a promise directed in particular to white men and activated in the election campaign and beyond, through violently racist and sexist 'banter'. Trump proposes that anyone can make it, and in his discourse, merit becomes the ability to parlay 'talent', anti-elitism and ostensible 'entrepreneurial acumen' with working hard to make it to the top (Elmer and Todd 2016; Ouellette 2016; Hearn 2016). His own vast privilege is simultaneously sidestepped and mutated into a discourse of being 'worth it'. Trump offers a corporate justice narrative which will work to siphon off more wealth for plutocrats, and increase inequality, whilst offering a meritocratic dream to his voters. Those who do not make it and who disagree with his prescription of rampant capitalism are, in his meritocratic discourse, 'weak'; over them hangs his violent threat of being punished. Political destabilisation is a state which can be seized upon by a range of different political interests, and at present the new right has been very good at using it to extend its own advantage.

## The journeys of meritocracy

This book has endeavoured to contribute to and extend the multifaceted, if often somewhat disconnected, conversation around meritocracy, to draw existing strands of divergent debate together and to contribute new forms of analysis and argument. It has attempted to do so by outlining meritocracy's historical genealogies in contemporary social theory and political rhetoric and its manifestations in popular culture. It has sought to offer theoretical resources to understand its shifting cultural formations and to analyse telling examples of how it is activated as a popular parable. Arguing that the ideological discourse of neoliberal meritocracy has been used over the past few decades as the key legitimating narrative for contemporary capitalism, this book has shown how it has been reproduced, popularised and extended.

Whilst meritocracy has a variety of genealogies, the book has argued that we can understand its more recent formation by tracing its journey as a term since it came into being in mid-twentieth-century Britain. As we saw in the first chapter, about the travels of the word in social theory, the word 'meritocracy' was initially used by Alan Fox as part of a socialist critique of 'merit'-based inequality. Michael Young's subsequent more famous elaboration was a social-democratic critique that was primarily oriented towards education and the dangers of building a hierarchical society around talent-based 'merit'. The social-democratic critique was less committed to anti-capitalism than its earlier phase, and this ambivalence enabled the incipient discourse of neoliberal meritocracy to take hold. Neoliberal meritocracy, which has presented meritocracy as a wholly positive discourse, became popularised from the late 1970s in social theory in work by academics including Michael Young's friend, Daniel Bell, the US cheerleader of the idea of the 'knowledge economy'.

I have argued that we need to understand neoliberal meritocracy in terms of its specific relationship to the movements and struggles for liberation around gender, race and class. As chapter 2 demonstrated, the capitalist rhetoric of neoliberal meritocracy which was developed from the 1970s directly addressed those with less social power, with what I term 'a meritocratic deficit', and has incited them into the neoliberal meritocratic dream of individualistic competitive striving with a particularly emphatic insistence. In doing so it selectively appropriated the aspects of liberation struggles that were compatible with capitalism in order to sell products, individualised modes of self-conduct and precarious labour as liberating and meritocratic. Neoliberal practice and discourse, mobilising its existing institutional power, has also attempted to cash in on these forms of structural injustice. What I term 'neoliberal justice narratives' recognise structural injustice but then offer to sell neoliberal meritocratic solutions for them. This is a discourse which puts the already disempowered under extra pressure, a double move which promises opportunity whilst producing new forms of social division.

This book has foregrounded how the meaning of neoliberal meritocracy was created through multiple contexts – social, cultural and political. Taking politics as it key object, the third chapter outlined how the UK's political sphere in the neoliberal period since the late 1970s has popularised the idea of meritocracy. It focused its discussion around the meritocratic messages different prime ministerial personas have variously projected, from Thatcher to Major, Blair to Brown, Cameron to May. Whilst the meritocratic mantra of equality of opportunity has been consistent throughout this period, it has been differently modulated: from the authoritarian anti-establishment version offered by Thatcherism, through socially liberal Blairism, through the castigation of a 'morally degraded' underclass by the ex-Etonian David Cameron, and on to the neoliberal justice narratives of potential redemption promised by Theresa May. This chapter's analysis showed how discourses of political meritocracy evolve and mutate within a given national context whilst being connected to other national and transnational narratives about meritocracy.

All these varied expressions of neoliberal meritocracy have primarily worked to expand the gap between rich and poor, even while some of their political strategies encouraged different groups of people to attempt to become rich. A wide economic chasm between rich and poor is a structural hallmark of neoliberalism. Chapter 4 examined how neoliberalism's wealth gap has been justified with recourse to narratives of neoliberal meritocracy starring the rich, whether in terms of specific plutocrats or as abstract entities and through a range of motifs from normcore plutocrats to kind parents to luxury-flaunters. In doing so it marked the shift in emphasis in the second half of the book from tracing genealogies to examining 'parables of progress' in popular culture. It foregrounded the rise of an image of the 'ordinary rich' as a key persuasive motif of our neoliberal times and related it to the selective poaching from liberation struggles that I discussed in chapter 2. In other words, the idea of the normcore plutocrat who struggles against the system is not only a hugely popular contemporary motif, but is structurally constitutive of a wide range of mediated fields including politics. It has become profoundly useful to a neoliberal economic system which wishes to extend the logics of profit-seeking, marketisation and competition whilst retaining an image of social fluidity and mobility.

Chapters 5 and 6 extended the book's analysis of cultural parables of progress and their challenges in more depth. Chapter 5 examined the racialisation of meritocracy. The Damonsplaining incident was analysed as an example of how the discourse of post-racial meritocracy was mobilised and rejected. Matt Damon simultaneously insisted that diversity did not matter and that he was the one who knew how to deal with it, a tautological framing which when performed through the attempted silencing of a highly experienced black producer provoked substantial media ridicule and outrage. As the chapter argued, the very vignettes and performative parables of meritocracy that reality-TV talent-search competitions have publicised so well are themselves a constitutive part of the problem of inequality; problems Damon, as producer and presenter, embodied. Here, the idea of a post-racial meritocracy was crumbling, was appearing ridiculous, was unbearable.

The emergence of the mumpreneur, as the last chapter outlined, is often presented as a solution for the recognised problems of inequality at work and inequalities over childcare at home faced by parents but disproportionately by mothers. As such the mumpreneur offers a highly gendered version of what I term a 'neoliberal justice narrative'. This chapter positioned mumpreneurialism in its historical context to clarify how it is being offered as an ostensibly meritocratic solution to these wider social failures to deal with the relationship between productive and reproductive labour, whilst extending the business of profit-seeking further into the home. In particular, it foregrounded the flip side of narratives of mumpreneurial triumph by highlighting a trope I termed 'desperate success', the insistence that people are winning even as the costs – online and offline, in and out of the home – of its multiple exertions are palpable.

As we saw in chapter 1, people are more likely to tolerate severe inequality, if it is suggested that, regardless of this fact, there is enough social mobility for everyone to succeed. But full social mobility simply cannot co-exist with extreme inequality. If there is not anything like a level playing field, to deploy another beloved trope of meritocracy discussed in chapter 1, the structural advantages given to the children of the rich and the extreme disadvantages constraining the lives of the poor simply negate the opportunities for social mobility *ad infinitum*. Meritocracy as a social system is therefore a structural impossibility, and, as a cultural discourse, it is a damaging fiction.

## What is the alternative?

Clearly, the language of 'equality of opportunity' has been used to restrict the possibilities of this outcome for the majority. As this book's title indicates, we need to name neoliberal meritocracy as a problem. We need to talk more loudly about how it functions as a figleaf for inequality. We need to foreground the variety of collaborations, solidarities and change needed to create a more equitable society and to discuss, strengthen and implement alternatives. We need to take the power away from the 1% and give it to the 99%. Ultimately this means finding techniques and strategies to undermine and dismantle neoliberal ideology and economics – phenomena which, as Doreen Massey pointed out, are intimately interrelated through the vocabularies we use – and to produce greater velocity towards economic equality, anti-capitalism, anti-racism, anti-sexism and environmentalism (Massey 2013).

In conventional political terms, then, I am arguing for 'equality of outcome' above and instead of 'equality of opportunity', as chapter 1 discussed. However, I also argue that it is crucial to understand the significance and salience of the languages of opportunity which are being mobilised. For what this neoliberal language of opportunity speaks to, in its most positive sense, is a desire for human lives and potential not to be constrained and to find occupations and/or outlets in forms of activity that match the abilities they have developed so far and enable them to flourish in a way which is not delimited by the precise context they were born into. It is a formulation which notices that what we are born into may be constraining; it is a formulation which recognises that the world is large and multifaceted and speaks to adventurous desire to extend our capacities to act, our capabilities. These facets of the desire for meritocracy and its often used political/academic synonym 'equality of opportunity' should not be minimised but recognised. They are recognised by plutocrats and the right. To put this in even simpler terms: we need to argue for economic equality and for social, environmental and cultural diversity.

But what does the alternative mean in practice? It is varied and multi-faceted, to be sure, but there are a lot of resources we can draw on here. Richard Wilkinson and Kate Pickett's book *The Spirit Level*, for instance, has used an array of disciplinary evidence to prove that the more equal income levels in a society are, the happier and healthier it is: the narrower the income gap, the more advantageous it is for all. They argue that greater equality and an end to the obsession with economic growth is the way – indeed the only possible way – to rein in consumerism, tackle global warming and improve the quality of life (Wilkinson and Pickett 2010). Like the 2015 film based on it, *The Divide, The Spirit Level* does an excellent job of foregrounding the critical importance of working towards economic equality for the good of all. Like an array of other theorists (Hall, Massey and Rustin 2013; Simms 2009; Wright 2010), they argue that to reduce inequality we have to expose the damage caused by, and jettison our attachments to, the idea of economic growth:

> We have seen that the rich countries have got to the end of the really important contributions which economic growth can make to the quality of life and also that our future lies in improving the quality of the social environment in our societies.
>
> *(Wilkinson and Pickett 2010: 272)*

At the end of the book Wilkinson and Pickett discuss a range of different strategies to move toward economic equality, such as using taxes and benefits or narrowing the difference in gross market incomes. They argue we need to use both (Wilkinson and Pickett 2010: 245).

Alongside economic inequality we need to reduce discrimination. As Stephen McNamee and Robert Miller put it, 'merit is in reality only one factor among many that influence who ends up with what. Nonmerit factors are also at work'. Discrimination is 'a major source of nonmerit inequality' (McNamee and Miller 2009: 215, 229). Education is of pivotal importance in addressing broader cultures of discrimination (Guinier 2015), as is the importance of legal regulation to deal with structural inequalities, including in the form of anti-discrimination laws. McNamee and Miller also promote affirmative action policies, through, for example, the use of quotas for women and non-white people in institutional contexts as a basic regulatory code rather than relying on the whims of the already powerful who tend to hail from a very limited demographic base. As Gary Younge put it: 'I am not in favour of quotas in general. They are a blunt instrument. But I am even less in favour of getting nothing done and I prefer blunt instruments to no tools at all' (Younge 2014).

Alongside strategies to redistribute wealth, and to tackle discrimination, we also need a greater amount of socialised provision (Gilbert 2013). The grossly inflated phenomenon of corporate power needs cutting down, and the potential of democratic employee share-ownership (Wilkinson and Pickett 2010: 255) and co-operatives (Sandoval 2016a, 2016b) expanding. Crucially there are forms of collective provision that we all need because of our interdependency: we need government spending on healthcare, education and transportation, as well as libraries and community centres. But I do not advocate extending *noblesse oblige*, or the altruistic philanthropy of the rich, to fund such forms of socialised provision (and here I depart from McNamee and Miller's otherwise excellent analysis). For as I have outlined above and explored at greater length in chapter 4, the rich have found plenty of ways through philanthrocapitalism to use donations to vastly extend their power and perpetuate new inequalities. Instead we need concerted actions to break down such concentrations of wealth. Where this theme is taken up at persuasive length is in Andrew Sayer's readable and thorough scholarly work *Why We Can't Afford the Rich*, discussed in chapter 4. Sayer presents an array of strategies to curb the wealth extraction produced by plutocratic rentiers, from radical reform of the institutions of finance capitalism, to a maximum wage, to tackling inheritance (Sayer 2016).

The potential of digital technology in sharing wealth is also critical. How we can maximise the benefits of new technologies, rather than prioritising profit for technology companies through planned obsolescence and create more efficient forms of solar power to share resources are all key issues (Wilkinson and Pickett 2010: 266). The potential of technology in democratising politics, in extending democratic decision-making and participatory politics, has been explored in a variety of works (Bria 2015; Fisher and Gilbert 2014). In *Inventing the Future*, for instance, Nick Srnicek and Alex Williams set out a way to think boldly about post-capitalist social and technological policy and potential: of combining a 'universal basic income' with a genuinely smart and social use of technology to minimise tedious labour and maximise sociality (Srnicek and Williams 2015).

There are then a wide array of strategies which could most definitely be used, in our lifetimes, to move away from the inequalities of capitalist meritocracy. But practical strategies are but one part of the picture. As this book has shown, the ideology of meritocracy has been the key justification for neoliberalism, and it has operated on multiple levels: through political narrative and strategy, through social theory, and through widely disseminated parables of popular culture. Undoing the power of neoliberal meritocracy therefore also has to work on multiple levels. Such alternatives need coherent and powerful forms of political representation and persuasion. They have to deal with a media landscape which is becoming increasingly right-wing. To win support, to gain broader, hegemonic power they need to be popularised within everyday discourse, through engaging media forms, and through organisational practices.

## Changing the cultural pull of meritocratic hope

Might we not retain the word 'meritocracy' to indicate the necessity for people to be able to move into spheres of work into which they were not necessarily born? We have social democratic meritocracy and neoliberal meritocracy: might we not have a diverse, non-authoritarian socialist meritocracy too? It is not completely inconceivable that there could be a strategic use of the term in this vein. But 'meritocracy' has, ever since it was first used and in all its different historical–political incarnations, meant a society where people are given far greater economic rewards according to their perceived merit. This creates a system of economic inequality, which means their children grow up in privileged circumstances. 'Meritocracy' is thus, as it has always been used so far, a tautology.

It is important to disaggregate the different components of discursive formations of meritocracy, as I have attempted to do throughout this book. What is worth keeping is a question which is a little different, for as we have seen there are different components or aspects of an ideology of meritocracy depending on which particular era, field and/or discursive formation it is part of. There is plenty that is good, admirable and useful about many of the separate components of the contemporary ideology of meritocracy. For instance: 'working hard'. Obviously this is articulated in the neoliberal ideology of meritocracy to capitalism, to the idea of overwork in the service of neoliberal capital, to working too hard for the further profit of the already wealthy. Yet working hard in the sense of focusing, putting in effort and persevering through difficult moments and tough times is, of course, not a bad quality unto itself. Indeed, it is an important and a crucial quality that needs to be cultivated and drawn upon in order to expand our potential (Wright 2010; Hesmondhalgh 2016). At the same time it is equally important to insist that it always needs to be accompanied by enough time for rest and recuperation. It is what 'working hard' becomes connected to, or what cultural studies calls 'articulated to', in the 'chain of equivalence' that is neoliberal meritocracy, which is the problem (Slack 1996; Hall 2016).

Similarly, aspiring to be involved in pursuits and work that is different from that pursued by people in the zone, the habitus, the locale you have grown up in or have become habituated to is obviously also not a bad thing. Aspiring to do and be something different is, of course, not problematic *per se*. Just as with focused hard work, pursuing such difference is usually a crucial and important part of living. Again, its potential for extending our capacities to act, for human flourishing and self/collective realisation is immense, and its ubiquity indicates why neoliberal meritocracy has power. It is important to recognise that these are key affective zones from which neoliberal meritocracy becomes fuelled. They are sources of power and emotional resonance, and their appropriation is a core reason why neoliberal meritocracy works. Orienting these powerful affects and attributes in different directions, through less individualistic and more co-operative pathways, is crucial.

Equally, it is not useful or credible to deny the importance of merit. It is, however, important to argue about what forms of merit are useful for what purpose, and to nurture them in their diversity. It is not useful, as Michael Young's satire pointed out all those years ago, to create an elite cadre of those deemed to have merit at the expense of others and of themselves (Young 2004). As Alan Fox said, why would you want to heap great wealth and prizes on the already prodigiously talented? Surely we should find better ways to share our skills (Fox 1956). Following in this vein, in this tradition of left sociology, I argue that the word 'meritocracy' has become too toxic for it to be recuperated. Instead, we should argue for economic equality combined with social, cultural and environmental diversity.

## Alternatives to the ladder

A variety of people opt out of the meritocratic race for one reason or another. Whilst, as we have seen in chapter 4, some elites, particularly those who have a public profile, often strenuously use discourses of meritocracy to justify their position, for other sections of the super-elite, meritocracy is simply an irrelevant discourse with which they have no need to be concerned. This is particularly the case with high earners in the financial industries for whom having a public profile is not a necessity (Freeland 2012; Mizruchi 2013). Similarly, although from a very different political angle, the meritocratic discourse that 'effort mobilising talent' will propel you to the top can be rejected by those sections of the working and middle classes who do not see any persuasive evidence for believing in the discourse of neoliberal meritocracy or believing that it is fair. Why bother with the rat race when the race is rigged? From downsizing lifestyles to dropping out, this is a palpably recognisable popular discourse.

A third constituency consists of those who are actively and self-consciously rejecting the individualistic, competitive foundations of the meritocratic myth by participating in politics or in co-operative, mutual or 'commons-oriented' activities instead. For instance, the UK co-operative Altgen was set up by a group of recently graduated students who realised that despite getting firsts in their degrees and doing internships, they could still not obtain the paid work in the industries they wanted to work in.[3] They founded Altgen (short for 'alternative generation') as a co-operative group which rejected the individualism of the career ladder, and which is oriented towards helping each other, working together and in association with other co-operative groups.[4]

As we saw in chapter 1, the ladder is the prime symbol of meritocracy: as Raymond Williams pointed out nearly seventy years ago, it 'weakens community and the task of common betterment', as its promise of individual rewards 'sweetens the poison of hierarchy' (Williams 1958: 331). One of Altgen's graphics depicts a ladder turned on its side, above the caption 'You don't need to climb the ladder' (Figure C.1). This is not just inviting other people to drop out and do nothing. It is inviting them, or us, to engage in constructing alternatives that involve working together and to share resources.

A key issue is what possibilities do and might exist for those who do not believe in neoliberal meritocracy and those who are actively trying to construct alternatives to it to connect together, in order to create and to popularise democratic alternatives to the individualised social ladder.

Within my lifetime, through neoliberalism, 'meritocracy' has become an alibi for plutocracy, or government by a wealthy elite. It has become a key ideological term in the reproduction of neoliberal culture, offering the false

**YOU DON'T NEED
TO CLIMB THE LADDER.**

**ALTGEN**

FIGURE C.1 Altgen graphic. Design by Constance Laisné for Altgen. Reproduced courtesy of Constance Laisné and Altgen via a Creative Commons License.

promise that the social ladder is consistent and there for us, if only we have enough nous and gumption to climb. It has achieved this feat by seizing the idea, practice and discourse of greater social equality which emerged in the first half of the twentieth century and by marketising it. Neoliberal meritocracy, as a potent blend of an essentialised notion of 'talent', competitive individualism and belief in social mobility, is mobilised to both disguise and gain consent for the economic inequalities wrought through neoliberalism. However, such discourse is neither inevitable nor consistent. It requires actively reinforcing and reproducing and can be augmented and shaped in a number of different places and spaces. The alternative to plutocracy-as-meritocracy is a more plural understanding of merit – which considers merit on a collective and not a purely individual basis – alongside mutual and co-operative forms of social reproduction which create greater parity in wealth, opportunity, care and provision.

## Notes

1 Todd 2015: 9–10.
2 The US business magazine *Forbes* estimated his net worth at $3.7 billion in September 2016 (*Forbes* 2017).
3 Personal communication, 2016. See http://altgen.coop. Accessed 1 December 2016.
4 Of course small, co-operative groups on their own are not the singular solution to all society's problems; the attempted extension of neoliberalism into new domains has attempted to include co-ops, through, for example, Cameron's 'Big Society' rhetoric in the UK or the encouragement of loose forms of domestic co-operation in Italy (Dowling and Harvie 2014; Muehlebach 2012) and it is hard to work in a small co-op and crack the problem of low-paid labour, for instance. But progressive strands of worker co-operativism are often aware of such issues, all co-operative activity cannot be reduced to it, and such activity can offer both a crucial alternative and important prefigurative politics (Sandoval 2016a, 2016b).

## References

Bloodworth, James (2016) *The Myth of Meritocracy: Why Working-Class Kids still get Working-Class Jobs*. London: Biteback Publishing.

Bria, Francesca (2015) 'D-Cent Tools for Social Participation and Political Change', *Nesta*, 7 December, www.nesta.org.uk/blog/d-cent-tools-social-participation-and-political-change. Accessed 10 December 2016.

Dowling, Emma, and David Harvie (2014) 'Harnessing the Social: State, Crisis and (Big) Society', *Sociology* 48(5) pp. 869–886.

Elmer, Greg, and Paula Todd (2016) 'Don't be a Loser: Or How Trump Turned the Republican Primaries into an Episode of The Apprentice', *Television and New Media* 17(7) pp. 660–662.

Fisher, Mark (2014) 'Fading Privilege', *New Humanist*, 3 June, https://newhumanist.org.uk/articles/4667/fading-privilege. Accessed 1 December 2016.

Fisher, Mark, and Jeremy Gilbert (2014) *Reclaim Modernity: Beyond Markets, Beyond Machines*. London: Compass, www.compassonline.org.uk/wp-content/uploads/2014/10/Compass-Reclaiming-Modernity-Beyond-markets_-2.pdf. Accessed 3 December 2016.

*Forbes* (2017), 'The Definitive Net Worth of Donald Trump', www.forbes.com/donald-trump/#70e64ba790be. Accessed 4 March 2016.

Fox, Alan (1956) 'Class and Equality', *Socialist Commentary*, May, pp. 11–13.

Frank, Thomas (2016) *Success and Luck: Good Fortune and the Myth of Meritocracy*. Princeton: Princeton University Press.

Freeland, Chrystia (2012) *Plutocrats: The Rise of the New Global Super-Rich*. New York: Penguin.

Gilbert, Jeremy (2013) *Common Ground: Democracy and Collectivity in an Age of Individualism*. London: Pluto.

Guinier, Lani (2015) *The Tyranny of the Meritocracy: Democratising Higher Education in America*. Boston: Beacon Press.

Hall, Stuart (2016) *Cultural Studies 1983: A Theoretical History*, ed. Lawrence Grossberg and Jennifer Daryl Slack. Durham, NC: Duke University Press.

Hall, Stuart, Doreen Massey and Michael Rustin (2013) (eds) *After Neoliberalism: The Kilburn Manifesto*. London: Lawrence & Wishart.

Hayes, Christopher (2012) *Twilight of the Elites: America After Meritocracy*. New York: Crown Publishing Group.

Hearn, Alison (2016) 'Trump's Reality Hustle', *Television and New Media* 17(7) pp. 656–659.

Hesmondhalgh, David (2016) 'Capitalism and the Media: Moral Economy, Well-Being and Capabilities', *Media, Culture and Society* 39(2) pp. 202–218.

McNamee, Stephen J., and Robert K. Miller (2009) *The Myth of Meritocracy*. Lanham: Rowman & Littlefield.

Massey, Doreen (2013) 'Vocabularies of the Economy', in Stuart Hall, Doreen Massey and Michael Rustin (eds), *After Neoliberalism: The Kilburn Manifesto*. London: Lawrence & Wishart, pp. 3–17.

Mizruchi, Mark S. (2013) *The Fracturing of the American Corporate Elite*. Cambridge, MA: Harvard University Press.

Muehlebach, Andrea (2012) *The Moral Neoliberal: Welfare and Citizenship in Italy*. Chicago: University of Chicago Press

Ouellette, Laurie (2016) 'The Trump Show', *Television and New Media* 17(7) pp. 647–650.

Sandoval, Marisol (2016a) 'Fighting Precarity with Co-Operation? Worker Co-Operatives in the Cultural Sector', *New Formations* 88 pp. 51–68.

Sandoval, Marisol (2016b) 'What would Rosa Do? Co-Operatives and Radical Politics', *Soundings* 63 pp. 98–111.

Sayer, Andrew (2016) *Why We Can't Afford the Rich*. Bristol: Policy Press

Simms, Andrew (2009) *Ecological Debt: Global Warming and the Wealth of Nations,* 2nd edn. London: Pluto Press.

Slack, Jennifer Daryl (1996) 'The Theory and Method of Articulation in Cultural Studies', in David Morley and Kuan-Hsing Chen (eds), *Stuart Hall: Critical Dialogues in Cultural Studies*. London: Routledge, pp. 112–130.

Srnicek, Nick, and Alex Williams (2015) *Inventing the Future: Postcapitalism and a World without Work*. London: Verso.

Todd, Selina (2015) *The People: The Rise and Fall of the Working Class, 1910–2010*. London: John Murray.

Wilkinson, Richard, and Kate Pickett (2010) *The Spirit Level: Why Equality is Better for Everyone*. London: Penguin.

Williams, Raymond (1958) 'Democracy or Meritocracy?', *Manchester Guardian*, October 30, p. 10.
Wright, Erik Olin (2010) *Envisaging Real Utopias*. London: Verso.
Young, Michael (2004) *The Rise of the Meritocracy* [1958], 2nd revd edn. London: Transaction Publishers.
Younge, Gary (2014) 'Diversity: What Can We Learn from America?', *Royal Television Society*, www.rts.org.uk/article/diversity-what-can-we-learn-america. Accessed 1 December 2016.

# INDEX

Abrahams, Jessica 93
Achola, Ella 149
Act for Change Project 63
Adkins, Lisa 195
Affleck, Ben 154, 164
'After the Family Wage' (Fraser) 183
Aitken, Jonathan 85
Allende, Salvador 79
Allen, Kim 125
Altgen (co-operative group) 222
American cultural imperialism 168
'Americanism and Fordism' (Gramsci) 205n12
*Annie* (film) 115, 137–8, 140n8–10
*Anyone Can Do It* (Bannatyne) 121, *122*
*Apprentice, The* (TV show) 1, 59, 121
Arendt, Hannah 1, 12, 25, 37–8, 100
aristocratic elite 124–6, 128
Armitage, John 134, 135
Armstrong, Heather 200, 205n13
Arnold, Matthew 172n6
art, canon formation of great 157–8
Asher, Rebecca 187, 203
aspiration 102
'Aspiration Nation' 13, 89–91, 92
Atlee, Clement 32
*Attic, The* (film) 106

*Baby Boom* (film) 180
Banet-Weiser, Sarah 199
Banks, Mark 62
Banks, Miranda 164
Bannatyne, Duncan 121–2, *122*
Barnett, Anthony 67, 88
*Battle of Algiers, The* (film) 158
Bechdel, Alison 173n8
Bechdel Test 163, 173n8
Beck, John 86, 88
Beck, Ulrich 183
'bell curve' thesis 156
Bell, Daniel 12, 25, 39–41, 215
Bell, Steve 83
'Benetton Britain' (Murray) 205n12
Benn, Tony 79
Berlant, Lauren 51, 90
*Better Call Saul* (TV series) 213
Beyoncé (singer) 69
Bill and Melinda Gates Foundation 131
Billig, Michael 127
*Birth of a Nation, The* (film) 158
*Birth of Biopolitics* (Foucault) 192
Black Lives Matter movement 153
Black Panthers 57
Black Power movement 69
Black Twitter 170, 171

Blairism 67, 86–8, 93, 105, 215
Blair, Tony 35, 85, 86, 87–8
Blanden, Jo 17n5
Bloodworth, James 7
blue-collar billionaires 94–7
Blunt, James 61
Boden (clothing company) 140n4
Bogle, Donald 158
Boliver, Vikki 53
Boltanski, Luc 58, 71, 123
Boone Issacs, Cheryl 171
Bradford, Barbara Taylor 196
Bradley, Milton 30
*Breaking Bad* (TV series) 213
Brexit 84
*Brief History of Neoliberalism, A* (Harvey) 53
Britain: as 'Aspiration Nation' 89–91; education system in 100–1; establishment 96–7; idea of 'self-help' in Victorian 104–5; Labour Force Survey 62; political representation 103; recession 89
Brown, Archie 105
Brown, Effie 14, 147–8, 160, 165–9, 171, 173n13
Brown, Gordon 89
Brown, Phillip 31
Brown, Wendy 192
Bryant, Chris 61
Buffett, Warren 115, 119, 139
Burrows, Gideon 203
Bush, George 84
Byrne, David 53

Cable, Vince 131
Caldwell, John Thornton 164
Cameron, David: 'Aspiration Nation' rhetoric 13, 89, 90–1; 'Big Society' project 72n8, 224n4; Brexit campaign and 96; on culture of low expectations 90; on education policy 102; hard work rhetoric 93, 129; on opportunity to succeed 1, 2; populism 106; resignation 97
Cameronism 105
Campbell, Beatrix 183
canon formation of great art 157–8

*Capital in the Twenty-First Century* (Piketty) 1, 118
capitalism: new forms of exploitation 58; social mobility and 27; *See also* philanthrocapitalism; welfare capitalism
Carter, C. 190
Catherine, Duchess of Cambridge *See* Middleton, Kate
Cattel, Raymond 4
*CEO Mums* (website) 201, *202*
Charles, Prince of Wales 124, 126
Charney, Dov 123
Chiapello, Eve 58, 71, 123
chief executive officers (CEOs) 121, 123–4, 140n3
childcare 186–7, 191, 203
child labour 182–4
Chilean coup d'état 79–80
Chiles, Perrin 160
Christie, Bridget 100
Churchill, Winston 117
Clancy, Laura 125
class: academic discussion of 66–7; ambiguities of meaning of 66
'Class and Equality' (Fox) 32
*Class and Stratification* (Crompton) 66
classlessness: idea of 67
class warfare 115, 139
Clegg, Nick 131
Clinton, Bill 87
Cohen, Phil 205n11
Comaroff, Jean 65
Comaroff, John 65
*Coming of Post-Industrial Society, The* (Bell) 39
Conservative Party (UK) 80, 84, 85, 131
consumerism 81–2
co-operative activity 222–3, 224n4
Cooper, Brittney 150, 151, 159
Corbyn, Jeremy: 'Aspiration for All' slogan 102–3; as leader of Labour Party 101–2, 103, 106n5, 107n6; political platform 103–4, 205n15
corporate justice 213–14
corporate populism 67, 88
creative industries: academic studies of 161; covert discrimination 62;

cultivation of image of being 'cool' 161; gender disparity 162–3; homosocial nepotism 62; informal networks 161–2; lack of diversity 62, 161, 163; profession paternalism 62; self-exploitation in workplaces 197; unequal employment 61–2, 63
'Crisis in Education, The' (Arendt) 37–8
Crompton, Rosemary 66
Crosby, Lynton 91
'cross-grading': as route towards greater equality 33–4
Cross, Steve 27
*Cruel Optimism* (Berlant) 51
'cruel optimism' 90
Curtis, Adam 106n3

*Daily Mail, The* (newspaper) 133, 169, 190
Damon, Matt: apology of 149–50; on diversity in production 14, 147–8, 155, 157, 164–5, 216; playing merit card 150–1; racial comments 154, 159, 166, 169
Damonsplaining incident: analysis of 216; as example of mansplaining 167; as example of post-racial meritocracy 14–15, 169; idea of merit 156–7; media coverage 168–9; post-racial discourse 154, 171; publicity 168; reaction to 149, 150–1; use of politicised hashtag 14, 169–70; white male privilege and 147–51
Dardot, Pierre 192, 193, 194
Davies, William 43
Davis, Viola 163
*Dear White People* (film) 147
*Democracy in America* (Tocqueville) 27
'demotic populism' of media forms 67
desperate success 182, 184–92, 216
Diana, Princess of Wales 124
digital technology 219–20
'discourse': meaning and use of term 9–10
diversity: merit as opposition to 151; notions of good and bad 152
*Divide, The* (film) 218
Donovan, Clare 44n9
*Dooce* (blog) 200

Dorling, Danny 5, 117
double egalitarian deficit 70
Douglas, Susan J. 186
Dowling, Emma 187
*Downton Abbey* (drama series) 115, 129–30, 131
*Dragon's Den* (TV show) 122
Drucker, Peter 193
Dunham, Lena 213
Durkheim, Emile 27, 35
DuVernay, Ava 173n11
DuVernay test 173n12
Dyer, Richard 200

Eagle, Angela 107n6
Earle, Liz 188
educational essentialism 37–8
educational system: in Great Britain 26; in the United States 37–8
Edwards, Michael 132
egalitarian deficit 13, 51, 69–72
Eikhof, D. R. 190
Ekinsmyth, Carol 188–9
Eliot, Charles William 155
*Elizabeth at 90: A Family Tribute* (BBC programme) 125
employment: erosion of working conditions 50; horizontal and vertical models of 55; inequality of 61–3; model of progression 55–6; no-collar labour 50; for people with autism 190–1; pros and cons of self- 185–6; status of professions 6–7
Elmer, Greg 95, 214
Enfield, Henry 81
enlightenment 'individual' 166
entrepreneurship: challenges of 191–2; competition and 193; gender and 15, 182, 192, 194–5, 196, 205n9; key characteristics of 193–4; male culture of 187; manifestations of success 190; in neoliberal theory 193; in reality shows 59–60; subcontracting and 195; as upper-middle class occupation 191
environmental movement 57
*Episodes* (TV show) 164

equality: economic 218; in media, discourse of 164; of opportunity 27, 40, 42; of outcome 27, 217–18; second age of 58
Equal Pay Act 56
*Ethnicity, Inc.* (Comaroff) 65
*Eve* (magazine) 189

family models 183–4
Farage, Nigel 94, 106
feminism 64, 68–9; *See also* magical femininity
film industry: canon formation 158; criteria of merit 159; gender and racial inequality 158, 162, 163, 164; lack of diversity 62–3, 165–6, 171; merit-based assessment 159; problem of access to 162
financial elites 136
*Finding Your Roots* (TV show) 154
Fisher, Mark 91, 213, 219
Fisher, Stephanie 62
Fordist Deal 52
*Fortunes of Feminism* (Fraiser) 64
Foster, Dawn 184
Foucault, Michel 9, 42, 192–3
Fox, Alan 12, 25, 32–4, 214
Foxx, Jamie 137
Fraiser, Nancy 64
*Framing Class* (Kendall) 134
Frank, Thomas 94
Fraser, Nancy 179, 183
Freeland, Chrystia 118–19
Friedan, Betty 189
Friedman, Sam 56
Friedman, Thomas 31

Gabriel, Yiannis 52
garment industry subcontracting 194–5
Gates, Henry Louis Jr. 154
Geena Davis Institute 163
gender disparities in media 163
George VI, King of Great Britain 127
Giddens, Anthony 12, 25, 43, 86, 87
Gilbert, Jeremy 87, 135
Gilles, Valerie 91
Gill, Rosalind 62, 64
Gill, Ross 198

Gilroy, Paul 65
*Girls* (TV series) 213
Glodthorpe, John 17n5
Goldberg, David Theo 14, 65, 151, 153, 154, 156, 168
*Goodbye Jimmy Choo* (Sanders) 189, 200
Goodman, Michael K. 135
*Got Talent* (TV show) 59
Gramsci, Antonio 205n12
Gray, Harold 137
Gray, Herman 164
Greening, Justine 100
Griffith, D. W. 158
Grosvenor, Gerald Cavendish 128
*Guardian, The* (newspaper) 169
Guilford, Guy 4
Guinier, Lani 156

Hall, Catherine 131
Hall, Stuart 5, 16n3, 48, 86
hard work rhetoric 92–3, 220–1
Harry, Prince of Wales 125–6
Hartley, John 60
Harvey, Alison 62
Harvey, David 53
hashtags 169–70, 171
Hayek, Frederich 193
Hayes, Christopher 58, 156, 172n4
Hays, Constance L. 123
Healey, Denis 79
Hearn, Alison 95, 198
hedonistic consumption, idea of 80
*Hello!* (magazine) 133
Hemsley, Jeff 170
Hesmondhalgh, David 161
Hicks, Marie 54–5
Hickman, Rebecca 3, 53
Hill Collins, Patricia 167
Hochschild, Arlie 187, 191
*Hollywood Diversity Report: Flipping the Script* (UCLA) 163
*Hollywood, the Dream Factory* (Powdermaker) 162
*Huffington Post, The* (news site) 169
Hughes, Robert 84
*Hunger Games, The* (film) 213
Hunt, Darnell 163

Hurricane Katrina 69, 153, 172n4
Hutchinson, Leslie 130

ideology: definition of 9
*Idol* (TV show) 1, 59
*I Don't Know How She Does It* (Pearson) 180
imperialism, justification of 131–2
income gap 218
indebtedness 136
individualism 29, 59
inequality: across countries 117; act of addressing 89–90; discrimination as source of 218–19; expansion of 139; relation to race, gender, and class 69–70; social mobility and 32–3, 217
*Inequality by Design* (Fischer) 4, 28, 156
intelligence: concept of 4–5, 35; IQ test 4, 156
International Monetary Fund 79
*In the Cut* (film) 147
*Inventing the Future* (Srnicek and Williams) 219

Jefferson, Thomas 26
Jerolmack, Colin 92
Johnson, Boris 92–3, 96, 119, 129
Johnson, Mark 30
Jones, Deborah 161
Jones, Mosey 180, 203
Joubert, Marc 166
*Just Another Emperor* (Edwards) 132

Kardashian, Kim 140n5
Karmel, Annabel *181,* 187, 188, 190, 201
Kendall, Diana 134
Kendall, Liz 102
*Keywords* (Williams) 23
Khan, Shamus 92, 119, 128
kind parent figure 129–33
*King's Speech, The* (film) 115, 127, 128
Kirst, Seamus 173n12
Kirzner, Israel 193
*Kitchen Table Tycoon* (Naik) 181, 188
Klass, Myleene 201
Klein, Naomi 53, 80

Kristol, Irving 39–40
Kynaston, David 32

Labour Party (UK) 103, 106n5, 106n6
ladder of opportunity 2–3, 8, 28, 70–1, 222, *223*
*La Haine* (film) 158
Laisné, Constance *223*
Lakoff, George 30
Land, Hilary 36
Lang, Tim 52
Lapavitsas, Costas 117
Latham, Mark 2
Laval, Christian 192, 193, 194
Lawler, Steph 66
Leadsom, Andrea 95
*Lean In* (Sandberg) 184
*Lean Out* (Foster) 184
Leavis, F. R. 157
Lee, Spike 171
*Leisure Class, The* (film) 165
Lentin, Alana 152
Le Pen, Marie 94
level playing field, idea of 30–1, 50–1, 64, 65, 85
Lewis, Patricia 189
liberalism *vs.* neoliberalism 42
liberation movements 56–8, 63–4, 65–6
*Lifestyles of the Rich and Famous* (TV show) 133, 134
Lim, Kane 134, 135
Lim, Peter 135
Lipsitz, George 147, 172n5
*Little Orphan Annie* (comic strip) 137, 140n7
Lowell, Lawrence 155
Luckman, Susan 191
luxury: environmental price for 135–6; luxury-flaunters 133–6; in modern era, status of 134–5; presentation of 133–4; vision of communal 135

Maastricht Treaty 84
McGuigan, Jim 67
McNamee, Stephen 4, 7, 92, 218–19
Macpherson, C. B. 28
McRobbie, Angela 59, 64, 184, 186, 197
*Made in Chelsea* (TV show) 133

Mad Men (drama series) 57
magical femininity 197–8
Mair, Peter 88
Major, John 83–4, 85
Mandelson, Peter 88
Mann, Jason 165
mansplaining 148
Marwick, Alice 134
Marx, Karl 27, 66, 135, 140n2
Massey, Doreen 217
material superabundance: spectacles of 133–4
Mayer, Vicki 161, 164
May, Theresa: cabinet re-shuffle 97; education policy 98, 100; first speech as prime minister 106n4; meritocracy language 16, 100–1, 106, 215; rhetoric of social inequalities 99–100; *The Sun* publication about 97, 98; sympathy to working-class people 97, 99; T-shirt espousing feminism 100; vision of neoliberal meritocracy 88
Medhurst, John 79
Media Diversified 63
Meek, James 94
*Men can do It!* (Burrows) 203
merit: ambiguous nature of 5, 88; debates around 35; *vs.* diversity 151, 157; importance of 221; Matt Damon on 150; plural understanding of 224; racialisation of 14, 151, 155–7, 157–8, 159–66; shift in notion of 95–6; of things 158–9; whiteness and 156–7, 166–8
meritocracy: alternatives to 36, 220; American Dream as promise of 26; aspirational 90; career advancement and 48–51; clarity and 23, 25; components of 220–1; consumerism and 105; in context of welfare state 41; contradiction to principle of equality 38; corporate justice narrative of 213–14; crisis of post-racial 168–72, 171; critique of 16, 33, 214–15; cultural pull of 11; definition 1, 2, 3, 8, 23–5, 34, 78; development of framework of 41–4; discourse of 85–6, 212–13; economic context 40; as engine of growth 41; evolution of concept 13, 25–6, 36, 43–4; and extension of privilege 115–16; five problems of 3–8; freedom to work 49; genealogies of 12, 214–17; as ideological discourse 7, 9–10, 11, 25; individualism and 105–6; interpretations of 40–1; ladder as symbol of 2–3, 5, 222; 'level playing field' 30; merit of 85; mutuality *vs.* 104–6; in neoliberal context 7–8, 41–4, 88, 89; plutocracy and 1–3, 222–3; political discourse and 78–9, 86; racialisation of 151–5, 216; social democratic 10, 34–8; and social inequality 41; social roots of 32–4; as social system 8–9, 10, 24, 25; study of 8, 11–12; super-elite and 221–2; symbolism around 30–1; as tautology 220; *See also* neoliberal meritocracy
Meritocracy (online job agency) 48–50, 72n2
*Meritocracy and the "Classless Society"* (Wooldridge) 41, 42–4
*Meritocracy Myth, The* (McNamee and Miller) 4, 7
meritocratic deficit 69–72, 215
meritocratic extremism 95
meritocratic feeling 13
meritocratic media bubble 165
Michaels, Meredith 186
Middleton, Kate 124, 125
Miers, Thomasina 188
Miliband, Ed 106n5
Miller, Robert 4, 7, 92, 218–19
Mills, Tom 93
Mitter, Swasti 194
Mixer, Tobias 5
*Modernity Britain: Opening the Box, 1957–59* (Kynaston) 32
mommy bloggers 199–200
*Mommy Myth, The* (Douglas and Michaels) 186
Moore, Michael 171
Morris, William 135
Mossack Fonesca law firm 136
Mountbatten, Edwina 130

multiculturalism 152
*Mumpreneur* (Karmel) *181,* 188
*Mumpreneur Dairy, The* (Jones) 203
Mumpreneur of the Year contest 190
mumpreneurs: awards and services 179–80; childcare and 180–2; life-work balance 187–8, 201; magical femininity 196, 197–8; in matron literature 180, 182, 189, 200–1; self-branding of 198–201, 200–1; skills required for 190, 197; social background of 188–9, 191; in women's magazines, portrayal of 180, 189
mumpreneurship: as aspirational activity 205n9; in context of social reproduction 182, 187, 203; co-operatives *vs.* corporations 203, 204; emergence of 179–80, 216; evolution of 194–5; feminist discourse 184; as form of desperate success 189–90, 216–17; popularization of 196; problems of 15, 201; as self-employment 184–5; as solution to inflexibilities of paid work 182, 201; studies of 11, 182, 195–6; types of enterprises and products 180, 191
Murray, Robin 199, 205n12
*Myth of Meritocracy, The* (Bloodworth) 7
*Myth of the Strong Leader, The* (Brown) 105

Nahon, Karine 170
Naik, Anita 181
Negra, Diane 180, 187
*Neoconservative Persuasion, The* (Kristol) 40
neoliberalism: feminism and 64; geographical developments 53; justice narratives of 67–9, 100, 215; language of opportunity 218–19; meritocracy and 43; post-Fordist 65–6; promotion of corporate power 79–80; racialised 65; relation to gender, class and ethnicity 64, 65, 194; wealth gap 215–16

neoliberal meritocracy: access to 71–2; connection to aspiration 89; contemporary studies of 13–14; as corporate liberation 49; discourses of 13, 25–6, 68, 69, 71, 212–13; egalitarian deficit and 51; emergence of 16, 39–41; externalised and internalised 171–2; idea of self-promotion 59; liberation movements and 215; link to capitalist market 41–2; meaning of 215–16; moralistic dimension of 106; political context 101–2, 215; popularization of 214–15; racialisations of 14, 153, 167; *vs.* social democratic meritocracy 10; socially liberal version of 87; social mobility and 50, 89; sources of power of 221
*New Entrepreneurs* (Valdez) 190
New Labour 85, 86, 88, 89, 91
Newman, Janet 195, 196
new rich 136–40; *See also* plutocratic elite
*New Spirit of Capitalism, The* (Boltanski and Chiapello) 58
*New Statesman* (magazine) 32
*New Way of the World, The* (Dardot and Laval) 192–3
Nuffield Mobility Study 52

Oakley, Kate 62
Obama, Barack 1, 153
O'Brien, Dave 62
Occupy movement 116–17, 119
*Off-Centre: Feminism and Cultural Studies* (Franklin, Lury and Stacey) 195
O'Grady, Frances 131
O'Neill, Essena 200
'On Meritocracy and Equality' (Bell) 39
Ortner, Sheri 162
Ouellette, Laurie 96, 214

Papachrissi, Zizi 170
parables of progress 12, 13, 51, 59–61
parental leave policies 205n16
parents overwork 204
Peabody, George 28
Pearson, Allison 180

philanthrocapitalism 131–2
Pickett, Kate 218
piece-work seamstress 194–5, 205n10
Piketty, Thomas 1, 95, 118
plutocracy 1–3, 223–4
plutocratic elite: *vs.* aristocrats 128; charitable work 131–2; evolution of 116, 118–19; media image 115–16; meritocracy discourse and 14, 120; normcore plutocrats 120–4, 216; private business interests 131–2; social types of 14, 120; wealth accumulation 116, 117, 118; *See also* super-rich
Pollock, Griselda 157
post-class 67, 69, 71, 72n8
post-democracy 127
post-feminism 64–5, 67, 68, 69, 71, 198
post-Fordist culture and society 39, 199, 205n12
post-race 65, 67, 68, 69, 71, 153, 154–5
post-work 204
poverty: criminalisation of 136
Powdermaker, Hortense 162
Pringle, Judith K. 161
Pritschet, Gloria 5
*Private Eye* (magazine) 131
*Production Studies* (Mayer) 161
*Project Greenlight* (TV show) 72, 147, 154, 158, 160, 164–5, 172n7; *See also* Damonsplaining incident
Protestant work ethic 58
*Public Interest* (journal) 39
public welfare systems 53
Puwar, Nirmal 166

race and racism 69, 151–3, 158, 168
Race Relations Acts 56–7
Ramon, Ana-Christina 163
Rattansi, Ali 159
Rawls, John 40
Reagan, Ronald 30, 31, 80
reality shows 59–61
reason and progress 159
Reay, Diane 179
Redmayne, Eddie 61
*Reflections of a Neoconservative* (Kristol) 40
Reign, April 171

rentier economy 118, 140n2
Richads, Lawrence 96, 97
*Rich Dad, Poor Dad* (Gilroy) 65
*Rich Kids of Instagram* (blog) 14, 115–16, 133–4, 135, 136
Riley, James Whitcomb 140n7
*Rise of the Meritocracy, The* (Young) 4–5, 12, 32, 34–5, 36–7, 41, 88
Roberts, Joanna 134
Robertson, John S. 140n7
Rojek, Chris 88
Ross, Andrew 136
Ross, Kristin 72n8, 135
royal family 125–6, 127

Saha, Anamik 161
Sandberg, Sheryl 184, 197
Sanders, Bernie 104
Sandoval, Marisol 203, 219, 224n4
Savage, Mike 34
Saville, Jimmy 96
Sayer, Andrew 116, 117, 133, 138–9, 219
Sen, Amartya 23, 25
*Sex in the City* (TV series) 213
*Shadow Elite* (Wedel) 136
Shah, Mona 190, 197
Sharma, Sanjay 171
*Shattered* (Asher) 187, 203
*Shock Doctrine, The* (Klein) 53
*Sight and Sound* (magazine) 158
Simms, Andrew 218
Skeggs, Bev 7, 60, 66
*Small Change: Why Business won't Save the World* (Edwards) 132
Simms, Andrew 218
Smiles, Samuel 26
Smith, Jada Pinkett 171
Smith, Owen 107n6
snakes and ladders board game 28–30, 29*fig*, 30*fig*, 44n3, 44n5
socialism: advantages of 135
*Socialist Commentary* (journal) 32
social ladder *See* ladder of opportunity
social media 170, 171, 199, 200
social mobility: comparative perspective 8–9; concept of 4; disadvantage factors 12–13; dissociation from support network and 56; grammar

school and 101; hard work rhetoric 92–3; ideological narratives of 27; inequality and 217; limits of 212–13; measurement of relative 53; opportunities for 5, 7–8, 17n5, 26, 52–3; as politically driven distraction 179; popularization of idea of 104–5; in post-industrial society 39; in public sector 52–3; studies of 56; upper middle-class values and 7
social movements 39
social order: transformation of 26–7
social reproduction 182–3, 204
Solnit, Rebecca 148, 172n2
Speaks, John 140n7
*Spirit Level, The* (Wilkinson and Pickett) 218
*Spitting Image* (TV show) 83
Srnicek, Nick 219
Standing, Guy 185
*Stranger in a Strange Land* (Younge) 168
*Stuart Hall Project, The* 16n3
Sugar, Alan 60, 119, 121, 123, 124
Summers, J. 190
*Sunday Times Rich List* 121
*Supermummy: The Ultimate Guide to Business Success* (McGee) 182
*Supernanny* (TV show) 91
super-rich: attacks on 139–40; idea of 1% of 116–17; internal differentiation 117; in media, presentation of 14, 115–16; positive representations of 139; profit without producing 117–18; as rentiers 117; wealth accumulation 118, 139; *See also* plutocratic elite
Surowiecki, James 123

Tannock, Stuart 31
Tasker, Yvonne 180
Taylor, Jessica 199
Taylor, Stephanie 189
*Telegraph, The* (newspaper) 169
Thatcherism: consumerism and 81, 82, 105; economic policy 79, 80, 81; enterprise culture 60; housing privatization 81; ideology of 79–83; meritocratic discourse 80–1, 215;
mumpreneurialism and 195; popular support for 82; social conservatism 81
Thatcher, Margaret 27, 80, 82, 83, 93
Tilly, Charles 162
Tincknell, Estella 196
Titley, Gavin 152
Tocqueville, Alexis de 27
Todd, Jennifer 160
Todd, Selina 212
*Tokyo Story* (film) 158
*Toms, Coons, Mulattoes, Mammies and Bucks* (Bogle) 158
*Top Model* (TV show) 59
Trump, Donald 16, 94–6, 106, 129, 140n3, 170, 213–14
Turner, Graeme 60, 67
*Twilight of the Elites* (Hayes) 58
*Two Cheers for Capitalism* (Kristol) 40
*Tyranny of the Meritocracy, The* (Guinier) 156
Tyler, Imogen 7

UK Independence Party (UKIP) 94
*Uncle Tom's Cabin* (film) 158
*Undoing the Demos* (Brown) 192
United Kingdom: Conservative-Liberal coalition government 89; educational system 26; expansion of democracy 26; individual entrepreneurship 185; inheritance rights 128
'Upward Mobility' (art installation) 5, 6
upward mobility phenomenon 53, 119
US New Deal 137, 138, 139

Valdez, Zulema 190
Valentine, Jeremy 140n2
*Voice* (TV show) 59
Von Mises, Ludwig 193

Wallis, Quvenzhané 137
Walters, Julie 61
wealth: accumulation of 118; displays of 115–16, 133–4, 135, 136; distribution of global 116–17, 132–3; ethnicity and 161; inflation of 118–19; redistribution strategies 218, 219–20; taxation 118, 119
Wedel, Janine R. 136

welfare capitalism 51–2, 53, 54, 56
West, Kanye 153
*We Were Feminists Once: From Riot Grrl to Cover Girl* (Zeisler) 68
*What Not to Wear* (TV programme) 64
*Where Now for New Labour?* (Giddens) 86
whitesplaining 148–9
*Why We Can't Afford the Rich* (Sayer) 117, 219
Wilders, Geert 94
Wilkinson, Richard 218
William, Duke of Cambridge 124
Williams, Alex 219
Williamson, Milly 60
Williams, Raymond 3, 23, 35, 78, 222
Willis, Paul 91
Wilson, Julie Ann 191
Winch, Alison 198
*Wire, The* (TV series) 213

*Woman of Substance, A* (TV series) 196
women: discrimination of 54–5; emergence of entrepreneurial 195–6; image of consuming 196–7; liberation movement 57–8; self-improvement strive 198; and technology 54–5; voting preferences 85
Wooldridge, Adrian 41, 42
working-class 62
*World is Flat, The* (Friedman) 31

Yasujiro, Ozu 158
Yochim, Emily Chivers 191
Younge, Gary 168, 219
Young, Michael 4, 12, 25, 32, 34–7, 40–1, 44n9, 214

Zeisler, Andi 68
Zuma, Jacob 1